Colonial Meltdown

NEW AFRICAN HISTORIES SERIES

Series editors: Jean Allman and Allen Isaacman

Colonial Meltdown

Northern Nigeria in the Great Depression

Moses E. Ochonu

OHIO UNIVERSITY PRESS
ATHENS

Ohio University Press, Athens, Ohio 45701
www.ohioswallow.com
© 2009 by Ohio University Press
All rights reserved

Printed in the United States of America
Ohio University Press books are printed on acid-free paper ⊗ ™

16 15 14 13 12 11 10 09   5 4 3 2 1

Cover art: *The Colonial Railway* by Oluwaseyi Babalola

Library of Congress Cataloging-in-Publication Data
Ochonu, Moses E.
   Colonial meltdown : northern Nigeria in the Great Depression / Moses E. Ochonu.
      p. cm. — (New African histories series)
   Includes bibliographical references and index.
   ISBN 978-0-8214-1889-5 (hc : alk. paper) — ISBN 978-0-8214-1890-1 (pbk. : alk.
paper)
   1. Nigeria, Northern—History—20th century. 2. Nigeria, Northern—Economic
conditions—20th century. 3. Great Britain—Colonies—Africa—Administration—
History—20th century. 4. Depressions—1929—Nigeria, Northern. 5. Depressions—
1929—Great Britain. 6. Nigeria—Colonial influence. 7. British—Nigeria,
Northern—History—20th century. I. Title.
   DT515.9.N5O25 2009
   966.9'503—dc22

                          2009023500

To my family

Contents

Illustrations

Acknowledgments

I incurred many debts in the course of writing this book. During my research I received enormous financial and moral support from various facilities at the University of Michigan: the Department of History, the Center for Afroamerican and African Studies, the International Institute, and the Rackham Graduate School. The staff of the University Library put up with my incessant requests and inquiries.

Equally deserving of my gratitude are the many archives and libraries that yielded the materials for this work. I thank the staffs of the following institutions for their help: the National Archives, Kaduna; Arewa House (Centre for Historical Research and Documentation), Kaduna; Northern Nigerian History Research Bureau, Ahmadu Bello University, Zaria; the Norcross Memorial Methodist Mission, Otukpo, Benue State; Rhodes House, Oxford; the British Library Newspaper Archive at Colindale; the School of Oriental and African Studies Library; and the Eleanor and Franklin Roosevelt Institute, Hyde Park, New York.

The book was finished with an International and Area Studies Fellowship sponsored by the American Council of Learned Societies, the Social Science Research Council, and the National Endowment for the Humanities. Their support is greatly appreciated. The board of the Roosevelt Institute was generous in funding a research trip to the institute's archives in August 2001. I also thank the American Historical Association for awarding me a Bernadotte E. Schmitt Grant to support research for this book.

Mamadou Diouf and Frederick Cooper, who guided me through the first life of this book as a PhD dissertation, offered profound, incisive advice throughout the research and writing. Their support and that of David Cohen, Elisha Renne, and Kevin Gaines, all of whom provided invaluable counsel, were crucial to this project.

In the long transition from dissertation to book, Stanford Griffith helped with proofreading and formatting, Sheri Swanson helped with proofreading, and Jeff Deason produced the maps and formatted the final version of the manuscript.

I thank the late Philip Shea, who read several versions of the book, offered expert advice, and remained a key intellectual influence on me till his unfortunate passing in April 2006. His intellectual imprints are discernible throughout this work. I am deeply grateful to Steven Pierce for mentoring me through identifying, researching, and writing on this subject. His intellectual friendship and the social support his family provided kept me grounded and helped sustain me throughout the project.

My colleagues at Vanderbilt University generously read and commented on versions of some of the chapters. Thomas Schwartz and Devin Fergus were especially helpful. Jane Landers was always a pillar of professional support. Other colleagues offered encouraging words.

The academic and social friendship of the following people was vital for the completion of this work: Vukile Khumalo, Ann Rall, Michael Hathaway, Leslie Williams, Lisandro Trevino, Kidada Williams, John Mbugua Gakau, Afshin Jadidnouri, Mawasi Keita Jahi, William Sutton, Ibrahim Hamza Apollo Amoko, Grace Davie, Allison Lichter, Rob Gray, Samuel Temple, Tijana Kristic, and Steve Nwabuzor. Some of them read various chapters and gave me very useful comments; others contributed by making my life as an educational immigrant in the United States easier.

My college classmates and close friends have remained fountains of encouragement and inspiration. Without the support of Abiodun Adamu, Farooq Kperogi, Emmanuel Taegar, Aliyu Ilyasu Ma'aji, John Kolawole, and others, this project would have been harder than it was. Adamu helped me at the early stages of my research, and Kperogi, an astute scholar in his own right, has been a valuable intellectual sparring partner.

I thank my fellow Northern Nigerianists for believing that this book had a contribution to make to the historiography of colonial Northern Nigeria. Thanks to the formal and informal inputs of Mohammed Sani Abdulkadir, Sean Stilwell, Shobana Shankar, Ibrahim Hamza, Susan O'Brien, Rudolf Gaudio, Brian Larkin, Douglas Anthony, and Novian Whitsitt, the book is now a reality.

I thank Julius Scott, who may never know how much of an intellectual influence he has been on me. In the last few years, two senior colleagues, Toyin Falola and Adebayo Oyebade, have become invaluable sources of inspiration. I appreciate their support.

My family provided the single most powerful stimulus for my scholarly pursuit. In particular, I thank my wife, Margaret, and my daughter, Ene, for making the sacrifices necessary for the completion of this book.

Above all, I am grateful to God Almighty for His sustaining grace, mercy, and love. Without Him, nothing is possible.

Crisis, Colonial Failure, and Subaltern Suffering

> No matter where it starts, an economic crisis does not stop at
> the water's edge. It ripples across the world.
>
> —Gordon Brown, prime minister of the United Kingdom
> (speech to joint session of U.S. Congress, March 4, 2009)

IN NOVEMBER 1933, W. R. Crocker, a British colonial district officer, traversed Idoma Division, a remote district of colonial Northern Nigeria, raiding villages and hamlets and confiscating the food, livestock, and property of tax defaulters. As his haul of goats and chickens increased—and the owners did not come forward to redeem them—Crocker wondered what to do with "the livestock that remains on my hands" and the property he would yet confiscate from other villages in default. He could auction it but, as he conceded in a rare moment of colonial frustration, "the people haven't enough currency to pay their tax let alone buy extra goats."[1]

The Idoma soon began a defensive campaign. They hid from the raiding parties in bushes and forests, set booby traps for the tax gatherers, and concealed their livestock. Colonial officials responded with more desperate and severe acts of social punishment, setting residential huts afire and destroying foodstuffs. Crocker's successor, H. P. Elliot, was more emphatic in his own moment of frustration, blaming the Great Depression and its effect on farmers' income for the embarrassing condition of British colonialism in Northern Nigeria.

This vignette portrays a weak, ineffective colonialism, a colonial project temporarily unable to extract profits and surpluses from Northern Nigeria, and which, as a consequence, resorted to financially unrewarding and politically embarrassing confiscation of property at the colonial grass roots. For scholars long used to the image of a powerful, ruthlessly effective colonial system, Northern Nigeria during the Depression decade (1929–39) is a puzzle. It was a weak colonial state that belied the notion of the colonial state as an omnipotent, all-conquering genius of exploitation, a notion that has informed much of

African colonial studies.[2] Exploitation is presented in this dominant narrative as a given, and the possibility of its absence, if only temporary, is discounted.

Economic exploitation presupposes and requires a consistent production of surpluses and profits that can be appropriated without harming the production capacity on which the regime of exploitation itself depends. As Michael Hardt and Antonio Negri argue, imperial conquerors, as producers and exploiters of surplus value, were not interested in eroding the productive capacity or disrupting the social organization of their subjects, since these elements were crucial to colonial capitalist accumulation.[3] It is true that this commitment to the preservation of the existing forces of production and the social cohesion of subject communities was rarely tested during years of economic boom. But, as has been demonstrated with regard to various colonial contexts, colonial intentions and calculations rarely survived the unforeseen turbulence of colonial and world markets and the survival strategies of the colonized. I contend that this colonial economic orthodoxy came under severe strain in times of crisis, when a dearth of surpluses and profits compelled colonial authorities to deplete rural productive capacities and to undermine existing social organizations in the name of generating revenue and maintaining law and order. This is precisely what happened in Northern Nigeria during the Great Depression.

Arguments about colonial intent to remove surpluses while preserving the productive institutions of colonies are founded on the notion that colonizers were efficient capitalists and power wielders, capable of ensuring the uninterrupted production of profits and surpluses. Like Hardt and Negri, several scholars of Africa's colonial history assume that surpluses and profits always existed or that colonial regimes were capable of squeezing out a surplus where none existed.[4] Implicit in this assumption is a notion of colonial power as all-controlling and all-powerful, a view of colonialism that has already been challenged in the political arena.[5] Because of these assumptions about the abilities and linearity of colonial power formations, periods of collapsing produce prices and dwindling profits—like the Great Depression—have not received much attention in the historiography of colonial Africa. Consequently, the important lessons that such periods hold regarding the limits and constraints of imperial power, the inversion of colonial paternalism by Africans, and the sociopolitical implications of imperial economic crisis remain largely overlooked.

The question that seems to drive assumptions about the consistency of colonial economic exploitation is, what happened when Europeans encountered or directed an African economy with profit-producing capacity? Rarely posed but equally important is the question of what happened when colonial powers suddenly found themselves ruling over an African territory with a collapsed export trade and an inability to generate surpluses and profits. In other words, what did colonial authorities do *to* their African colonies when they could no longer—by fiat or suasion—eke out nonexistent export profits? How, in turn, did Africans respond to this momentary absence of colonial exploitation? How did the British seek to manage an economy that could no longer be exploited, and how did Northern Nigerian colonial subjects react to this new regime of colonial economic management?

These are some of the questions that drive this book. Such questions should force us to rethink the possibilities for colonial exploitation across time and space and to more seriously consider the limits of colonial power, the importance of African agency in shaping colonial destinies, and the many unforeseen factors—global and local—that complicated colonial aspirations and goals. I will implicitly argue against the paradigmatic assumption that colonialism was consistently about exploitation and that colonialists were always successful in exploiting their African subjects.

Scholars have sought in other geographic contexts to explain how colonial authorities reacted to economic crises in their domain and what they did *to* colonial subjects in the process of responding to such crises. Catherine Boone contends, for example, that in Senegal the "Depression cast the economic weaknesses of the . . . [state] in sharp relief" and forced French colonial authorities to deepen the implementation of imperial preference, which denied African subjects access to competitive prices for their exports and manufactured imports, causing widespread impoverishment.[6] As the incomes of peasants fell and the prices of imported consumer goods rose in francophone Africa, colonial authorities responded by taxing Africans even more heavily in a classic colonial strategy of economic self-insulation and in the spirit of transferring the burdens of recovery to colonial subjects.[7] In Burundi and the Belgian Congo, colonial authorities' insistence on balancing their beleaguered budgets at the expense of Africans' economic well-being sparked revolt among the peasants of both colonies.[8]

Such strategies of imperial economic self-cushioning at the expense of subjects' welfare and even survival were neither novel nor invented by the guardians of the new empire in Africa. Their dramatic fallouts and the violently instructive local reactions they elicited had precedents in earlier imperial encounters. As Mike Davies informs us,[9] the British in India had, a few decades earlier, perfected the imperial strategy of responding to famines, depressions, and other economic disasters in ways that, while absolving Britain of the financial responsibilities of recovery and relief, exacerbated colonial subjects' suffering while leaving death, disease, and despair in their wake.

Through the prism of a debilitating economic crisis, I shall trace the unpredictable and volatile unraveling of colonial power and claims in Depression-era Northern Nigeria, with particular focus on the consequences of such crisis-driven projects. The Great Depression was one period that highlighted the inability of the British to effectively exploit their African colonial subjects, maintain social order, and preserve the myths of British colonial paternalism. The impacts of this momentary colonial inability to exploit Africans were profound. This decade-long failure to exploit, as well as the responses of Northern Nigerians and British colonialists to the resultant economic shifts, were just as serious and instructive as were the consequences of colonial exploitation in years of economic boom.

This work is set against an academic climate of intense debate over whether or not, or to what degree, colonialism was exploitative—a debate that often revolves around the unspoken issue of how Africans and other colonized peoples fared under European colonialism.[10] It is important to transcend the simplistic premise of these contentions by stressing that British colonialism was just as disruptive to Africans' lives when it failed to exploit them as it was when it did. The temporary absence of exploitation did not mean a temporary absence of African suffering. Both sides in the debate often assume, wrongly, that only colonial exploitation and its coercions caused hardship to Africans and underwrote violent intrusions into their lives—or that subaltern suffering occurred only in the context of exploitation—hence the vigor of the debate over whether or how exploitative colonialism was. This erroneous assumption fails to recognize the range of policies and behaviors that colonial officials brought to bear on Africans because of the absence of profits and surpluses and their effects on local institutions and livelihoods. It also ignores Africans' many strategies of surviving and coping with such novel colonial policies. As I shall demonstrate, the fleeting colonial failure to remove profits from Northern Nigeria authorized policies and practices that caused suffering and dislocation in many communities. The colonial frustration and anxiety arising from the dearth of profit and surplus inspired far-reaching colonial interventions that generated as messy an outcome and had as profound an impact on Africans as did colonial exploitation in economically favorable times.

The story of a colonial failure to exploit is intimately connected to the consequent recourse by colonial authorities to politically risky low-level exactions and ineffective administrative behavior at the colonial grass roots. Rattled by its financial troubles, the Northern Nigerian colonial state insisted on collecting taxes and other fiscal exactions from local economies already stripped of profits and surplus. These exactions produced devastating outcomes for Northern Nigerians. As one reflective British official noted at the height of the Depression, "taxation of non-existing profits is a rank poison."[11] This book is an exploration of the far-reaching political, social, and economic fallouts from these novel colonial responses to economic crisis.

The new British colonial order that the Depression produced in Northern Nigeria was more modest in its claims, rhetoric, and goals. But British colonialism was also made more violent by the collapse of the Northern Nigerian economy and became committed merely to the nurturing of a semblance of British control—to the maintenance of British colonial pride. The economic crisis of the 1930s did two interrelated things. It exacerbated the violence, protectionism, and strategic elimination of Africans' choices often inherent in the British colonial order; and, more interestingly, it focused attention on colonial routines that often went unchallenged and undebated in normal economic times.[12]

Contrary to what some scholars have argued regarding this period in Africa, the contraction of the goals, ambitions, and rhetoric of British colonialism during the economic crisis does not imply an intensifying exploitation.[13] Rather, it illustrates the collapse of preexisting infrastructures of exploitation and the British attempt to adjust accordingly. The commitment of British colonial technocrats to the mere preservation of the British presence did not lead to stagnancy or to a lull in economic and political encounters between Northern Nigerians and the British. As colonial encounters became more volatile and politically charged, Northern Nigerians' practices of self-preservation intensified, further straining colonial power relations. In fact, the British attempt to freeze previously declared colonial ambitions, obligations, and responsibilities pending economic recovery generated local protests, demands, and violent attacks that, together, make the Depression an important period in the history of colonial Northern Nigeria and Africa. The anticolonial expressions of this period, the labor troubles, and the violent confrontations between disgruntled locals and edgy British officials are important backdrops for understanding the origins of the nationalist struggles after World War II.

NORTHERN NIGERIA AND COLONIAL CAPITALISM

The Great Depression of the 1930s was not the first worldwide depression to affect Nigeria. The economic depression of the 1870s ultimately led to the conquest of Northern Nigeria (1900–1907). The downturn cut deeply into European profit in the Niger River trade and heightened competition among European traders. The ensuing rivalry between small and large British firms on the one hand and between British traders and African middlemen and German traders on the other contributed to the conquest of Nigeria. It informed the proactive and perhaps preemptive British effort to "protect" the interest of British traders by buying out non-British European firms and bringing Africans in the Niger area under the jurisdiction of the British crown.[14]

Nonetheless, three key differences mark the way in which the two depressions affected Nigeria. First, the ramifications of the depression of the 1870s were limited to the coastal areas and areas in the hinterland directly connected to coastal trade. The depression of the 1930s and the subsequent reaction of the colonial state affected the entirety of Nigeria, as British rule had already been fully established and consolidated throughout the country. Second, the depression of the 1930s prompted the British to initiate an economic recovery program. The social, political, and economic crises triggered by that program constitutes the central concern of this book. Third, while Nigerians did not participate in the political conversations that preceded and followed the depression of the 1870s, they did join in the robust public debates and discussions of the government's economic recovery policies of the 1930s (see chapter 4). While the British reacted to the depression of the 1870s unilaterally—realigning their interests and involvements on the Niger River to protect their economic foothold—they had to temper their unilateralism in the 1930s with their need for African cooperation and support for a controversial economic recovery program.

With the unilateral British effort to alter the commercial status quo on the Niger came the "pacification" of territories on both sides of the river. But British colonial economic reengineering in Northern Nigeria did not end with the conquest; in many senses the conquest marked the beginning. Under Frederick Lugard, the first British high commissioner of Northern Nigeria, the British venerated the socioeconomic and administrative model of the precolonial Islamic Sokoto Caliphate, especially its elaborate system of taxation and economic regulation and sought to preserve and extend it to other parts of Northern Nigeria. In addition, the British sought to organize, codify, document, and, where necessary, modify the fluid and malleable systems of land tenure, agricultural production, and revenue that existed in the protectorate. These spheres and practices attracted profound British intervention.

The British tried—with little, or at best mixed, success—to create an economic *system* that was discernible, coherent, and codifiable.[15] Lugard sought to create a land tenure system in which ownership was vested in chiefs, a supposed continuity with the precolonial past that would enable an agricultural aristocracy—and agricultural wage labor—to emerge. His successor, Sir Percy Girouard, reversed Lugard's land tenure reform, articulating and codifying a land tenure system vesting control in the state and only supervision in African rulers. This system took hold and engendered the emergence of an export-oriented agricultural peasantry in the former territories of the Sokoto Caliphate.[16]

In the revenue domain, Lugard's Native Revenue Proclamation of 1906, which imposed a variety of taxes and levies by invoking the discourse of continuity with antiquity, helped codify a system of colonial revenue for Northern Nigeria. Subsequent modifications of that system preserved the core principles and types of exaction that inhered in the original legislation.[17] Agricultural production was similarly reengineered where possible. The British Cotton Growers' Association set out to promote cotton cultivation, and the increasing demand for butter substitutes in Europe transformed groundnut cultivation in Northern Nigeria into an export-oriented agricultural system, with the colonial government using a mixture of incentives and coercive measures to promote their cultivation.[18]

Although founded largely on ecological and ethnographic data collected on the Sokoto Caliphate, the British applied these economic reforms to the entire Protectorate of Northern Nigeria, disregarding the history and cultural divergence of the significant population of noncaliphate peoples in the protectorate.[19] The outcomes of the economic reforms differed markedly from district to district, and the degree to which they were implemented varied from province to province. But the British never gave up their effort to create a local agricultural economy suitable for colonial economic objectives.

By the eve of the Great Depression, the peoples of Northern Nigeria had found their place in the British imperial economy—and by extension the world economy. They produced primary products and sold cotton, groundnuts, palm produce, and, to a much smaller extent, beniseed (sesame) to British industries through British merchant firms. Completing the colonial economic configuration of Northern Nigeria, the region emerged in the first decade of the twentieth century as a major producer of tin, a product that, because of its use in the ammunition industry, had been classified by the U.S. Department of State as a strategic product after World War I.

CRISES AND COLONIALISM

The onset of the Depression in Northern Nigeria, as early as December 1929, first manifested in the form of falling export prices for crops and tin, and in declining trade profits and revenues, as British firms either ceased importing European manufactures or sought tax relief. These developments took an immediate toll on the income of Northern Nigeria's peasant cultivators—the majority of the region's population. Declining revenue rattled a colonial state long accustomed to balancing its budget, extracting agricultural raw materials and minerals cheaply and profitably, and accumulating "reserves" in London from the taxes of colonial subjects.

In response to these signs of crisis and to the directives issued from the Colonial Office in London, the Northern Nigerian colonial authorities crafted a broad policy of austerity resting on pay cuts, retrenchments, broadening taxation, an aggressive revenue drive, and the suspension of public works. Other aspects of the economic recovery policy included expansion of export crops, direct money transfers to Britain, and, to a smaller extent, price controls. Lastly, the British vigorously enforced imperial preference, a system of tariffs designed to discourage both the sale of colonial raw materials to non–British Empire buyers and the importation of manufactured goods from outside the empire.

A people's integration into the world market neither sufficiently explains their vulnerability to the vicissitudes of global interconnections of trade and finance nor is it an automatic channel for the distribution of economic crisis. Thus, I will first examine the convoluted ways in which the Depression traveled to Northern Nigeria's peasants and to the colonial financial bureaucracy. I then examine the economic recovery policies put in place by the colonial state, their messy and volatile implementation in colonial urban centers and at the grass roots, their multilayered repercussions, and the reactions of chiefs, workers, peasants, and elites to those policies.

I posit three interconnected theses in this book. First, the Northern Nigerian colonial government's response to the Depression aimed to promote export by incorporating more Africans into the export economy, but it ended up alienating colonial subjects already disillusioned by the instability of that economy, forcing them to seek alternative socioeconomic platforms of survival. Second, my analysis suggests that instead of viewing the Depression (and the interwar period) simply as an era of stagnancy, unbridled exploitation, and colonial inactivity, the volatile colonial encounters of the period should be understood as catalysts for the seminal anticolonial struggles of the Post–World War II era. Third, the events, incidents, and encounters described and analyzed in these chapters point to one inescapable conclusion: in spite of appearances to the contrary, the Northern Nigerian colonial state, like its counterparts in other parts of Africa, was fundamentally weak and its politico-economic sway over Africans tenuous at best. The British resort to familiar-but-heightened and novel forms of coercion to extract revenue and control subjects during a time of economic hardship and uncertainty illustrates this contention about colonial power.

The stories told here advance an understanding of Africa's incorporation into the global economy that takes into consideration the simultaneous manifestation of events and processes that exacerbated and threatened incorporation. Specifically, during the Depression the British colonial authorities implemented a contradictory policy of both incorporation and imperial closures—of colonially mediated globalization and deglobalization. Colonial authorities urged Northern Nigerians to either participate or increase their participation in the world market through export-crop production and by patronizing and complying with colonial economic institutions and obligations. But an aggressive campaign of imperial preference reduced, for instance, the flow of cheap Japanese textiles into the region. As a result, Northern Nigerians had to bypass the colonial state to both insert themselves in desired and beneficial economic processes and remove themselves from state-imposed connections to the global economy. These local strategies of self-preservation entailed a selective participation in both the global trade system and the colonial economic bureaucracies that mediated it.

The incorporation of African peasant producers into the world market has typically been seen as one of the most successful colonial policies, removing millions of Africans from the comfort and stability of subsistent and semi-subsistent production and placing them in the web of an uncertain, volatile, and exploitative world market. This perception has been sustained largely by the discourse of dependency, underdevelopment, and allied concepts, which denote the systematic subjugation of raw-material producers to the forces and vagaries of the world market.[20] Seen within this paradigm, the Depression experience in Africa represents a deepening of the incorporation of African producers into the world market.[21]

These conceptual understandings, whether they are articulated in the form of unequal exchange, structural-Marxist core-periphery inequities, and similar dualisms, ignore the power of actual, on-ground colonial relations and colonial struggles in the making of economic experiences.[22] They also seem to ignore how the incoherence of colonial power and periodic colonial anxieties, as well as the quotidian decisions and actions of colonial personnel and those of African subjects, shaped the ways in which African peasants experienced and engaged with the world economy. Also sidestepped in these notions of structural determinism are the ways in which the proactive and reactive actions of Africans and others located outside the developed world constrained the workings of the world capitalist system.

Although radical historians quibble with neoclassical economic analysts of colonial capitalism about whether colonial policies spread poverty or prosperity in African colonies, the two groups of scholars unwittingly agree on one point. Both are invested in the notion of colonial economic success, the notion that colonial power formations consistently created and removed surpluses and profits from African colonies. They differ only on the question of who benefited from this economic "success." This unlikely consensus assumes a linear trajectory for colonial economic policy implementation and a structural coherence in the formulation and pursuit of colonial economic priorities. More important, it overlooks the creative and disruptive agency of Africans and their strategies of economic self-preservation in the face of colonial economic schemes.

The concept of a subaltern economic and political experience already (and consistently) determined and constrained by the forces of the global and imperial economy ignores the struggle, negotiation, and mobilization that sudden changes in colonial policy often unleashed. Colonial extractive policies during the Depression contracted an economy where the circuits of colonial economic activity were already functioning badly and in which Northern Nigerians were trying to develop alternative strategies of economic survival. Such novel forms of extraction (and the problems that inspired them) did not result mechanically from the relationship of Northern Nigerian agricultural peasants to the world economy. Rather, they emanated largely from on-ground British responses to the crisis as well as from multiple maneuverings and struggles among and between African farmers, trade brokers, laborers, chiefs, and British merchants and officials.

This analysis broadly echoes the works of anthropologists who insist that on-ground colonial encounters, the actions of local peoples, and local institutions could and do remake and complicate the workings and forces of the world economy, and that "the varied responses to the penetration of capitalist institutions of work, consumption, and leisure reveal a variety of strategies not predictable from the imposed system."[23] The story here depicts how colonial politics, local culture, and individual and group choices constrained the Depression experience in Northern Nigeria and produced outcomes that neither Africans nor British colonialists could have predicted.

Another important point along these lines is that a contradictory duality underlay the encounters of British economic recovery agents with Northern Nigerian peasants. While the colonial state, as part of its program of economic recovery, sought to increase the production of agricultural exports by bringing nonexport farmers into the export system (and by extension into the world market), its aggressive implementation of imperial preference took Northern Nigerians out of global economic interactions by circumscribing them in rigged imperial ones. However, this duality cannot simply be explained by an invocation of the concept of colonial exploitation. For what was happening during the Depression was not an expansion of the colonial economy or of African participation in it. Rather, the economy was contracting and many Northern Nigerians rejected its tightening strictures. The agricultural economy of Northern Nigeria underwent a variant of what Clifford Geertz calls "involution"[24] — increasing peasant crop production with extra labor but ultimately harming the value of produce and the capacity to produce. The Northern Nigerian colonial economy decreased in size because it was feeding on its own productive capacity. It was not supporting what would seem on the surface to be an unprecedented level of colonial exploitation.

The concept of colonial exploitation has been a terrain of vigorous debate. It has become a retrospective designation for a range of practices that colonial powers across Africa engaged in. However, such "exploitative" practices were part of missions that were authorized by political doctrines that deny or rationalize exploitation. Most scholars of colonial Africa, especially those who seek to write colonial African history from an African perspective, flatten a variety of ideological and practical colonial projects into the concept of colonial exploitation. To read exploitation backward into the economic policies of colonial states is to sidestep the discursive formations and ideologies of rule that authorized some of these policies. It also refuses to acknowledge the mutual coexistence of what we call exploitation and what colonial powers saw as a civilizing mission.

The term *colonial exploitation* is often deployed as a stand-in for complex social and economic practices and realities of the colonial period. Indeed, even my assertion that exploitation, in its strict definition, was almost impossible in Depression-era Northern Nigeria employs a notion of colonial exploitation that is ahistorical. I use *exploitation* purely as a point of departure, a heuristic device to illustrate how the concept breaks down when juxtaposed with real colonial events. For not only did colonialists not call what they were doing exploitation, the outcomes of "exploitative" policies did not always bear out official economic expectations.

The British concept of the dual mandate of colonialism and the French doctrine of *mise en valeur* encapsulate, however problematically and at least in theory, the colonial disavowal of unbridled exploitation as an overarching strategy of colonial economic management.[25] The British often formulated economic and social policies on the theoretical and rhetorical premise that such policies would advance both the colony and the metropole and that they would improve Africans' standards of living enough to keep them from revolting. The French, as Alice Conklin has argued, went even further in trying to erase the incongruity between French republican ideals and coercive exploitation. Mise en valeur, or rational economic development, represented a French attempt to advance development and social uplift as the foundation of colonial rule in French West Africa.[26] These two colonial doctrines represent an ideological acceptance, however shrewd, of the impracticability of unbridled, unabashed exploitation.

The notion that colonial peoples could and should be rationally ordered toward social improvement, even through coercion and compulsion, never actually departed from the vocabulary of colonial policy, French or British. When the British therefore sought to increase the production of export crops in Northern Nigeria in the midst of the Depression, and engaged in an unprecedented and violent revenue drive, they did so not simply on an extractive premise. Such self-interested colonial exactions also occurred in the context of a protodevelopmentalist conception of colonialism—what Catherine Coquery-Vidrovitch calls "predevelopmentalist colonialism."[27] This precursor to the so-called developmental colonialism of the post-Depression period was, to be sure, accompanied by intrusion, repression, and violence. But it was explained within the imperative of progress, not of exploitation.[28]

The dual mandate of British colonialism was pursued with more theoretical fervor than with practical enthusiasm. Often the British employed dual-mandate rhetoric as a defense against charges of unconscionable exploitation and not as a platform for colonial policy. In fact, at certain junctures colonialism embraced "civilization" and "development" only because the pressures of African activism and demands (see chapter 4) and metropolitan politics required it. Nonetheless, the dual-mandate philosophy of British colonial rule cleared a limited space theoretically for African participation in the advertised benefits of the colonial project. The dual-mandate consensus of the pre-Depression era also recognized that, although permissible, excessive coercion and violence had an endpoint after which it was counterproductive. The unprecedented use of violence to pursue colonial economic recovery aims during the Depression must therefore be understood as a desperate departure from the norm. Of course, the dual-mandate rhetoric rarely interfaced with policy and practices on the ground, but it meant that crude plunder was rarely permitted. What happened before the Depression was therefore not the unbridled exploitation and plunder advanced in orthodox African colonial history but a necessarily limited effort by Britain to appropriate surplus produce and profits from Northern Nigeria in a period when both expanded.

This basic point about pre-Depression limitations of colonial exploitation makes the argument that the Depression caused a temporary break in the ability of the British to exploit the resources and profits of Northern Nigeria's export agriculture easier to comprehend. The failure to exploit was a shift rather than a rupture. Moreover—and this is the overarching point here—exploitation as an all-explaining concept occludes the effects of colonial "exploitative" schemes on average Africans at the colonial grass roots, for it almost forecloses discussion on the microlevel of African engagements with colonial policy. These grassroots receptions of colonial policy are much more important and productive to investigate than the restrictive and reductive concept of exploitation. The Depression marked an important period in African colonial history, not so much for how or whether colonial responses to it led to the exploitation of already impoverished Africans as for its diverse socioeconomic implications for different segments of the African population. As a consequence, the crisis produced diverse responses and engagements from Africans. These differences in predicaments and responses reveal infinitely more interesting insights than does the blanket question of whether—or how much—exploitation accompanied the government's economic recovery policy.

To problematize and historicize colonial exploitation is not to deny its analytical utility. But by unpacking the concept and pointing to its recent origin in discourses of colonial critique and anticolonial struggles, one gets a better sense of its temporal and spatial limitations. Such a reflection also helps illustrate the fact that a colonial economic project already circumscribed by pragmatic concessions to Africans (and by colonial doctrine) could not have become more exploitative during the economic crisis of the 1930s. The cessation of public works and of socially beneficial projects by the

Northern Nigerian colonial government—despite growing local clamor for these colonial benefits (chapter 4)—does not indicate an intensifying colonial exploitation. Neither does the collapse of the colonial educational project in Idoma Division (chapter 5). The colonial state cited a lack of funds as the reason for these retreats from the dual mandate of exploitation and development. To the extent that pre-Depression colonial social projects—limited as they were—operated with the surpluses and revenue extracted from local peasants, the dwindling of these social projects during the economic crisis indicates that surpluses, profits, and revenue extracted by the state contracted rather than increased. The dual-mandate principle rested on the rationale that beneficial social projects would offset or mitigate the pains of colonial exploitation on the minds and bodies of Africans. The relative absence of profits and surpluses to exploit during the Depression removed the need for the second, constructive part of the dual mandate—the need to fund schools and build social infrastructure like roads, bridges, clinics, and dispensaries. A nuanced understanding of the limits and problems of colonial exploitation recognizes the effort of Africans who, as groups or individuals, complicated and sometimes defeated the envisaged outcomes of colonial economic policies.

The diverse engagements of Africans with the self-cushioning economic strategies of colonial authorities during the Depression and the combustive interaction of Africans' strategies of self-preservation with European colonial recovery schemes contradict the dominant scholarly representation of the 1930s and by extension the interwar period in African history. A number of Africanist economic and social historians have posited that the Depression decade represents a "lost period" marked by an unremarkable stagnancy and unprecedented exploitation of African resources.[29] It is further argued that retrenchments and pay cuts as well as the availability of surplus labor led to a decline in African laborers' bargaining power and permitted various forms of worker abuse and exploitation during and after the economic crisis.[30] The Depression years have, therefore, been rightly described as the worst years for African colonial workers.

One could untangle the fates of various social segments of the African population under the Depression and make accurate observations about how they fared under the colonial state's economic recovery policies. But Africanist historians have often shunned such a fine-grained analysis in favor of a holistic representation of the Depression years as a period when nothing happened—a period to be skipped in the chronology of African colonial history in order to get to the more interesting and consequential period of World War II and beyond. This historiographical orthodoxy has colored the way that African colonial history is taught in African and Western colleges and graduate schools.

Arguing against the unprecedented exploitation paradigm, the narratives and analyses presented here shift the focus from absence to presence. The absence of colonial projects and the scaling back of colonial infrastructural ambitions did not lead to a lull in the colonial encounter between Africans and the British in Northern Nigeria. On the contrary, it opened the way for important struggles and encounters that made colonial power somewhat more pervasive and intrusive, not less. The Depression was a tumultuous period characterized by monumental struggles, tensions, labor troubles, and multiple maneuverings that collectively transformed British colonialism in Northern Nigeria, Britain's most populous and elaborately governed colony in Africa. Therefore, to understand the succeeding periods of African history—World War II and the postwar period—one must understand what happened in colonial Africa in the 1930s.

The 1930s also represent a pivotal moment for understanding the nature and operations of the African colonial state. Scholars of state power in Africa have provided invaluable insights into the evolution and unraveling of power formations across Africa. Mahmood Mamdani and Achille Mbembe have offered illuminating documentary excursions into the patterns and constants of colonial power and its operation in Africa.[31] The economic turmoil of the 1930s and the additional anxieties of control and extraction that it placed on Northern Nigerian colonial authorities led to a stripping away of some of the civil pretensions of colonial power. British colonialism in Northern Nigeria became even more colonial, and indirect rule—the British policy of ruling Africans through their own institutions and symbols of authority—more direct and coercive. The emergence of a more direct and coercive form of indirect rule during the economic crisis—the baring of the fangs of colonial power—had far-reaching consequences for African colonial subjects at the colonial grass roots in Northern Nigeria.

The stories in chapters 3, 5, and 6 bring these fallouts of the Depression into sharp relief. At an epistemological level, the analysis of the reemergence and legacies of coercive colonialism reinforces Mamdani's and Mbembe's postulations about the ambitions and illusions of ubiquity that colonial power formations often harbored. It also demonstrates the shifting contours of colonial power ambitions and control mechanisms and how those shifts tended to correspond to crisis and fractures in the colonial system as well as to the degree of discontent and strain in grassroots colonial power relations.

The stories in these chapters demonstrate the weak and tenuous condition of colonial state power. An understanding of this fundamental colonial ineptitude allows us to view the weaknesses and failures of the contemporary African state as a product of economic and relational dynamics and not of a radical break with a supposedly strong and coherent state structure inherited from colonialism. This understanding should also complicate the view that colonial states were focused, determined, and powerful, and that those qualities enabled them to be consistently successful in achieving colonial economic objectives. Both neoclassical and dependency theorists of African colonial economics subscribe to this flawed notion of colonial power.

Postcolonial African states inherited some of the fundamental failures and weaknesses of the colonial state, especially in the area of mismanaging Africans' economic expectations, anxieties, and aspirations. Many African states portray a picture of stability while the predatory appropriation of revenue and surpluses remains undisturbed, only to be unsettled and exposed by economic crisis. As in colonial times, it sometimes takes economic and social crisis to highlight the tenuousness of the state's power. Like colonial regimes, postcolonial African states are often unaccustomed to dwindling revenue and incomes and the resultant discontent, demands, criticisms, and disappointment of citizens. With the illusion of paternal omnipotence discredited by deteriorating economic conditions and growing citizen unrest, many postcolonial African states have resorted, like their colonial predecessors, to more exactions, brutality, and crudely direct forms of exercising power and engineering consent among the populace.

THE STORY IN BRIEF

The vigorous enforcement of imperial preference curtailed the economic choices of Northern Nigerians and hampered Northern Nigeria's economic recovery by restricting the sale of the region's most lucrative export, tin, to British and British Empire buyers. However, protectionism as a mechanism of economic recovery was counterproductive in a contracting productive space with little or no economic incentive. It reflected more the economic anxieties of the state than it did an economically sound commitment to recovery. Protectionism failed to cure the problem of collapsing prices and contracting trade. Other elements of the colonial state's economic recovery policy also provoked reactions and engagements that were both unexpected and harmful to British interests. The self-cushioning actions of Northern Nigerians contributed substantially to these complicated outcomes.

In theory, economic recovery measures were designed to cushion the colonial state and to enable it to support recovery in Britain. Those measures, however, produced their own set of dilemmas. Those dilemmas required careful handling as they threatened the viability of British rule. Pay cuts, when applied to chiefs, curtailed their commitment to vigorous collection of taxes and proved to be an incentive for extralegal exactions and extortion (chapter 2). Those extortions eroded the legitimacy of chiefs and undermined indirect rule. British officials disciplined and removed chiefs who sought to make up for the pay cuts by extorting money from their subjects, further damaging British authority, destroying the relative harmony between superintending British officials and African rulers, and heightening local resentment of British rule. Chiefs who were seen by their subjects to be working too hard to help the colonial state collect revenue became the targets of local wrath.

While helping in the transfer of some wealth to Britain, aggressive revenue drives at the grass roots caused food shortages and full-scale famines in several districts, the fallouts of which hardly seemed worth the meager rewards of such invasive revenue expeditions. Famines devastated whole villages as the agents of an avowedly bankrupt state watched helplessly. This colonial paralysis in the face of local suffering called into question in Africans' minds the paternalism at the heart of the dual-mandate ideology of British rule. As tax raids became more sustained and more uncompromising, in tandem with deepening state fiscal anxieties, they inevitably eroded the productive base of local agriculture in several Northern Nigerian provinces, leading to several violent antitax revolts that targeted local chiefs, scribes, and other local agents of the state's economic recovery efforts. These uprisings undermined what the British had always taken for granted: the loyalty of subjects and the legitimacy of chiefs.

Retrenchments similarly had a multipronged unintended consequence. Retrenched workers congregated on tin mine compounds on the Jos Plateau and on the railway, engaging in a wide array of criminal and subversive activities, including the sale of children, child labor trafficking, and the stealing and vengeful sabotaging of railway track components. These disgruntled colonial subjects also helped spread practices that bordered on "criminal self-help," such as currency counterfeiting and uttering. More important, some retrenched workers began to radicalize workers retained on the mines and on the railway, initiating, for the first time in Northern Nigeria, labor organizing and strikes and heightening the volatility of the economic situation in the region. Many retrenched workers returned to their villages of origin with no money or economic hope, straining food resources and family finances. No longer accustomed to farming, many of them became a burden to wives, mothers, and other female relatives who had become both breadwinners and tax payers. Women's expanding role in the management of household economies underscored the precarious position of males in the Depression-era economy. As some of the retrenched men began to migrate to Lagos and other commercial centers in search of paid employment, they relied on female relatives for initial sponsorship money and for the maintenance of the household in their absence. Women also had to increasingly engage with ruthless colonial tax gatherers, devising and perfecting strategies of child concealment, among other trickeries, to reduce household tax obligations. What seemed like a period of unintended empowerment for women in fact produced novel burdens for them. The social crises caused by these local reactions to retrenchment—and the time, money, and material devoted by the British to fighting these local acts of defiance—outweighed the fiscal benefits of retrenchments and increased exaction.

Economic hardship made Northern Nigerians innovative as retrenched workers sought economic reprieve in gold prospecting. Similarly, farmers took steps to wean themselves from dependence on the world market by cultivating more food crops. The state encouraged these innovations, touting traditional self-help, communal support, individual resourcefulness, and the exploration of latent resources as bulwarks against destitution and as a stand-in for a hoped-for—and costly—governmental welfare intervention. While these innovative strategies of economic self-preservation on the part of some Northern Nigerians, and the state's support for them, succeeded in boosting the economic hopes of these groups of colonial subjects, the increasing refusal by new gold-prospecting entrepreneurs and innovative farmers to let the state regulate, monitor, and tax their activities further heightened tensions in colonial power relations. In the end, the state's support for African innovation and self-help, while fiscally wise, essentially undermined British power. It inadvertently encouraged Northern Nigerians to wean themselves off state control and to escape the formal economy and the fiscal nodes through which the state sustained and replenished itself.

Women weavers led one of the most significant innovative enterprises in response to the economic crisis. Historically dominated by women, the Kabba and Okene cloth industries had always maintained a small market for itself in the face of cheap European and Japanese textile imports. The persistence of ceremonies, rituals, and other performances requiring the wearing of local cloth kept the women weavers of the Okene-Kabba axis employed. During the economic crisis, the prices of imported textiles increased, remained at their pre-Depression levels, or decreased by only a slight percentage not commensurate with the sharp drop in local incomes. As this disparity registered with Northern Nigerians, and as colonial officials enforced a ban on the importation of cheap Japanese textiles as part of the policy of imperial preference, Northern Nigerian consumers turned increasingly to Kabba and Okene cloth for their clothing needs. The women cloth makers expanded production to satisfy this demand, and new female entrepreneurs rose to take advantage of this new economic reality. Throughout the 1930s, the Kabba and Okene cloth industries experienced steady growth, with colonial officials urging more expansion and commercialization in the hope that it would ease the financial anxieties of locals, whose purchasing power had been diminished by the pervasive cash crunch. Although such hopes never fully materialized, the growth experienced in the sector and the wealth accumulated by women textile makers in a period of acute financial crisis inaugurated a new, if fleeting, psychology of female economic empowerment.

The reactions of different groups of Northern Nigerians confounded the simplistic economic assumptions of anxious British officials, as locals increasingly focused on the quotidian dimensions of the economic crisis in disregard of the grandiose imperial economic projections of British colonial crisis managers. Members of Northern Nigeria's embryonic elite—many of them retrenched from their positions in the colonial civil service and from British mercantile companies—responded to their plummeting personal finances and loss of patronage and privileges by turning against the colonial system. They articulated a strident anticolonial and nationalist rhetoric through newly established anticolonial newspapers and petition writing.

In Northern Nigeria's best-known colonial backwater, Idoma Division, where the institutions of colonial economics—currency, export-crop production, taxation, and trade—were tenuous at best at the onset of the Depression, the implementation of the state's economic recovery policy was particularly fraught with crisis and mutual recrimination between colonizers and the colonized. As the British moved away from an expensive project of preparing the "backward" Idoma for indirect rule through missionary education, the Idoma, to the dismay of colonial administrators, demanded schools and more government investment in Western education as a pathway to economic stability. Unable to squeeze cash out of Northern Nigeria's economically least viable and most depressed zones, colonial authorities raided villages for goats, chickens, grain, and any other items of stored wealth they could find. The raids devastated the Idoma countryside, causing social dislocation and demographic chaos. But the raids also helped the Idoma to perfect their skills of escaping colonial control and exaction. To resist and reject these invasive economic harassments, the Idoma hid themselves, their chickens, goats, and other valuables in Idoma Division's thick forests, away from raiding parties. They also began to aggressively disobey colonial directives and to reject the institution of colonial taxation as a whole.

The choice of Idoma Division as a case study reflects the need to extend the analysis beyond the Muslim provinces and divisions—the most visible targets of British economic and political policy. The discussion of the Idoma experience of the Depression illustrates the effects of the state's economic recovery policy on a colonial administrative unit largely neglected in previous colonial schemes because of what officials saw as the extreme backwardness and insularity of its people. The people of the division had, before the Depression, neither fully adopted the British currency nor joined the export-oriented agricultural economy of Northern Nigeria. Because of that prior British attitude toward the division, the Idoma area provides a site for a particularly intriguing Depression experience.[32] The Depression-induced attempt to integrate the division into the revenue generation schemes of the Depression produced instructive encounters and lessons in colonial power relations.

The conjuncture of global economic and political forces, imperial decisions, regional colonial peculiarities, and local colonial encounters presents major structural and analytical challenges for a work like this. It is difficult to bring together and sustain within the same analytic frame the global, imperial, regional, and local forces and events that shaped the Northern Nigerian Depression experience, given that these various elements were always in conversation and in creative tension with one another throughout the Depression. But I have sustained this vertical alchemy of forces in my analyses.

This important analytical choice helps capture the several levels on which the economic crisis manifested, as well as its messy and convoluted trajectory. These geographically disparate forces of global, national, regional, and local socioeconomic and political dynamics appear through all the chapters to demonstrate how they reacted with one another in shaping Northern Nigerians' experiences of the Depression. The crisis did not trickle down in a linear trajectory from the centers of the world economy to Northern Nigeria and its various districts. Rather, it is my contention that because of the incoherence and inconsistencies in British colonialism, and in the face of local maneuvering and strategies of survival, the effects of the Depression and of imperial economic recovery schemes were a lot more incoherent, convoluted, and a lot less predictable than officials at the imperial metropole might have hoped.

Similarly, the Depression experience in remote districts of Northern Nigeria and the implementation of the economic recovery program of the government in those districts did not always conform to the economic and political calculations of regional colonial authorities in Kaduna. This differential manifestation of the crisis originated with the economic, ecological, and cultural realities in each district. It was also a backlash against the homogenizing idealism of British economic recovery polices and the ignorance and arrogance of petty British grassroots officials.

Idoma Division represents a key illustration of the grassroots backlash. The division did not conform to the dominant export-oriented colonial agricultural economy of Northern Nigeria. The cultivation of food crops was the mainstay of the Idoma economy. The division was indirectly and tenuously connected to the regional, imperial, and global economies—through intermittent food and labor export to the Jos tin mines. At the inception of colonial rule in the division in the 1910s, the British undertook a campaign to bring the division within the economic and administrative mainstream of Northern Nigeria. They even imported a class of Hausa Muslim political and economic colonials to help spread the colonial message of trade, export-crop production, and indirect rule among the Idoma. When all these efforts failed to transform the production, exchange, and leadership configurations in Idoma Division, the British retreated into a rhetoric and practice of regarding the division and other non-Muslim administrative units of Northern Nigeria as a periphery of the "core" North—a domain to be left to the devices of weak local rulers and unfortunate British officers. This disengagement however included a determined program of cultural uplift conceived through a colonial missionary desire to educate as many Idoma as possible.

During the Depression both the policy of constructing Idoma Division as an economic and political periphery and that of culturally civilizing the Idoma people through colonial missionary education came back to haunt the British. The move complicated the implementation of the state's economic recovery program and caused unprecedented friction in colonial power relations, constraining the Idoma experience of the Depression. This became painfully obvious as the British sought to rediscover the economic utility of Idoma Division as a revenue-yielding domain, while applying the full force of colonial austerity to the division.

The fall in produce prices and the government's rather novel revenue campaign dramatically, if not uniquely, affected Idoma Division. In the ensuing engagement with the state's economic recovery actions, some segments of the Idoma sought to make sense of the economic difficulties and to weather them by reinventing the concepts of settler and stranger. These restructured concepts acquired valences that enabled them to function more and more as tropes of economic, political, and ethnic exclusion. The Idoma blamed the fall in produce prices and the resulting hardship on the involvement of non-Idoma "settlers" and "strangers" in local agriculture, substituting this local explanation for the globality of the economic crisis. The reinvention of these categories during the Depression has continued to have implications for interethnic relations in Northern Nigeria's Middle Belt. More important, it illustrates the ways in which a global economic crisis informed local dynamics that in turn fed on preexisting social and economic tensions and ultimately but inadvertently helped to discursively decouple the global and the local.

These remote consequences of the Depression illustrate the uncertain trajectory of economic and political crisis. The economic disaster of the Depression in Northern Nigeria could not have been discerned or predicted from its manifestation at the colonial metropole. Its socioeconomic implications for Northern Nigeria and for the colonial experiences of Northern Nigerians were shaped by colonial economic recovery policies and by vigorous local reactions to them.

Local reactions to the government's economic recovery measures did not break down neatly along gender, ethnic, and class lines, although differing fortunes dictated somewhat different coping strategies. But the Depression brought women into the forefront of colonial engagements. Before the crisis, the British and their African auxiliaries had dealt with women through a Victorian prism—as entities incidental to colonial economic and political calculations and schemes. The Depression changed that perception temporarily in the non-Muslim zones of Northern Nigeria, where women historically took on more central roles in the household than in the Muslim zones. As males were displaced by economic turmoil or chose migration and transience over the harassment of tax collectors, colonial officials increasingly had to deal with women—wives, sisters, mothers, grandmothers—who became, for a moment, household heads and breadwinners. For instance, tax collectors increasingly had to deal with women's inventive effort to reduce tax obligations through the strategy of child concealment, which reduced a household's assessed tax.

This is only one example of the way in which, once economic crisis travels, it sets off struggles that play out dramatically in the context of preexisting relational, political, and economic dynamics. At the heart of the Northern Nigerian Depression experience lay tensions, fissures, and assumptions of colonial and household relations preordained by colonial priorities and ideologies of rule. Northern Nigeria's experience in the Depression is, in the final analysis, a crisis of colonialism and of the difficulty of maintaining colonial control in the face of crisis and translating colonial paternal idioms into workable policies at the colonial grass roots.

A NOTE ON METHODOLOGY AND GENDER

Much of this book is written from a close textual reading of a variety of colonial documents, Nigerian newspaper articles, petitions to colonial authorities, and oral interviews. At the onset of my research, I set out to produce a significantly oral-historical work. My preliminary inquiries convinced me that that was practically impossible. In the research field I found that remembrances and memories of the Depression were scattered, chronologically unreliable, and too general to be used specifically to recover the suffering and encounters of the 1930s. As a result of low life expectancy in Nigeria, poor health, and illiteracy, I had little success in locating Northern Nigerians old enough to remember or who kept mental notes of the specific events and problems of the Depression.

The preponderance of written sources in this book is a product of this early methodological disillusionment. I made a choice after my pilot research. Instead of writing an oral history of the Depression, I would make up for the dearth of useful African memories of the Depression by using as many colonially generated and African-generated written sources as possible and incorporating oral testimonies where and when they were available. The preeminence of written sources in this book is therefore a methodological necessity. I have, as much as possible, made up for the sporadic presence in this work of unmediated African voices with a determinedly critical reading of colonial documents, as well as a consistent attention to contradictions within and between these documents. I have teased out substantive dissonances between colonial rhetoric and policies and the on-ground grassroots encounters and intrusions into Africans' lives that they authorized. I also probed the policy idioms, propaganda, and the claims of Northern Nigerian colonial authorities on the economic crisis vis-à-vis their interventions in Africans' lives and Africans' strategies of evasion and self-preservation. The use of the ultrasecret colonial intelligence reports, in particular, helped me access self-indicting colonial admissions outside the official, publicly communicated rhetoric. These reports provided an unvarnished representation of African suffering and colonial exaction.

My main focus in all this effort is to provide a context for a central thrust of the book: the strategies of survival, resistance, and self-interested engagement devised by Northern Nigerians during the crisis. But it was difficult to fully capture the peculiar experiences of Northern Nigeria's different demographic groups in the economic crisis. While I covered the experiences of chiefs, laborers, farmers, colonial auxiliaries, and the unemployed to the extent allowed by the specificity and experiential differentiation in the sources, in many cases the sources did not mention women. This presented a methodological and interpretive problem. In my analyses of women's experiences and encounters during the crisis, I therefore resorted to recovering their struggles and strategies of coping by deduction and inference. Because colonial authorities dealt mostly with men, the colonial archive mostly reflects that gender bias, obscuring the role of women in stabilizing the household, in sponsoring husbands migrating to earn cash, and in creatively protecting what was left of family wealth from the predation of colonial revenue hunters. I based my analyses of women's experiences in these events as much on a reading of silences in the archive as on a vigorous extrapolation of presences. Only in one instance—the economic empowerment of female textile entrepreneurs in the Okene-Kabba axis—did a fortuitous convergence of direct oral testimony and colonial sources enable me to make a definitive, evidence-based analytical statement about the experiences of Northern Nigerian women in the Depression.

I intend these methodological disclosures and disclaimers not just as a guide but as an explanation of the methodological and analytical choices that underpin this book. They should also broach the methodological dilemma that continues to face Africanist social historians, who, on the one hand, value direct African voices and consider them integral to social historical reconstruction but, on the other, must be pragmatic enough to accept the chronological limitations of accessing such voices for distant colonial events and periods. Social historians also have to reconcile themselves to the fact that the sociopolitical strictures of colonialism mediated, constrained, and still constrain many African voices. Finally, their quest for African voices, for the early and mid-colonial periods especially, is often undermined by the political economy of memory recovery, which in Africa is often determined by issues of health, poverty, life expectancy, and illiteracy. Readers will notice that I wrestled, at several junctures, with these tensions and problems.

ORGANIZATION OF THE BOOK

Each of the six chapters deals with a separate issue or set of issues relating to the Depression experience in Northern Nigeria, although themes and arguments overlap considerably among them.

Chapter 1 analyzes the vehicles through which the Depression traveled to Nigeria, the crafting and initial implementation of a national colonial economic recovery policy aimed at cushioning a fiscally challenged state, and the early African receptions of these policies. It argues that the economic anxieties of Nigerians were incidental to the economic recovery schemes and that as Nigerians groaned and complained under the weight of the new policies, official discourse justified them with the rhetoric of African traditional self-help and nativist communalism. Chapter 2 details the implementation, contradictions, and consequences—intended and unintended—of the state's economic recovery program in Northern Nigeria. It argues that the aggressive enforcement of revenue generation—a cardinal plank of the recovery measures—was ultimately self-defeating, as it undermined indirect rule by eroding the legitimacy of chiefs and their ability to persuade their subjects to pay taxes and levies.

Chapter 3 deals with two issues in the Depression experience in Northern Nigeria. I first examine the phenomenal rise in crime in the 1930s, which was linked to the policy of retrenchment and pay cuts adopted by the colonial government and British firms. I argue that the crime wave, the rise in vagrancy and militancy on the railway, and the escalation of currency counterfeiting created new social challenges for the state and are a window into the widespread adoption of criminal self-help, subtle subversion, and labor agitation as strategies of self-preservation. Second, I consider the range of creative economic responses and innovations that Northern Nigerian women and men devised to cope with the Depression, arguing that these strategies served both to create islands of wealth creation and to wean their proponents from the formal colonial economy.

Chapter 4 analyzes the rhetorical strategies adopted by the emerging Northern Nigerian elite to criticize the colonial state's economic recovery policy, highlight its unsavory consequences for Northern Nigerian colonial subjects, and decry what it saw as the state's neglect of its social obligations to an impoverished and suffering people. I contend that in articulating a strident anticolonial critique founded on the hardships brought on by the Depression and the government's responses to it, members of the Northern Nigerian elite were driven as much by their own anxieties about the momentary cessation of colonial exploitation (which paradoxically provided them jobs and patronage in pre-Depression times) as by the imperative of indicting the economic failures of the state.

Chapter 5 examines the Depression experience in Idoma Division. I argue that the incongruence between colonial efforts to reorganize Idoma Division in the interest of revenue generation and a strategic colonial disavowal of earlier obligations and promises drew a backlash as the Idoma demanded roads, bridges and, more importantly, colonial missionary schools that they thought would give Idoma men and women a path to a more stable economic existence. I also argue that the Idoma took their own economic recovery into their own hands, migrating to the relatively solvent cocoa-producing regions of Western Nigeria to earn cash, a migratory flow which ultimately spurred the development of wage labor in Idoma Division.

In chapter 6, I analyze the violent encounters between the Idoma and the British as the latter pursued revenue generation through tax raids in the Idoma countryside. Particularly, I examine the use of tax raids and property confiscations by petty colonial officials to exact revenue. I argue that the sheer unfamiliarity of the tax raids unsettled the social fabric of the Idoma countryside, engendering fear but also eliciting crafty strategies of escape and concealment that frustrated the revenue expeditions. Rather than bring the Idoma into the vortex of colonial revenue generation, the tax raids antagonized and alienated them further from the institutions of colonial control, underlining, once again, the paradoxical fundamental weakness of a desperate, violent, and invasive colonialism in a period of hardship.

1 ↷ From Empire to Colony
The Great Depression and Nigeria

AT THE ONSET of the Depression, British economic recovery policy in Nigeria focused on the strict implementation of austerity measures approved by the Colonial Office in London, whose prescriptions, in turn, were inspired by the economic recovery consensus in Britain. But as my analysis will demonstrate, the economic recovery plan of the Nigerian colonial state existed merely to maintain a semblance of economic and sociopolitical stability. Already in financial crisis, with dwindling trade surpluses and profits, the state found its ambition to remove surpluses and resources from Nigeria in peril. Colonial exploitation was thus a foreclosed proposition, and the state became preoccupied with less ambitious but equally disruptive alternatives.

By enforcing the policy of imperial preference vigorously, the state curtailed Nigerians' buying choices and made sure that their purchases benefited Britain. It cut the pay of African colonial auxiliaries and collected income taxes with a new enthusiasm. It retrenched many Nigerian colonial auxiliaries, worsening an already bad unemployment problem. To boost revenue and the state's capacity to lubricate its administrative machinery, colonial officials intervened robustly in the domain of export agriculture.

These actions resulted from the colonial state's own financial anxieties, and officials saw Nigerians' economic interests and suffering as merely incidental to the state's. This was not exploitation at work, but a desperate, cynical colonialism committed, temporarily, to self-preservation for its own sake. These economic recovery measures intensified Nigerians' suffering and economic insecurities, to be sure, but their victimhood remained incidental to state recovery efforts. More important, the unsavory effects of these efforts masked the state's own economic insecurities, which threatened to expose and undermine

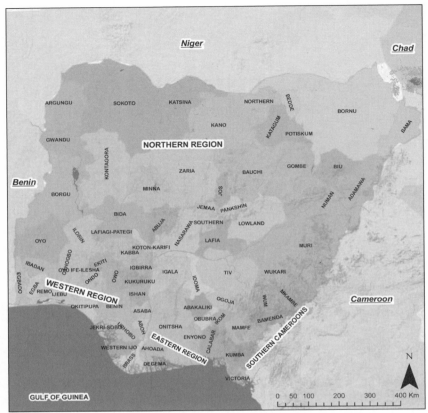

Colonial Nigeria

British colonialism's paternalistic machismo. The pursuit of economic recovery carried the theoretical possibility of propping up state finances, thus helping officials maintain an illusion of administrative stability and political control. But it also carried the risk of exposing the state to Nigerians' anger, frustration, and distrust. Furthermore, it intensified a fundamental, preexisting weakness of the state: precarious political control.

BRITAIN, DEPRESSION, AND EMPIRE

The Great Depression was marked in Great Britain by acute unemployment, an unusual decline in exports, and a drastic reduction in the volume of new investments. By September 1931 the problem of the overvaluation of the pound in world markets had become obvious, taking a toll on British industries. Britain departed from the gold standard in the same month, reverting to a free-floating exchange rate, which, while good for export-oriented industry, opened the way for a currency crisis, panic, and an aggressive quest for precious metal that would engulf Britain and the empire.

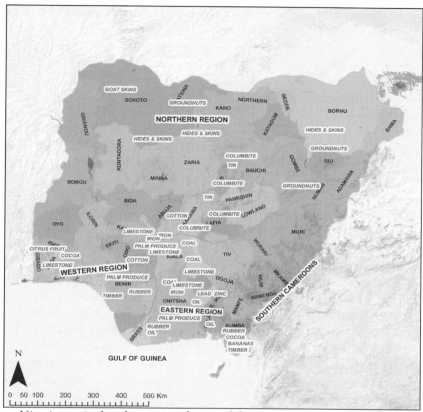

Nigerian agricultural exports and mineral deposits

A long history of recessions helped shape Great Britain's experience of, and reaction to, economic downturns, leaving it remarkably sensitive to sudden economic changes. The Depression inaugurated a new period of economic nationalism in Britain. That nationalism was, however contradictorily, bound up with a novel economic solidarity that operated along the lines of empire. In 1929 local desperation for recovery led to institutionalized mechanisms for survival and inspired a heightened consciousness about the economic importance of empire and of shared imperial economic fates. The economic recovery measures that emerged in Britain maintained this new idea of empire, emphasizing empire as a safety cushion during hard times, a domain to be isolated from global economic competition in the interest of Britain.

From the late 1870s Britain went in and out of recession, and the cycle of boom and bust began to register on the national consciousness.[1] The depression of 1921 to 1923 firmly entrenched what some would call a depression mentality in state officials and gave authority to policies bordering on economic protectionism and solidarity of the empire. During the early 1930s this British preoccupation with economic crisis led a minority of mostly non-British commentators to wonder, somewhat cynically, if Britain was not "generically in a Depression" or at least getting what it had always planned for.[2] Most Britons adjudged the preemptive and reactive economic policies justifiable by the seemingly unique economic vulnerability of their country. Within Britain any efforts calculated to bring succor to British citizens during the Depression met with an overall favorable reception. The consensus in Britain favored both familiar and novel ways of managing economic crisis. In this atmosphere of heightened economic desperation, imperial solidarity and colonial outposts became fulcrums of economic recovery.

IMPERIAL SOLIDARITY TO THE RESCUE

British economic recovery measures focused largely on imperial solidarity. A shift toward protectionism and economic territorialism enabled and sustained the decisive shift toward an empire-based economic recovery. Globally, economic territorialism had become an acceptable, if problematic, way of responding to the Depression. In the words of Arthur Schlesinger, "Every country tried to seal itself, tried to contain the economic consequences of Depression, tried to prevent other countries from exporting their own troubles."[3] As Britain struggled to incorporate the empire into its domestic efforts to mitigate the economic damage of the prevailing hardship, the emerging trend toward economic isolationism compelled it to further rally the empire around a common principle of economic solidarity. Germany, France, Austria, Italy, Japan, and other Western economies crafted nationalistic responses to the Smoot-Hawley Tariff of 1930, which closed American markets to foreign goods. The ensuing tariff war merely aggravated the Depression. Britain's acutely protectionist response reflected the contours of empire. Its empire-based economic recovery measures included retaliation against the Americans and a desire to inoculate itself against the perceived disruptive effects of free trade. Britain's rather unique position as the guardian of a large empire, which had long functioned, however loosely, as an economic unit, shaped this new policy of protectionism.

Few British voices condemned protectionism altogether, and fewer still berated the creation of a protected empire market as a bulwark against the vicissitudes of global markets.[4] For the most part, the British public remained agreeable to all measures deemed necessary to protect them from the Depression, including those that promoted economic recovery through the sacrifices of people in the British Empire. Protectionism gradually became a tolerated item on the economic emergency menu—not as an accepted economic virtue but as a cushion against the unsavory outcomes of global market turbulence. From this consensus of imperial economic solidarity emerged lobbies and pressure groups to champion the concept of imperial sacrifice in Britain.[5] After the second imperial economic conference in Ottawa, Canada, in 1932, Britain and the empire formally entered into a period of economic cooperation that would last through the Depression. The groups that lobbied for the conference remained active and constantly defended the principles behind the Ottawa tariff agreements. These agreements all but closed the empire to nonempire goods, while promoting exports and imports, even at uncompetitive prices, between empire countries. Some groups even called for "a common monetary policy throughout the empire."[6] The doctrine of "recovery through empire,"[7] which was popular in the economically desperate period after World War I, enjoyed a renaissance during the Depression as a slogan that encapsulated Britain's focus on economic recovery.

The Ottawa agreements, which formalized British commitment to imperial preference as a tool of economic recovery, understandably led to a trade war between the United States and Britain. The former needed the raw materials of the British Empire; but under the terms of Ottawa it would have to contend with prohibitive tariffs. Short of smuggling, the United States could no longer import mineral raw materials directly from British Empire countries. This had serious implications for Nigeria and Britain, especially because the U.S. War Department had classified tin as a strategic commodity after World War I. Ninety-five percent of the world's tin was produced in the British Empire—Northern Nigeria, Malaya, and the British East Indies. British tin-mining companies had benefited enormously from U.S. patronage before Ottawa. The terms of the Ottawa agreements changed that transaction to the disadvantage of the United States.

Imperial-preference tariffs and the effort of Britain to boost dwindling tin prices through production cuts seriously affected a tin-producing colony like Nigeria. In an era of falling prices, price gains from production cuts did not keep pace with the economic repercussions of closing mines that had become a source of livelihood and a market for thousands of Nigerian farmers. Tin was not only a major export from Northern Nigeria, it also gave rise to and sustained a vibrant trade in foodstuffs and a culture of migrant-labor remittances that sustained the economy of a large area. The manipulation of tin output and the subsequent reduction in tin mining destabilized the equilibrium of local patterns of exchange and economic sustenance in the tin-mining areas of Nigeria. The use of tariffs to block the entry of competitively priced goods from outside the empire economically punished the consumers of Nigeria.

Imperial preference ensured that Britain cornered most of Nigeria's market for manufactured goods, while shutting out rivals. During the Depression the bulk of Nigeria's major import—textiles—came from Britain. In 1932, 85 percent of Nigeria's imported textiles originated from Britain; the rest came from Japan, Italy, Germany, Holland, France, and India.[8] The preferential tariffs and the quota system put in place by Ottawa protected the flow of British imports, which were priced above products from rival countries, especially Japan. British officials moved more vigorously against Japanese textiles because Japanese products were the least expensive and therefore more attractive to smugglers.[9] Imperial preference also secured the Nigerian market for tobacco and salt. While the policy limited the range of choices open to Nigerian consumers, it helped keep British merchants in business.

British merchants and British industries took advantage of the Depression to increase their gains from Nigeria in other ways. The colonial authorities imposed new export duties on palm kernels, cocoa, groundnuts, and other Nigerian exports in late 1929. While designed to increase the government's revenue base at a time of contracting revenue, the new duties inadvertently supplied British merchants, long schooled in the art of manipulating local producer prices, a platform to exact more monetary concessions from Nigerian agricultural producers. Although some European mercantile firms initially protested the new duties imposed by the government, it soon emerged that their protests were most likely designed to make up for a practice crafted by the mercantile firms that was equally detrimental to the interests of Nigerian producers. In response to dwindling earnings during the Depression, British shipowning merchants formed combines all over West Africa, through which they set uniform produce-buying prices and freight charges. They set the former conveniently low and the latter high.[10] This arrangement between the shippers and the produce-buying merchants reduced the average income of the local producers of groundnuts, cocoa, palm kernels, and cotton.

The new system transferred new charges to local producers, reducing their earnings and engendering discontent. At the United Africa Company (UAC), which specialized solely in buying produce from the Nigerian hinterland (and was therefore closer to producers), officials quickly observed the level of resentment and began as early as 1930 to advocate dismantling the shipping combines. The UAC disliked the virtual freight monopoly that Elder Dempster, the major shipping line in British West Africa, and other companies of the conference shipping lines, had over West African trade, charging that the shipping monopoly was "exacting exorbitant and unconscionable charges from producers, merchants, and traders." The UAC argued that this amounted to "penalizing producers and purchasers of African products by causing low prices to be paid for produce and high prices to be paid for European goods in [West] Africa."[11]

The UAC's position was not entirely altruistic, though; the company hoped to exploit competition among the various shipping companies to its advantage. As the biggest produce buyer in West Africa, it would reap considerable benefits from a competitive shipping regime. However, the vehemence with which it pursued the campaign—threatening to stop all dealings with the shipping combine—mirrored the pressure it may have incurred from local producers and merchants, who ultimately bore the brunt of the freight charges. Few if any alternatives to the combine existed. Patronizing small independent shipping companies tended to be more expensive and riskier than patronizing the combines. Caught between two unfavorable options, British produce buyers simply passed on the excessive charges to local producers. Moreover, as one contemporary Nigerian commentator argued, competition during the Depression hardly resulted in cheaper shipping charges or higher buying prices.[12]

Such was the plight of the Nigerian producer during the 1930s. Interestingly, while accusing the newly formed Elder Dempster shipping monopoly of excessive charges, the UAC ignored its own previous shipping monopoly (while trading as the Great Niger Company) along the banks of the Niger, which now came under question.[13] A group of Nigerian merchants published an article (a rejoinder to the UAC's well-publicized indictment of Elder Dempster's alleged exploitative practices) that accused the UAC of hypocrisy. The merchants admitted that, "by these excessive freights, producers have been badly paid for their produce" and that "there had been abuse of ship owners' monopoly," but they questioned the motive of the UAC—itself no stranger to the practice of transferring its financial distress to local producers and merchants.[14]

A contemporary Nigerian newspaper columnist succinctly captured the importance of the shipper-merchants' conspiracy. He remarked cynically about the British merchants, "These intellectual giants overlooked the fact that the West African consumer would be unable to purchase Lancashire goods unless he obtained a reasonable price for his products." He urged the colonial government to fulfill the wishes of "the people of Nigeria who have suffered from an unexampled Depression" and are looking forward "almost despairingly" to the government to "destroy monopoly and open the markets of West Africa to equitable competition."[15] This columnist touched on the poignant dilemma inherent in the self-cushioning practices of British shipper-merchants and the acquiescence of colonial authorities. He distilled the problem into one crucial point: that an excessive disregard for the economic stability of local producers could hurt Britain in the form of dwindling demand for British goods. The issue, for him, came down to what was more important, shipper-merchants' profits and charges or a steady demand for British goods.

The self-cushioning practices of British economic actors in Nigeria undermined the financial incentive for local participation in the export economy in the long run, taking revenue away from local producers already suffering from the effects of diminished profits and increased familial obligations. Incompatible with the export promotion goals of the colonial administration, this situation portended the abandonment of the institutions of the colonial export economy by Nigerians for less complicated alternatives that gave producers more control—like food crop production. This was a fundamental contradiction in the government's economic recovery policy. Its stated goal, as we shall see, was to incorporate more Nigerians into the world export market by expanding export crop production where it already existed and initiating it where subsistence or semisubsistence agriculture was the norm. The effect of the government's policy and of the self-insulating practices of expatriate merchants contradicted the government's ambition by discouraging Nigerians from participating in a colonially mediated world export market.

THE ONSET OF THE DEPRESSION AND OFFICIAL RESPONSES

As early as December 1929 the colonial authorities in Nigeria began to feel the impact of the Depression. They watched helplessly as revenue drives ran into unforeseen difficulties following a sudden reduction in household incomes caused by falling produce prices. In June 1930 the government sent a circular to all branches and departments of the colonial regime to reaffirm two earlier directives from the chief secretary ordering them to "exercise the most stringent economy in expenditure." The circular lamented the state of the colony's finances and the government's poor revenue projections and urged that "every possible avenue . . . be explored of reducing expenditure."[16] The rush to cut expenditure and the cost of running the country mirrored and expressed the anxieties that the collapse of economic indicators engendered in colonial circles. The economic downturn arrived in Nigeria through preexisting economic interconnections.

Long before the Great Depression, Nigerian agricultural systems had become intricately interwoven with the imperial economy and, through imperial connections, with the world economy. Groundnut cultivation in Nigeria fed a variety of British manufacturing operations, especially in the production of household consumer goods. Nigerian cotton exports supplied the cotton mills of England. Palm oil from Southern Nigeria and parts of north-central Nigeria was used to make detergents, lubricants, and as an additive in the manufacture of a variety of consumer products. Cocoa, a lucrative export, had already helped build a vast commercial farming operation in southwestern Nigeria. Rubber, timber, and tin completed the lineup of Nigeria's exports to the British Empire and beyond. These exports, and British imports, tied the economic tastes, fortunes, and destinies of millions of Nigerian peasants and workers to the performance of the world commodity market. In addition to these connections, British shipping firms, capitalized in Britain and traded on the London Stock Exchange, controlled shipping operations between Nigeria and the world, while several British merchant giants invested heavily in produce buying and land transportation operations in Nigeria.

Because of these connections, the Nigerian economy promptly felt the reverberations of the global economic downturn. The price of tin, a major mineral export, fell to less than half its pre-Depression level.[17] Further, the colonial government entered into an international agreement in 1930 to cut tin output in order to raise its price. This led to the closure of at least 80 percent of the tin mines on the Jos Plateau.[18] The tin mine closures had profound effects on solvency in and around the tin-producing areas.

As bad as the tin situation was, officials worried more about the state of export agriculture, since the bulk of Nigeria's export earnings derived from agricultural products. The drastic fall in the price of cocoa, groundnuts, cotton, palm produce, and lesser agricultural exports undermined the personal economies of peasant producers, diminishing their ability to pay taxes and their capacity to produce more. The price per pound of seed cotton in Southern Nigeria, for example, fell from 2½–3d. in 1928–29 to ⅜–¾d. in 1931–32.[19] The same price collapse affected the American cotton variety cultivated in Nigeria. The average buying price per ton of groundnuts fell from £11 6s. in 1928–29 to £6 16s. in 1932–33.[20] Increases in the output of these goods sometimes matched the downward slide in prices. Apart from areas where peasants had only recently begun to engage in export crop production on a major scale (like some areas in Benue Province), the trend during the Depression saw producers of major export crops initially increase their output. Only later, disillusioned with deteriorating prices and a lack of market competition, did they revert to cultivating more food crops in place of export crops. The falling prices made the expansion of production irrational except when necessary to meet tax demands and unforeseen family economic needs. Since cotton and cocoa beans could not be eaten, the partial shift to food crops remained a rational option open to farmers. Contrary to the expectations of the colonial authorities, tax obligations and ad hoc needs guided whatever expansion occurred in export crop production. As the Depression progressed, Nigerians seemed to abandon even this limited, tax-induced expansion. The resulting fall in cotton and cocoa production became a source of serious concern to the British authorities. By gradually increasing the acreage of food crop cultivation and reducing that of export crop cultivation, many farmers were choosing food security over colonial tax obligation and increasingly elusive export crop profits.

In Eastern Nigeria most of the palm produce came from so-called wild, or bush, plantations. But the fall in prices diverted efforts from harvesting the kernels to food crop cultivation. The fall in palm kernel output worried colonial authorities as much as the fall of cotton and cocoa prices. Only groundnut cultivation continued at pre-Depression levels.[21] The reason for the relative stability in groundnut output was that groundnuts doubled as both export and food crop. They were and are still a staple in many Nigerian diets.[22]

The collapse of agricultural produce prices undermined the revenue projections of the government and forced authorities to craft new solutions, approaches, and rationalizations. Both familiar problems exacerbated by the Depression and unforeseen problems brought on by the downturn needed solutions. This was the premise of the state's economic recovery policy. Revenue generation and financial tinkering gradually came to constitute the core activities of colonial officials in Nigeria.

The problematic economy necessitated a special session of the Nigerian colonial legislature in July 1931. Addressing the session, the governor of Nigeria, Sir Donald Cameron, laid out the bleakness of the financial situation for the gathered European and African members of the legislative council. The governor repeated his promise, made the previous month: "The financial problems of Nigeria which I believe to be grave [will] receive my immediate attention."[23] He took the delegates through the balance sheet of 1930 and 1931, lamenting the shortfall in collected revenue but praising the reduction of infrastructure and recurrent spending, which saved the government £267,000. He criticized the current budget, which had a built-in deficit of £1,565,000, and declared the need for "drastic action" to defeat deficit budgeting. The governor then outlined a four-pronged approach for achieving this goal. First, he proclaimed that the government would charge expenditure on important infrastructural projects or improvement—such as the trade-facilitating railway—to a loan account maintained in London. Second, he would defer projects he deemed unimportant, mostly public works projects. Third, he required that government departments reduce their overheads by retrenching staff, while also scaling back their operations to reduce recurrent spending. The final measure would "widen the resources of the revenue," a euphemism for expanding taxation. The governor quickly rationalized this last measure by contending that the savings from the cuts in both infrastructure and recurrent expenditure were not enough to ensure a balanced budget.[24]

The speech went on to emphasize the importance of boosting exports over internal trade. Here the governor proposed what seemed like a resolution to the problem that confronted colonial authorities during the Depression. As exports fell the internal trade in foodstuffs and crafts appeared to become vibrant as farmers moved away from the cultivation of labor-intensive, and now poorly priced, export crops. Officials faced the dilemma of whether to encourage, regulate, and tax this growing internal trade or to allow it to continue unregulated. This was a hard question for colonial officials, especially if they retained the familiar colonial commitment to export crops and export trade. The retrenchment of colonial officials as part of the effort to cut expenditure made regulating the widespread, fluid, and sometimes informal patterns of local exchange unfeasible. The governor simply sidestepped the problem, explaining his decision in terms of economic priorities. He argued that "the value of our domestic trade—the transit trade of Nigeria—is not important." The governor concluded that in the pre-Depression years government departments and colonial officials could spend money liberally on governance and on projects because "money was too easily obtained." "In the next few years," he warned, "money is going to be exceedingly difficult to obtain."[25]

The measures outlined by the governor became the cornerstone of the colonial government's economic recovery policy. In the next few months the government retrenched hundreds of workers—mostly Africans—from government service, swelling the ranks of the unemployed and the disgruntled. Due to scant statistics, it is hard to determine the extent of retrenchment from European-owned firms, but retrenchment from the colonial service approached 40 percent of the entire workforce.[26] In fact, in 1935 when the government deemed it necessary to study the unemployment problem and ordered a census of the retrenched, about three thousand men between eighteen and fifty years old turned out in Lagos alone.[27]

If the July 1931 speech of Governor Cameron was colored by desperation and vagueness, his speech to the Nigerian Legislative Council in February 1932 unmasked his financial anxiety. He began, "During the year [1931–32] the severe and continued Depression in the prices of the primary products, which alone Nigeria has to export for sale overseas, and the consequent grave effect on the public finances have caused great anxiety to my government." With these words, he introduced the context in which to advocate the intensification of the policy of austerity and emergency restrictions. He argued that the budget could not be balanced "without further retrenchment of staff . . . unless the yield from the revenue improves."[28] Cameron envisaged an improvement in revenue from a new income tax on civil servants, chiefs, and other personnel engaged temporarily or permanently in the colonial civil service, as well as from further reductions in the allowances paid to colonial staff. In arguing his case for the new income tax, the governor contended that the reductions in allowances of the previous year had been "felt more by junior [African] than the senior officers," and that the planned graduated income tax would "have the effect of equalizing the sacrifice . . . between various grades of public service."[29]

The governor invoked the idea of disproportionate sacrifice for strategic reasons. First, he hoped to preempt and assuage the grievance of the African legislative council members, who had come to the meeting embittered by the extent of sacrifice expected from them and their colleagues—the African colonial clerks. Second, the governor wanted to rally the African members around the income tax agenda and prevent a closing of ranks between African and European civil servants for the purpose of scuttling the plan. In the end, however, the rhetoric of equal sacrifice remained just that: a convenient rhetoric. In practical terms, the governor needed neither the acceptance nor the support of the African clerks and European colonial officials. Aware of the expectation to act in line with the economic recovery consensus in Britain, the governor knew that the objection of African council members would not practically hamper his efforts. Eventually, he dropped all pretenses to deliberative consultation and invoked the power of the secretary of state for the colonies. While putting the additional emergency economic proposals across to the council members, Governor Cameron told them that "the secretary of state for the colonies [in London] had approved these proposals" and that the Colonial Office was happy with the way the government was "handling this unprecedented situation." The invocation of metropolitan authority stifled any dissent.

The governor's manner engendered suspicions of deception and manipulation. He had claimed in a dispatch to the secretary of state in August 1931 that nonimprovement of revenue would result in further retrenchment. However, despite reducing the allowances of workers and legislating a new income tax on workers and artisans—measures that assured an improvement in revenue—he argued in February 1932 before the council that further retrenchment "had become imperative," claiming that "the service was generously staffed." He claimed further that both the Association of European Civil Servants and the Nigerian Civil Service Union had accepted that "some retrenchment was inevitable."[30]

It is not clear if indeed African workers acquiesced to the intensified retrenchment exercise or supported its inevitability, as alleged by the governor. The invocation of the secretary of state's authority in the effort to propagate emergency economic measures, while effective in foreclosing debate and dissent, frustrated most African members of the legislative council. Despite their status as unofficial members, they had to sit through purportedly consultative and consensus-seeking speeches and contrived debates. An apparently frustrated council member from Egba Division lashed out: "Whenever we have come before this council and have had something to say against any item of expenditure, government has always thrown it in our faces that it was a ruling of the secretary of state. I certainly think we ought to make a stand; let the government know that we do not want rulings of this sort and that we should be allowed to make criticisms on the expenditure, on which government shall take action."[31]

Another council member, from Calabar, questioned the tendency of government to resort to the explanation that "expenditure on a certain item had been authorized by the secretary of state. If we are bound by what the secretary of state wishes to do, then I would ask, what is the object of our being here . . . if matters have already been settled beforehand by the secretary of state

and we are not allowed to make any alteration in his decisions? I submit, that
. . . it would be useless to put them [measures and proposals] before us and
say that we must endorse them when the secretary of state has already given
his consent."[32] These unusually candid statements from African council members highlighted their frustration at the top-down impositions of economic
recovery measures. The African clerks and the government had different ideas
about what governmental responsibilities and priorities should be in a period
of economic hardship.

Overwhelmed by the economic situation, Governor Cameron kept going
back to measures he had rejected. Although he rejected the idea of imposing
a temporary levy on the salary of workers in 1931 and 1932, finding reductions in
allowance and income taxation sufficient sacrifices for workers, he reversed himself in 1933, imposing levies of various percentages on the salaries of Nigerian
workers.[33] Either the governor had underestimated the economic problem or
he had become overzealous in his pursuit of financial solvency. In either case
the policy reversals resulted in an increased burden for African workers, artisans, and clerks.

AUSTERITY, EXACTION, AND IMPERIAL PREFERENCE

In deference to the governor's economic recovery recipe, the government
canceled planned welfare projects. It deferred some to a future date, when the
economy would have regained solvency. Other projects deemed productive,
such as the re-laying of the Kaduna-Minna section of the Nigerian Railway,
found funding from metropolitan loans that carried high interest rates. To
conform to imperial preference, the acting chief secretary to the government,
the head of the Nigerian colonial civil service, directed all government departments and native administrations to purchase all their imported goods from
within the British Empire.[34] This marked the official inauguration of imperial
preference in Nigeria.

The unusually high price of British imports in this period made this a particularly difficult directive to implement. Not only were heads of departments,
residents, and district officers under enormous pressure to reduce expenditure
while providing basic administrative needs, they were required to import supplies exclusively from the British Empire. Nigerian taxpayers were essentially
subsidizing British manufacturers of products desired by different branches of
the colonial bureaucracy. A more liberal import policy would have allowed
for cheaper importation of supplies from nonempire countries. But while
such a policy would have conserved funds, it would have violated the policy
consensus in British colonial officialdom. Imperial preference presented
several dilemmas during the Depression, but that did not stop the British from
expanding the policy into the realm of consumption.

Between 1931 and 1932 the government imposed a series of import duties on cheap Japanese cotton textiles, which had become popular with Nigerians as substitutes for British textiles, whose prices either rose or stagnated as the incomes and purchasing power of Nigerians plummeted.[35] The 1932 duties, just authorized by the Ottawa conference, were more ambitious. The onset of the Depression, in 1929, had focused new attention on Japanese competition with British textile exports to African colonies. Aided by a combination of cheap labor, the devaluation of the yen in 1931, and export-promoting fiscal policies, the Japanese could produce cotton and silk textiles more efficiently than did British factories. From about 1911, Japanese merchants flooded the markets of British West Africa with a variety of cheap products that became popular with Nigerian consumers. Japanese textile exports to West Africa grew during the Depression as demand for expensive British cotton goods dropped, threatening the cotton industry of Lancashire.[36]

In Nigeria the Japanese textile competition, as Marion Johnson notes, became a particularly serious concern after 1932.[37] Clearly the protective duties had failed to curb the popularity and availability of Japanese textiles. Legal exporters of Japanese textiles could pay the new protective duties, price their product well below the products of Lancashire, and still make a profit, rendering the duties only modestly successful. Moreover, smugglers took advantage of the Anglo-French Free Trade Convention of 1898 to smuggle Japanese cotton goods into Nigeria through the vast borders with the French colonies of Cameroon, Chad, Dahomey, and Niger. Previously, Japanese merchants had taken similar advantage of the 1884–85 Congo Basin Agreement. They flooded East African markets with cheap Japanese textiles, leaving Britain unable to impose any restrictions without flouting international law and jeopardizing its trade in Belgian and Portuguese territories.

The Anglo-French convention covered much more of British West Africa—especially Nigeria and Ghana—than did the Congo Basin Agreement, making it much easier to implement the provisions of the Ottawa conference in Nigeria than in British East Africa, with its greater legal and economic repercussions of imperial preference.[38] Though the Japanese exported more textiles to British East Africa than it did to West Africa because of the free trade environment created by the Congo agreement, the British acted faster and more vigorously in West Africa than they did in East Africa. To stem the influx of Japanese textiles, the Nigerian government imposed strict quotas in May 1934. In 1936, France denounced the Anglo-French convention, freeing the Nigerian government to clamp down on smuggling across the border and impose full-scale general trade discrimination in favor of British goods. These measures proved very effective in curtailing the importation of Japanese textiles into Nigeria, thus restoring the dominance of expensive Lancashire goods in the Nigerian market.

Practically, the restrictions on Japanese textiles curtailed the consumption choices of Nigerians in an area of necessity: clothing. Not only did imperial preference make the Japanese textiles more expensive, they also inaugurated a period of artificial textile scarcity that drove up prices. As Kweku Ampiah notes, "The quota system applied against Japan . . . left a [supply] vacuum that Britain and other competitors [were] not able to fill."[39]

Another economic recovery policy targeted taxation. The scope of taxation increased even though income tax rates either remained intact or were modestly reduced in many districts. In 1932, for instance, the expanded taxation regime yielded an estimated £253,000 in additional revenue,[40] the most significant one-year increase since the boom of the mid-1920s. While the breadth and practice of taxation expanded, officials reviewed its legal basis to accommodate the revenue generation priority of the Depression period. In particular, they reviewed the Native Revenue Ordinance—enacted in 1927 to make taxation a more formal institution—to criminalize tax default. They enforced the ordinance more vigorously, targeting African traders, urban artisans, and clerks—all of whom before 1927 had escaped taxation altogether and after 1927 had benefited from the inchoate nature of the ordinance.[41] The government remained determined to pursue the twin policies of expanding revenue while drastically reducing government spending. In late 1931 it imposed additional customs duties on imports.[42]

By 1936 the aggressive pursuit of revenue expansion appeared to have succeeded, as had the suspension of public works. In response the government gave a few cautious and self-congratulatory indications of recovery. Western-educated Nigerians soberly reacted to the proclaimed successes of these economic recovery measures. They knew that what little recovery had ensued came on the backs of Nigerian peasants and workers. Letters and articles in the nascent Nigerian press conveyed the prevailing discontent.[43] To what extent such local criticisms shaped government's actions, we may never know. Some of the government's actions, such as the decision in 1931 to start taxing the income of immigrant Syrian, Lebanese, and Libyan merchants, may have come in response to complaints of Nigerian traders and artisans, who competed directly with Levantine immigrants in various vocations. Nigerian traders had protested that, despite being impoverished by the Depression, they were being taxed at a higher rate than their Arab and Levantine counterparts.[44]

THE AGRICULTURAL ADVENTURE

Despite local outcries, the government's actions during the Depression reflected its own anxieties and not the appeals of locals. The government did not set out to exploit Nigerians more during the Depression. Exploitation had become all but impossible due to the contraction of the export economy. However, it intervened in the export economy in ways that were just as destabilizing for peasants as the removal of surpluses and profits before the Depression. In the pursuit of its primary objective—assuaging its economic anxieties—the government remained indifferent to the effect of its interventions on Nigerians. This became especially clear with regard to its intervention in export agriculture. Officials feared that the fall in exports in the first few years of the Depression might erode the basis of the colonial economy. As falling produce prices led to reduced earnings from export agriculture, the colonial authorities began to make what they considered progressive and modernist interventions in agricultural practices with the aim of increasing crop yield.

Agricultural interventions in pre-Depression Southern Nigeria had been confined to the distribution of government-approved seed varieties. In the desperate economic atmosphere of the early to mid-1930s, the colonial department of agriculture assumed a more intrusive role. Authorities could no longer leave farmers to their own agricultural practices, only advising them to adopt better-yielding crop varieties. Instead the very basis of Southern Nigeria peasant agriculture came under scrutiny. Suddenly, "Nigerian farmers' methods of growing cocoa [were] open to criticism": "plantations are often too thick, nothing is done to replace what is taken from the soil, and little care is generally devoted to measures of plant sanitation to protect the trees from diseases."[45] Above all, "the communal land system constituted a brake, rather than a bar to planting." The colonial conflation of a wide variety of land rights and usage arrangements under the rubric of the communal land system authorized various interventions in land matters. These interventions were at variance with the multiplicity of land use systems at work in pre-Depression Western Nigeria.[46] The disruptive new system inspired efforts to enforce a colonial vision of land ownership. The cocoa-producing areas of Western Nigeria also became a site for the "educative work . . . of the Agricultural Department," which educated farmers on "modern" farming practices such as the "correct method of [cocoa] preparation."[47]

In Eastern Nigeria, where palm produce constituted the major export crop, the Agricultural Department also criticized "the communal system of land ownership," which it described as "constituting a considerable handicap to the enterprising farmer who wishes to establish a small plantation of palms." After a number of "experiments," the department concluded that plantation palm trees were better yielding and easier to harvest than "wild" palms.[48] The entire process of palm produce preparation—from cultivation to palm oil extraction to kernel preparation—subsequently came under similarly intense supervision and tinkering. The production data for 1930, 1931, and 1932, show a significant expansion in the acres of palm plantation.[49] It is not clear whether this directly resulted from the colonial government's intervention or from local initiative born out of local agricultural dynamics. But the government promptly credited itself for this modest improvement in Eastern Nigerian export agriculture.

In Northern Nigeria, where cotton and groundnuts constituted the main export crops, the need to increase yield at a time of collapsed prices provided a platform for implementing agricultural measures that the British had conceived earlier but whose necessity was questionable in the boom years. Though mentioned in scattered official documents of the Agricultural Department before the Depression, in 1930 the British began to promote one of these measures, mixed farming, as a solution to the poverty of rural peasants.[50]

More determined intervention occurred in areas of Northern Nigeria where export crop production either did not exist or existed at a nascent stage. In Benue and Kabba provinces an aggressive campaign to induce local farmers to cultivate cotton commenced in 1930. Convinced that an export crop culture was the key to survival in depressed rural economies and the solution to the rampart tax default in peripheral provinces, colonial administrative officials took on the added role of agricultural proselytizers. They distributed cotton seedlings and dispatched agricultural extension workers to carry the campaign of export crop cultivation to rural cultivators.[51]

In addition to the promotion of export crop cultivation, the colonial authorities encouraged farmers to increase their cultivation of crops with export potential. The Northern Nigerian Agricultural Department promoted one such crop, ginger, through the distribution of "good seed-ginger," and the "demonstration of the correct (and rather difficult) method of preparation, and [the] grading [of] produce offered for sale."[52] The Agricultural Department also intervened in the cultivation of sesame, which Nigeria exported in small quantities. The department worked vigorously in Benue Province, the center of sesame production, to eliminate "inferior species" by producing and distributing "pure seed," which it exchanged for "adulterated seed."[53]

Livestock farmers in Northern Nigeria also came under unprecedented supervision and their livestock was subjected to intense veterinary attention. The 1930s "was an unfortunate [period] for the stock owner as owing to the economic Depression only very low prices have been obtainable for stock and the various animal products."[54] Adamawa Province became a target of official efforts to boost yields because livestock was the major cash earner for the people of the area.

The colonial government's interventions in agriculture took different forms in Southern and Northern Nigeria. Measures conformed broadly to the crops and the methods of cultivation in each region. The objective, however, remained the same: boost both export agriculture and peasants' ability to remit much-needed taxes. Some of these interventions did not progress beyond the level of intrusive inquiry and preliminary investigation. Though pursued vigorously, others failed to stimulate any significant expansion in export crop production.

It is tempting to attribute this to a generic African resentment of an intrinsi-
cally exploitative export market. On the contrary, the relative ineffectiveness
of these interventions derived largely from a gradual loss of confidence in an
increasingly risky world market made even more volatile by the self-interested
mediation of the government. Until the Depression, Nigerians needed little or
no colonial intervention to participate or expand their participation in the export market. The collapse of prices and colonial economic recovery practices
undermined the efficacy of colonial incentives and interventions as mediums
of agricultural export proselytization.

THE TRANSFER OF WELFARE OBLIGATIONS

For the British in Nigeria, the so-called decade of financial embarrassment
meant that in order to sustain colonial rule they would have to *practically* divest
it of traditional colonial claims of uplift and state-driven economic progress even
while maintaining rhetorical commitment to them. Officials devised ingenious
ways to deflect African expectations of state economic paternalism. An invocation of cultural relativism and nativism partly underpinned the effort to absolve
British colonialism of its vaunted paternal obligations in a time of economic
crisis. Confronted with severe hardship among Nigerians, unemployment, under-
employment, and despair, the colonial state reified and valorized aspects of
urban and rural Nigerian life previously construed in colonial policy discourse
as causal indicators of African backwardness. The focus on African modes of
socioeconomic resilience was a strategy calculated to absolve the state of the
responsibility of economic relief so that it could be transferred to Nigerians.

Unable and unwilling to invest in the welfare of distressed colonial subjects,
the state sought ideological justification for noninvestment in Nigerians' welfare,
while advancing the efficacy of "traditional welfare arrangements." "Native culture" became a tool of this official effort to justify austerity. For colonial officials,
"the people of Nigeria have not advanced to that state of civilization where it has
become necessary for the state to make provision for its destitute members."[55]
Instead of relying on the social responsibility of government to deliver welfare
benefits to impoverished and unemployed Nigerians, officials found it more
prudent for Nigerians to rely on "the family or clan [, which] is still a very vital
force" because "its members look after and support one another, in sickness,
old age, or any other misfortune." The government further elaborated on the
theme of self-help by fleshing out its repository of anthropological knowledge.
The "title" and age-grade societies of the southeast and the *egbe* societies of
Western Nigeria as well the cooperative-credit system of *esusu* and their mutual
support and communal economic cooperation mechanisms were advanced as
institutions that could be exploited by economically vulnerable Nigerians and
were strengthened to mitigate their vulnerability to the economic crisis.[56]

In addition to broaching the concept of self-help, officials situated the prevailing hardship in a way that implied that the economic crisis affected only certain individuals and not whole communities. If the economic downturn did not impoverish everyone, then self-help institutions could not be overwhelmed with destitute applicants. Officials argued that "many of these [ethnic] associations . . . assist members who find themselves in financial difficulties." The implication of such seemingly straightforward but subtly ideological statements are clear: individuals either bore partial responsibility for their economic situation or, as unfortunate victims of normal economic vicissitudes, should explore traditional avenues of economic support.

The campaign for self-help and a welfare system rooted in local, nonstate institutions received official mandate in 1933, the year the Depression hit the hardest. Early in November the chief secretary to the government released a memorandum on the issue. Aiming to enable the government to "extend the system of co-operative societies in this country,"[57] officials embarked on a nationwide tour later in the month to educate rural cultivators, artisans, and traders on the importance of economic cooperation.

This effort was inspired by a colonial insistence on placing both the cause and the solution of the prevailing hardship on Nigerians. The governor believed that the root of the debt crisis and the hardship in rural Nigeria lay in "extravagance [and] improvidence" and the lack of thrift. His prescription was simple: strengthening the indigenous mutual-benefit and savings societies and extending their reach would enable "farmers, craftsmen, or other classes of the community" to make "wise use of the money or other wealth . . . gained." Cooperation among Africans should not be for amusement and social recreation only, he argued, but "should aim at economic and social improvement." The economic crisis made it "necessary to lend positive support and constructive assistance to Africans in building up a social framework (no less an economic machinery), which will be adequate to the needs of the present day." Here, Europe with its public-welfare institutions could not serve as a model or paradigm because, as the secretary posited, the "growth of civilization has been long and continuous" there.[58] Examples of the kind of economic cooperation and cooperative welfare that the government envisioned existed in India, Java, and Japan. In those countries, the objectives of cooperative societies as well as "thrift and the repression of extravagance"[59] had been perfected. Officials prescribed the two approaches as antidotes to rural poverty. In this colonial economic recovery vision, African "traditions" of self-help and cooperation interfaced conveniently with a global impulse to advance cooperatives as a modified, acceptable version of socialism.

The chief secretary's perception of the economic situation in rural Nigeria either conveniently or naively played down the role of the Depression. But it also reflected a tendency, long entrenched within British colonial officialdom, to reduce economic problems to cultural causation. Once officials pointed out the cultural impediments to economic progress, they could more easily prescribe cultural interventions as an alternative to solving economic problems economically.

The government's plan to foster economic cooperation as an alternative welfare system during the Depression straddled a fine line between reifying a specific aspect of social organization in Nigeria's rural areas—cooperative societies—and condemning cultural practices like marriages, funerals, and ornamentation as incentives for and examples of extravagance. For the "crux of the rural problem," as the chief secretary saw it, was whether, "now that the excitement of a past time (war, witchcraft, secret societies) have been removed or reduced," there was "any desire in life as distinguished from personal ornaments and comfort." It seems clear that the secretary considered lethargy to be the primary cause of the prevailing scourge of rural poverty, a problem worsened, according to him, by the absence of economic institutions that encouraged savings and discouraged extravagance. For him, the problem resulted from a prevalence of "frivolous litigation, excessive drink, [and] harmful superstition." What the British needed to do was to "find in one village a group of persons who could work under supervision to rouse public opinion in their village against any selected one of these evils."[60] The cooperative societies that the government envisaged would promote the work ethic and economic values that the British had identified as lacking in rural Nigeria, values deemed capable of reducing rural poverty and dislocation during an economically difficult period. In an effort to deflect aspirations for governmental monetary or welfare intervention, British officials responded to the effects of the Depression on rural Nigeria with this elaborate ideology of self-help and directed economic cooperation.

The extent of the government's intention to avoid spending money during the Depression is illustrated not only by the contradictory project of cultural economics that it sought to entrench but also by the economic dilemma that characterized its Depression-era financial policies. Confronted with a choice between increasing social spending in order to expand the market for British goods and withholding spending and engaging in the crude extraction of revenue, the government opted for the latter. With surpluses and profits dwindling to a trickle, this amounted to crude colonial revenue generation and not colonial exploitation as we know it. Its danger was precisely that it did not deplete nonexistent profits but rather production capacity.

Aware that the infrastructure of the extractive economy had to be reinforced, the government made provision for spending that bordered on "productive" projects. Thus, a distinction between productive and nonproductive expenditure emerged, a distinction elaborated in the July 1931 speech of the governor to the legislative council and upheld throughout the Depression as the principle for government spending. This principle led to the completion of the bridge over the Benue River in 1932. It also enabled the government to initiate the re-laying of the Kaduna-Minna section of the Nigerian Railway,[61] a crucial transport infrastructure to the export crop industry, the major foreign exchange earner for the government. But adherence to the distinction also exacerbated a growing economic panic while deflecting the legitimate economic expectations of Nigerians.

~

The Nigerian colonial state's responses to the Great Depression primarily originated with its own economic anxieties rather than the concerns of Nigerians. The state wanted to extricate itself from a financial crisis and to pursue the holy grail of British colonial economics—a balanced budget. The colonial actions and reactions that these state goals inspired did not represent a new regime of exploitation. They did not result in an unprecedented incorporation of Nigerians into the world market, nor did they result in an increased exploitation of Nigerians, as there was hardly any profit or surplus to be exploited. Rather, they produced mixed and contradictory outcomes, arguably discouraging more Nigerians from the world market than they brought into it.

To be sure, these colonial economic recovery policies had the effect of burdening Nigerians already struggling with the collapse of prices and other economic indicators. But that effect was not the product of any enlargement of British organs of exploitation or of a new agenda of impoverishment. On the contrary, the colonial economy contracted, as did Nigerians' participation in it, endangering the economic goals of the British. The additional burdens for Nigerians came from the worsening of an already dysfunctional colonial economic system and from a combination of state economic recovery policy and the manipulations of expatriate merchants. Local concerns and fates mattered little to British colonial bureaucrats. The incidental outcomes of a British obsession with recovery, rather than of a deepening British exploitation, found Nigerians shouldering the new burdens of economic recovery. The transfer of wealth from the Nigerian economy, the retrenchment of workers, the wage cuts, and other economic recovery measures no doubt intensified Nigerians entanglements in the hardship of the Depression. But they also undermined the foundation of the colonial economy, leading to local resentment and protests and causing local producers to lose confidence in the colonial export economy. As we shall see, many Nigerians spent much of the 1930s seeking escape from the very economic institutions into which the British economic recovery policy sought to incorporate them.

2   The Depression and the Colonial Encounter in Northern Nigeria

THE CRISES SET off by the state's pursuit of revenue at the Northern Nigerian grass roots, as well as the unintended consequences of economic recovery policies, undermined the administrative system of indirect rule in a region that scholars regard as its cradle and laboratory. This weakening of indirect rule was particularly harsh on its most important legitimizing institution—chiefs and their traditional legitimacy. The economic crisis and British responses to it transformed the exercise of colonial power in Northern Nigeria. The increasing impatience of British colonial interlocutors in the maintenance of solvency and economic order made indirect rule more direct. In charting a course to economic recovery, British officials undermined—rhetorically and practically—the main thrust of the indirect rule system, which was central to British claims to legitimacy and power: respect for indigenous political institutions.

The maintenance of economic austerity and the aggressive pursuit of revenue came with a social cost, too: it generated enormous tension between local rulers—whose powers were reinforced to enhance their new role in the state's emergency revenue schemes—and their subjects. These tensions sometimes erupted into violence and, as a result, colonial authorities also found themselves trying to maintain social order. The chiefs' alleged misuse of the new powers given to them for revenue generation purposes compounded the state's problem. While strengthening the hands of local rulers and seemingly reinforcing indirect rule, the economic recovery regime actually dealt a blow to that system of rule, and to the power and prestige of chiefs. That outcome is similar to what James Genova argues for French West Africa during the Depression. The transition from "traditional chieftaincy" to an "administrative," revenue-generating, and fiscally obligated chieftaincy led to revolts against

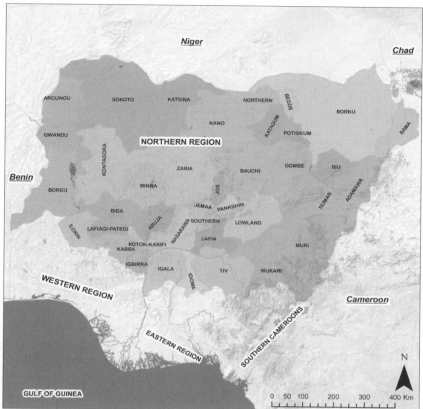

Colonial Northern Nigeria

the chiefs' colonially sanctioned exactions as well as to their imprisonment, public humiliation, and replacement by colonial authorities.[1] In Northern Nigeria chiefs who refused to wholeheartedly commit themselves to the new revenue generation campaign were subjected to unprecedented official scrutiny and punitive measures. Conversely, those who demonstrated loyalty to the government's emergency revenue drive lost legitimacy in the eyes of their suffering subjects. Both cases undermined what the British had taken for granted as a necessary condition for indirect rule: the loyalty and traditional legitimacy of chiefs.

The implementation of the revenue generation component of the economic recovery policy also caused enormous social and economic dislocation. It displaced African commodity traders and caused widespread famines, food shortages, and jurisdictional squabbles among chiefs. Additionally, it elicited antitax protests and innovative tax-evading techniques like strategic nomadic mobility, intraregional migrations, and the hiding of children from tax assessors. These volatile outcomes resulted from the inability of the Northern Nigerian

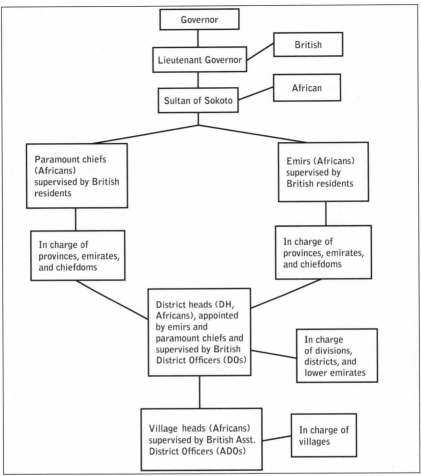

The colonial administrative hierarchy in Northern Nigeria

colonial authorities to continue to extract surpluses and profits from peasants without disrupting their lives and violating their already limited freedoms. The resulting rural exaction generated tense encounters in Northern Nigeria's colonial grass roots. In the end, the myth of British colonial control and paternal economic altruism became the main casualty. The desperate and ad hoc nature of British colonial actions in this period underscored this new reality.

SITUATING NORTHERN NIGERIA'S VULNERABILITY

Northern Nigeria's geographical position rendered it vulnerable to the effects of the Depression. As an inland colony with no direct access to the coast, Northern Nigeria sustained a minimal, informal, and loosely unregulated internal trade. Apart from tin mining on the Jos Plateau, the colony's economy depended on the exportation of agricultural products, which required transportation to the coast for shipment to Europe. When tin prices collapsed in early 1930, leading to the closure of most of the mines on the Jos Plateau and the retrenchment of most of the mine labor, the region relied even more heavily on its agriculture trade. This process of disruption came to a head in 1931, when Nigeria joined the international tin agreement—designed to stabilize prices by restricting the country's output of tin.[2] This agreement led to further mine closures, retrenchments, and immense income loss for many Northern Nigerian districts that subsisted on labor migration or food exports to the mines.

The Depression exacerbated dependence on agricultural incomes, which ensured that Northern Nigeria continued to secure the bulk of its revenue from direct taxation of farmers' income while coastal Southern Nigeria contributed the bulk of theirs from the export and import duties.[3] At the onset of depressive conditions, the government did not seek to disturb this distribution of revenue responsibility between Northern Nigeria and Southern Nigeria. The state remained content with the status quo, which located the center of direct taxation in the North and the center of indirect taxation in the South. While most people in Northern Nigeria had paid taxes from the inception of British administration at the turn of the century, the people of Southern Nigeria began to pay income tax only from 1927, when authorities enacted the Native Income Tax Ordinance. But even with the extension of income taxation to Southern Nigeria, tax rates remained markedly higher in the North. And while women had long paid taxes in certain provinces of Northern Nigeria, they rarely had in the South. The Aba Women's War of 1929 had made the practice virtually unacceptable in the South.[4]

Regionally differentiated policies regarding direct taxation probably reflected the belief in colonial circles that Southern Nigeria, which, through customs and export duties, contributed about 60 percent of Nigeria's total revenue, should not shoulder an income tax at par with the North's. The justification for this policy consensus is not as important as its legacy during the Depression: it placed Northern Nigeria firmly at the center of the emergency revenue schemes of the government.

In the 1933–34 tax year the government collected more than 10 percent of Northern Nigerian farmers' gross income (translating to more than 30 percent of their net income) as income tax. Taking into account the fall in prices and the increase in population, the government took 12.9 percent of Northern Nigerian farmers' gross income.[5] In the 1928–29 tax season, the government took 5 percent of Northern Nigerian farmers' income as tax, against 1.5 percent from Southern Nigerian farmers in the same period. The government's income tax revenue from Northern Nigeria was £1.455 million, against £0.674

million collected from Southern Nigeria.[6] These figures illustrate the asymmetrical distribution of direct income taxation between North and South.

Throughout the Depression, authorities maintained this asymmetrical distribution of the burden of direct taxation between North and South. With the introduction of women's taxation having been unequivocally rejected in the South and the income taxation regime there hanging precariously in the balance, the North became the key site for the aggressive revenue drive of the Depression. The government preserved the status quo in Southern Nigeria, which was characterized by a loose tax assessment regime, irregular collection, and regular concessions to tax-resisting farmers and artisans. Attention shifted to Northern Nigeria, which had a more firmly entrenched system of income taxation. There, the "traditional" political structures exploited in the service of British administration and taxation had proved stronger, more legitimate, and, for the new priorities, more coercive.

The statistics for the 1933–34 tax season show that the farmers of Northern Nigeria paid more than 30 percent of their net income as tax. This not only contradicted the limit of 10 percent of net income recommended by Frederick Lugard's *Political Memoranda*—regarded as the canonical reference for administrative and taxation policy in colonial Northern Nigeria—it far exceeded the 2½ percent taken from Southern Nigerian farmers' income as tax in the same period.[7] One concerned colonial official pointed out that the tax rates in the Northern Provinces[8] in 1933–43 were "too high" when compared with the assessment of 1928–29, the year before the Depression: "The Northern Provinces cannot at prices prevailing in 1933/34 pay more than £1 million in direct taxes, without exceeding the 10 percent maximum in the aggregate and probably very much exceeding it in particular areas. The Direct taxes proposed for the Northern Provinces for 1933/34 were 1.3337 Million, or nearly 35 percent too much."[9]

Before prices collapsed, tax rates had not previously caused much trouble, except when taxes were being collected from a district for the first time. At any rate, this Depression-era tax regime endured because it was sustained by an economic recovery logic founded on the primacy of revenue generation and the creation of financial reserves in London. As taxation became reenvisioned as a means of lubricating the colonial state, Northern Nigeria found itself absorbed more deeply into the vortex of income taxation, rendering the region's economy peculiarly vulnerable to the Depression.

Two facts underscore this vulnerability: price fluctuation and tax burdens. Prices of agricultural products—especially staples, on which many Northern Nigerian farmers depended for income—fell more in the North than they did in the South. In 1930 the price of beans was 2s. 2d. in the North, against 6s. 8d. in the South. The price of cassava was 1s. 2d. in the North and 9d. in the South.

In Northern Nigeria guinea corn commanded less than half, and maize and yams about half their Southern Nigerian prices.[10] The burden of income taxation, more than 60 percent of which came from Northern Nigeria, fell on every able-bodied male and, in some provinces, female. In the South the burden of indirect taxation—custom and export duties—fell mostly on Southern Nigerians who either participated in or patronized the import market: government workers, middlemen, and businessmen.

Both the emirate North[11] and the nonemirate areas[12] of Northern Nigeria occupied precarious positions during the Depression. Despite the raging debate between neoclassical and neo-Marxist scholars as to whether the penetration of European colonial capitalism did or did not lead to capitalist farming in Northern Nigeria,[13] a loose consensus recognizes that the rarity of large-scale capitalist farming in colonial Northern Nigeria makes it analytically insignificant.[14] Small-scale agricultural cultivation was the norm in Northern Nigeria. In an agricultural economy where production (and, to a large extent, reproduction) was anchored in the ability to mobilize household labor, a downturn in the agricultural produce market often disrupts the base of that economy. So too, as shall be discussed, can a string of disasters that coincide with a Depression in the agricultural commodity market. Both forces could have more serious repercussions than a mere temporary impoverishment caused by shifting ecological cycles, which can easily be absorbed by adjusting household work patterns. This was the fate of Northern Nigerian agriculture during the Depression.

In fact the downturn of the 1930s and the economic encounters it triggered gave rise to a cycle of impoverishment and debt that threatened the viability of the region's agricultural infrastructure and, of course, the reproduction of agricultural labor. This part of the Depression story in Northern Nigeria is buttressed by the fact that the level of indebtedness and poverty compelled many households to begin hiring out labor to a few wealthy rural farmers in order to raise cash for tax payment and for other cash needs.[15] This reality raises the question of whether revenue extraction from rural areas at rates not commensurate with falling prices was disruptive or regenerative. The question of how the persistence of obligatory cash extraction from insolvent rural sectors could contract rural productive capacity and ultimately undermine colonial quest for profits always stalked the government's economic recovery measures in the peasant sector. Colonial anxiety inspired isolated official acknowledgments of harsh taxes, as the state's economic recovery imperative undermined the mainstay of colonial revenue generation—rural agricultural production.

THE "BLIZZARD" HITS HOME

In March 1931 the acting chief secretary to the government of Nigeria, Sir Alan Burns, sent a confidential circular to the secretary of the Northern Provinces outlining what he expected of the Northern Nigerian colonial authorities with respect to the government's quest for financial stability.[16] The circular directed the secretary of the Northern Provinces to provide an estimate for budget cuts for the 1931–32 year and the resulting savings. The missive further requested that Northern Nigerian authorities report on savings made from the reduction of European staff as well as on "consequential savings under other charges as will follow the reduction of staff." As for African staff in the Northern Nigerian colonial service, their fate remained equally precarious under the new economic configuration, bound up as it was with the new priorities of the colonial regime.

The memo directed authorities not to fill vacancies and to terminate "the appointment of unconfirmed officers." They were required to report any savings from this and from the "reduction of Travelling and Transport allowances" of officials. Finally, the circular issued what amounted to carte blanche on the issue of savings. The colonial authorities in Northern Nigeria received permission to carry out "substantial economies under other charges and special expenditure" so long as they indicated "the amount that can be saved under each item."[17] The circular reminded the Northern Nigerian colonial officialdom of the ideological foundation of the new measures: "I am to impress upon you that the need for drastic economy is a very real one, and that His Excellency is confident that he will have the full co-operation of every Head of Department in this matter."[18]

This circular conveyed the first official directive from Lagos, the Nigerian colonial capital, to the Secretariat of the Northern Provinces, in Kaduna, articulating clear-cut measures and their objectives during the Depression. As revolutionary as the directives may appear, a few months earlier, colonial officials—residents and district officers (DOs)—had already started exercising their initiatives to achieve the objectives conveyed by the circular. Thus the Lagos directive became merely an official endorsement of the policy predilection of the Northern Nigerian colonial administration. It was already understood in Northern Nigerian colonial officialdom that development, loosely defined, and administrative efficiency must give way to austerity. Austerity was seen as the logical antidote to an acute fiscal crisis. But how severe was the financial problem of the Northern Nigerian colonial government?

A report from Adamawa Province for 1930 described the province's economic situation as "precarious" and cited the "collapse of the groundnut market" as the major cause.[19] Similarly, the annual report on Igbirra Division in 1930 spoke of an unprecedented fall in the price of cotton. It stated that "merchandise trade has seriously declined" and went on to recommend a reduction of "indents [purchase orders] and forward shipments" because "there seems to be no sign of a return to normal trade conditions until prices of produce harden."[20] It is clear then that before the authorities in Lagos authorized officials in Northern Nigeria to combat the Depression, colonial administrators at the grass roots had already begun grappling with the challenges of governing economically depressed polities. This distinction between preexisting portrayals of crisis and the official acknowledgment conveyed by the circular underlines the ways in which grassroots colonial officials helped *create* official economic anxiety through their discourses and lent observatory credence to the economic worries of higher colonial bureaucrats. In the process, they authorized and secured official endorsement for measures already contemplated or implemented at their own discretion.

Subsequent memos from Kaduna instructed districts to invest half their yearly revenue in a reserve fund "as precaution against emergencies." Another reserve, kept in a bank or in the native treasury, would serve as working capital. Additionally, Kaduna officials required all districts to invest £3,000 of their revenue in the crown agents in London.[21] In both theory and practice the scheme limited the discharge of colonial obligations in the area of providing social services and funding public works. It not only placed a limit on the percentage of revenue available for investment in public works, but, by recommending vaguely that "it might be advisable to place similar limitations upon other heads of expenditure," it portended the suspension of spending on infrastructure and urban utilities. The aim was after all to "maintain financial equilibrium within an Emirate." In addition to foreclosing the possibility of social spending, the memo from the secretariat urged "limitation along broad lines" with respect to the wages of government workers.[22]

State economic recovery policy had suspended public works and the building of infrastructure for the duration of the economic crisis. But the Northern Nigerian authorities allowed for impressionistic and cosmetic investments in intangible projects and in inexpensive schemes that could enhance British revenue collection. The memo's recommendation of artisan education instead of projects that yielded "material results alone" reflected this strategic exception.[23] As the secretary of the Northern Provinces argued, "There is a certain danger both financially and politically in forcing the pace [of material development]." This policy negated the foundational claim of colonialism as material uplift. It marked a retreat, albeit momentary, from the colonial promise of economic progress.[24]

Remarking retrospectively on the effects of the Depression on Northern Nigeria, a former colonial official in the Northern Nigerian Colonial Education Department captured the multifaceted devastation that falling prices of primary produce wreaked on Northern Nigeria:

> The price of groundnuts in 1931 slumped to £6 a ton from £36 a ton in the previous year. Reduced revenues meant reduced services—

many expatriate officers were retrenched. Salaries were cut by 10 percent and wages fell—Unemployment became a major problem amongst migrant labour forces, for example in the Plateau minefields the number of labourers fell from 37,000 to 12,000 and the wages of the latter from between 7/- and 9/- per week to 1/6d. to 2/- per week. Farmers were unable sell their produce and thus many people were unable to pay tax.[25]

This synopsis represents the tone of reports from different districts, including districts where crops other than groundnuts and cotton earned the majority of revenue. Between 1930 and 1934 colonial officials reported extensively on the economic damage produced in their districts by the slump. In Adamawa Province officials listed the main problem of African colonial subjects as "economic." Low prices "caused difficulty in collecting tax." In 1931 "the price of cattle was less than half of that of 1930."[26] From Bauchi Province, they reported on the "great lack of cash," which persisted because "market prices were very low."

Colonial authorities found the economic situation so serious that while urging official secrecy and restraint in the reporting of economic distress, they directed the colonial intelligence bureaucracy to investigate the extent of the problem. Intelligence did so, extensively, in the form of quarterly reports. Initiated to locate potential causes of grievance and anticolonial sentiment, the intelligence reports revealed the growing economic anxieties of farmers and livestock producers, as well as facts and statistics on deteriorating economic conditions in districts and villages.

The March 1930 edition of *Quarterly Intelligence Reports* spoke of discontent among producers of groundnuts in Kano Province, sentiments fueled by the "fluctuations in the already low price." The Kano peasants' dependence on groundnuts for their food needs had led to a concomitant reliance on grain from neighboring provinces. As prices collapsed, compelling these provinces to sell more of their crops to raise cash, the quantity exported to Kano diminished. As early as 1930 the problem had become crippling for Kano producers, who had to pay more for scarce grains while getting less for their cash-earning groundnut crop. "The difficulty," as the intelligence report stressed, arose from the reduction in the Kano peasants' purchasing power "owing to the trade Depression."[27] The emir of Kano found the predicament grave enough to "consider advising District Heads to encourage the farmers to return to the larger cultivation of cereal crops in view of the unsatisfactory price offered for groundnuts by European firms."[28]

Such dilemmas of local producers would become an albatross for the colonial authorities. On the one hand, officials had to recognize that producers could, as Frederick Cooper puts it, seek escape from markets not favorable to them.[29] On the other hand, they could choose to either educate locals on the larger forces responsible for the price slump or recognize and deal with the excesses of European produce-buying firms. Farmers in many other provinces had few if any choices. As prices of export crops collapsed, foodstuffs had already become a commodity sold in unusually large quantities for cash. But the price of foodstuffs was abysmally low. Between 1931 and 1932 "provinces generally state[d] that the price of foodstuffs [was] abnormally low." For instance, the price of guinea corn, a regional staple, "fell as low as 30lbs. for one penny."[30] As a result, producers faced a shortage of cash. The despairing representations of the crisis by on-ground officials portended what was to come, for fiscal problems would soon become one major element in a spiral of disasters that caused devastation, famine, and death.

THE YEARS OF THE LOCUST

The locust and grasshopper invasion of the early and mid-1930s exacerbated the prevailing economic conditions. Throughout the region, locusts devastated farms and destroyed potential harvests. By coincidence, this disaster continued apace with the steady fall in the prices of export crops and foodstuffs. As insects devoured potential harvests, earnings from what was spared continued to plummet.

In 1930 locusts invaded Zaria Province, causing "food shortage in Zaria and Birnin Gwari, whose crops of Iburu and Acha [grains similar to sorghum] were practically destroyed."[31] Other provinces recorded similar incidents. In 1931 the scourge increased in both intensity and breadth. In Bornu Province, "hoppers" made "their appearance in every direction." An eyewitness spoke of "an immense swarm of locusts . . . coming from the North and moving off towards the South."[32] This followed a similar wave of crop destruction by the ravenous locusts in 1930. Crops suffered "serious" damage, especially in the agriculturally fecund region of Lake Chad. In the same year, locusts attacked and destroyed crops in Gwaram District, in Kano. But the worst of the locust menace occurred, arguably, in 1932. The massive invasion completely overwhelmed all efforts to combat it. Eyewitnesses described a swarm so big it prevented the passage of trains in Kaduna. Residents heeded a proclamation that everyone should go out and kill the locusts, but even that proved ineffective, as "the hoppers were too numerous to be overcome entirely."[33]

In 1932, recognizing the seriousness of the situation, colonial authorities acknowledged the infestation as a regional problem. A government news release noted that "flying swarms of locusts are . . . to be seen in most of the Provinces." The large-scale invasions, the release noted, most severely affected the Zaria area.[34] The authorities' worries stemmed not only from the potential damage to revenue collection but also from the possibility of an embarrassing food shortage or famine. Top colonial officials in the region continued to discuss that disturbing possibility in secret. As early as March 1930 intelligence reports spoke of anticipated food shortages in some districts.[35] One such analysis, in September 1930, more explicitly predicted famine, drawing parallels between the biblical plague of locusts and the situation in Northern Nigeria: "the plague of locusts is said to portend the death of kings and a famine in 1931." The report "regarded with anxiety" the weeks preceding the harvest.[36]

LOCUSTS, TAXES, AND FAMINE

Locusts continued to wreak havoc, upsetting harvest projections up to 1935.[37] The invasion disrupted normal agricultural cycles. To continue to meet tax demands and other cash requirements, peasants sold much of their crops at declining prices, leaving them with no reserves for the difficult months preceding the next harvest. As Michael Watts has argued, the European buying firms cashed in on this situation to offer farmers credit against the yield of their crops.[38] In pre-Depression years farmers could still keep a reserve for feeding the household after paying off the buying agents with crops mortgaged earlier. Such reserves sustained the household in the few months of the rainy season before the first harvest. During the Depression the collapse of prices forced farmers to mortgage more crops to produce merchants than normal. Those who sold for cash similarly depleted their reserves for the preharvest months. Thus at the onset of the Depression farmers' economic fates already verged on impoverishment. When a farmer lost a crops to the elements or the locusts, as did most farmers during the infestation years, he or she relied on traditional support systems and local emergency mechanisms to stave off starvation and famine. Those mechanisms, sometimes stretched too thin, did not always function.

The fortuitous alliance between locusts and price slump dealt a crushing blow to the fortunes of Northern Nigerian farmers. It further exposed them to the unsavory nexus of colonial revenue systems, European produce buying firms, and Levantine, Arab, and African produce-buying middlemen. Colonial authorities recognized the connection between food shortages—reported widely in many provinces—and the mix of locusts and price fluctuations as early as 1931. Mention of it appeared in both a telegram from the resident of Benue Province and in a memo by the resident of Niger Province in that year.[39] In the same year the secretariat of the Northern Provinces asked all residents to report the extent of food shortages in their provinces. The responses from residents acknowledged the prevalence of shortages, though they claimed that "local measures [were] proving adequate."[40] Reports from Sokoto, Niger, Kabba, Zaria, and other provinces echoed each other. These vague, face-saving responses masked a deeper scourge of food shortages that would result in full-blown famine in certain districts, embarrassing the colonial authorities.

As food shortages continued to cause problems in most provinces, the government had to devise relief measures to help communities in distress. But the overarching need to avoid what colonial officials deemed as nonproductive expenditure (expenditure that would yield no tangible or immediate return for the government) compromised relief efforts. Plateau Province presented a clear case of the connection between the payment of taxes, the official reluctance to invest in relief, and the prospect of starvation. The resident there reported in March 1931 that the "locust depredations" had made famine imminent in the Wana area of the Southern Division of Plateau Province, adding disturbingly that twenty thousand people would "be on the starvation line towards the end of April."[41] He went on to propose a relief plan involving the purchase and distribution of food from the financial reserve of the district. Only when he proved that the people of the district had paid their taxes in full did he receive approval to withdraw money from Wana's fixed-deposit account. Taxation had become a mechanism of subtle blackmail, standing between starving peasants and food relief.

The peasants had a simple choice: pay taxes in full and starve or evade or partially pay and continue to eke out an existence. In Wana, residents who had lost their projected grain reserves to the locusts still could not get a holiday from colonial taxation. The eventually approved relief proposal carried one caveat: authorities would add the cost of relief to the future tax assessment of the Wana people. The secretary of the Northern Provinces even turned down a request by the resident to grant the relief food free passage on the railway because "it would involve the railway in a loss of revenue at a time when they can ill afford it."[42] Again, the Northern Nigerian colonial bureaucracy had wittingly or unwittingly trapped itself in a web of financial constraint. Once the regional colonial authorities got themselves into the language and practice of economic austerity and thrift, even an avowed outrage at the embarrassment of food shortages could not break their resolve. In general this determination stemmed from the fear that direct involvement of government in food relief would create a dependence that the government might have to continue to satisfy but that might compound state financial woes.[43]

The secretary of the Northern Provinces wisely warned residents to keep correspondences regarding the food shortages strictly confidential. The demands of the British policy of financial prudence threatened to further exacerbate a potentially explosive situation. The enormous social cost of maintaining and tightening the strict financial measures of the Depression meant that the colonial authorities had to be prepared to manage any resulting crises and tensions. Colonial authorities could not ignore the facts. With locusts on the rampage and with little respite from tax-collecting agents, circumstances could easily lead to starvation. In June 1931 the resident of Zaria Province reported that despite distributing 115 tons of food in the province, the population still faced an acute food shortage. However, the government insisted that the province pay for the food distribution, albeit at a subsidized rate. Communities like the Zangon Kataf, "who . . . have now reached the stage where their food supply is exhausted and . . . have no money with which to purchase even their bare necessities" were supplied with "free" food in exchange for work on a road project.[44]

The official discourses on food shortages tended to focus, understandably, more on the locust invasion as a causative factor than they did on taxation. Once again, British officials maintained the pattern of de-emphasizing the government's culpability in the prevailing economic travails. The locust invasion upset the structure and cycle of agricultural production that provided relative protection against starvation. But the tax collection campaigns—either carried out at harvest (compelling farmers to sell off their stock at prices lower than the Depression-era average) or after planting (thereby forcing farmers into a cycle of debt)—most directly caused the food problems. Middlemen gave cash advances to farmers, which took the form of "middlemen paying the producer's tax and withholding the receipt until crop delivery."[45] Some estimate that middlemen absorbed "at least 20 percent of the total price for export commodities" in addition to the profits from their transactions with farmers.[46]

Louise Lennihan adds yet another level to this hierarchy of extraction. Drawing on colonial records relating to rural poverty in the 1930s along the Bauchi Light Railway, Lennihan concludes that "30–42 percent of all rural [export] producers could not get through an annual agricultural cycle without borrowing." She adds that one of the most important ways of obtaining a loan was "through the mortgaging of unharvested crops to local . . . traders for a quantity of grain (or sometimes its cash equivalent in order to circumvent the Koranic prohibitions against usury)" at an interest rate of nearly 100 percent.[47] Additionally, European produce-buyers (as well as Arab, Levantine, and African middlemen), nudged on by the indifference of the colonial authorities, quickly identified profit-making opportunities in the exceptionally low prices of export and food crops. Depleted food reserves caused economic desperation and compelled farmers to seek credit, which in turn produced an opportunity for both European and African produce buyers to make good profits. A cycle of peasant indebtedness and impoverishment ensued.

The government had a difficult time regulating these diverse interests and managing this huge field of economic opportunism in which several economic actors—local and foreign—sought to profit from the economic downturn. Sometimes these skirmishes became a battle of economic wits. Local middlemen and British merchants went to great lengths to maneuver for succor and opportunity in the narrowing economic environment. With their self-interested actions, they turned economic adversity into an opportunity to entrench themselves more firmly in local trade. The profound struggle for a limited and constricting economic space brought both success and failure to actors.

The problem resulted largely from the entry of European, Levantine, and Arab merchant firms into the trade of foodstuffs. In pre-Depression times, these firms bought groundnuts, cotton, gum Arabic and other exportable products, with only a few sparsely capitalized Arab and Levantine firms trading in foodstuffs.[48] The Depression reduced the profit from the trade in export products, prompting the major European and Arab firms to enter the foodstuff market. At the same time, the Arab, Levantine, and African merchants who had carried on a small trade in foodstuffs (mainly in the emirate part of Northern Nigeria before the Depression) expanded their foodstuff operations. They expanded their buying network to virtually all parts of Northern Nigeria, including southern Kabba and Benue provinces.

The aggressive and opportunistic buying of food stocks for trade removed food from one area (leaving it impoverished, without cash reserves and food) and sold it in desperate, starving areas under the credit-buying system. In this way the Arab, Levantine, and African traders controlled the foodstuff trade, using its proceeds to make up for Depression-induced shortfalls in their export transactions.

The colonial government was aware of this but initially remained ambivalent. Colonial officials recognized that the Depression had paradoxically provided an opportunity for traders—Arab, Levantine, and African—to short-change local producers. However, because the traders were adept at anti-British propaganda, colonial authorities hesitated to act. To escape indictment and possible colonial persecution, the traders tried vigorously to sway local opinion against the ubiquitous United Africa Company, the biggest British produce-buying firm. They put out word among rural producers that the UAC was responsible for the impoverishment of farmers and for the widespread food shortages.

The entry of the United Africa Company into the buying of foodstuffs in early 1931 in the burgeoning climate of anti-British feelings confirmed, for good or ill, the propaganda claims of the Arab, Levantine, and African traders. Worse, once the company began direct produce buying, it diluted the role of African middlemen, whom local farmers trusted more. The African middlemen played their mistaken reputation of benign and sympathetic trade brokers to the hilt, spreading word that the UAC strove to secure a monopoly over all local produce to enable it to further exploit farmers.[49] Local farmers seemed to believe that the prevailing shortages and the level of rural indebtedness and poverty derived ultimately from the company's produce-buying practices.

This perception dovetailed, however inaccurately, with the fact that the farmers already associated the UAC with produce buying through its ubiquitous trading infrastructure and notoriously manipulative trading practices.[50]

Even the colonial authorities noticed the depth of Northern Nigerian dissatisfaction with the UAC's direct involvement in the foodstuff trade. A 1932 intelligence report lamented the "amount of resentment" engendered by the "persistent efforts of the United Africa Company to capture all trade" and to handle all its business by itself.[51] The report recognized that the "native middlemen in particular" had suffered a blow by the company's expansion into the foodstuff trade. The British regarded the situation as volatile, one that threatened the fabric of a fragile colonial order in Northern Nigeria. Smoldering since 1930 (when the company began its Depression-induced operational overhaul), an uneasy tension evolved between the UAC and British officials regarding the company's direct participation in the foodstuff trade. In August 1930 the company felt compelled to address the "local rumour" that it held responsible for the "misunderstanding" concerning its decision to get directly involved in the foodstuff trade. The company intended to use the confidential memo to the chief secretary to dispel the government's anxieties and to "make our position quite clear."[52] The company argued that its trade in foodstuffs would "relieve scarcity of supplies" by buying from areas of abundance and selling in areas of scarcity to "secure a reasonable margin of profit for our trouble." Unwittingly, the memo appeared to strengthen the hands of the company's detractors—mainly the African, Levantine, and Arab traders and brokers. The company's practice of buying foodstuffs cheaply at harvest to sell to areas of scarcity at high prices (a practice the company saw as a legitimate trade practice and as a part of its own economic recovery innovation) only fueled local anger and resentment. In a situation of increasing food insecurity, colonial officials worried that, if unchecked, the quest for profit might lead the UAC to overbuy foodstuffs from cash-strapped and indebted farmers and jeopardize social stability and economic production in rural areas.

The UAC memo responded directly to the charge that the company sought to hoard produce in order to create scarcity and maximize profit. The company maintained that its "interest is, and always has been, to be helpful to the general interests of the community."[53] It offered to withdraw from the trade because of what it saw as misrepresentations about its intentions. The chief secretary's response expressed the government's acceptance of the company's offer: "In view of the combination of circumstances, however, which are assisting to depress trade and prices generally and which are probably beyond the comprehension of even the literate minority of the people, His Excellency thinks that your decision to withdraw your activities in local foodstuffs for the present is a wise one."[54]

The authorities may have agreed with the position of the UAC. However, officials clearly regarded the UAC's operations as a liability and a source of local misgivings. At the same time, officials empathized with the UAC. It was an empathy founded on the economic kinship between the administrative and mercantile branches of British colonialism. But in such a volatile socioeconomic environment that empathy took a back seat to the imperatives of keeping a restive subject population calm and of preventing the intensification of inter-racial economic tensions. The chief secretary argued that the trade methods of the UAC seemed sound "from the European point of view" but that they "cannot escape the suspicion—however unjust—of exploitation."[55] Specifi-cally, the government feared an uprising like the Aba Women's War of 1929, which a government inquiry revealed had partly resulted from the introduc-tion of "modern trading methods."

Instead of leading to a closing of ranks between colonial administrators and British merchants, the economic crisis drove a wedge between them, fueling suspicion in both camps and undermining intracolonial economic solidarity in spite of shared economic interests. More than anything else, this tension underlined the major dilemma of Depression-era colonialism in Northern Ni-geria: British officials could no longer protect or defend their own merchants' practices, which African farmers perceived negatively in the context of the prevailing hardship. Whether officials admitted it or not, the Depression and its fallouts were causing enormous strain in the tenuous solidarity between colonial administrators and colonial merchants.[56]

As it turned out, the offer by the UAC to withdraw from food-buying opera-tions was only rhetorical; the company had no intention of quitting the highly profitable foodstuff operations. It had consolidated this success through a process of strategic cooperation with its biggest rival, John Holt & Company Limited, to avoid competition and maximize profits. The perceived price fix-ing that resulted from this cooperation enraged farmers in Tiv Division in 1931. They blamed the low price of beniseed (sesame), Tiv's only export crop, on the UAC's merger with John Holt. The Tiv farmers earned the sympathy of colonial officials, who endorsed the farmers' protest against the European buying conglomerate.[57]

In the wake of this incident, the UAC responded with a determined campaign to convince the government of its trading methods—which it saw as beneficial, fair, and socially safe—and of its lofty intentions. The company claimed that the bad impressions created about its operations emanated from a conspiracy against it by an alliance of African and Arab traders and Levantine middlemen, who, it claimed, rhetorically exploited local hardship for strategic economic gains.

The company shifted the blame for the scourge of rural indebtedness and food shortages to local traders, who it claimed "have exploited local difficulties on which they have flourished in the past." The African middlemen were "taking grave responsibility in opposing . . . sound modern trading methods."[58] It accused the Arab and African traders of speculation; they were men "whose outlooks were confined to the making of an immediate profit and whose operations are not on a scale which induces them to make their main motive the building of a commercial structure of permanent service." The company blamed the existing "dissatisfaction" among local farmers on the "low prices which they are today obtaining for their produce due to the period of Depression in [the] world market from which we are all suffering."[59]

Here the UAC presented itself not only as a company that understood and sympathized with local economic grievance but also as a cosufferer of the Depression. Its rhetorical strategy was elaborate self-exoneration; local farmers' "ignorance of the world market and the factors playing thereon" made them receptive to anti-UAC propaganda: "A certain amount of hostility having been successfully created, rumours as to the sinister intentions underlying the extension of a certain branch of the United African [sic] Company's activities are sure to find a receptive audience."[60] Despite the UAC's best efforts at explaining its operations, farmers and African trade brokers continued to causally associate the UAC's trade in foodstuffs and its method of buying export crops with the poverty of farmers and the dwindling fortunes of African middlemen. This perception led to more efforts by colonial authorities to distance themselves from the company and to urge it to scale back its operations while the Depression lasted.

Bob Shenton has suggested that the Northern Nigerian authorities consistently supported the UAC and other expatriate trading firms and that the government backed the UAC's antimiddleman propaganda and actions during the Depression.[61] This is not entirely accurate. In the face of growing anti-British sentiments at the colonial grass roots, the colonial authorities in Northern Nigeria, fearing social upheaval, recoiled somewhat from their traditional support for British firms, to the disappointment and dissatisfaction of the firms.

FROM FOOD SHORTAGE TO FAMINE

In the midst of the UAC's involvement in the foodstuff trade and the aggressive tax-collection measures of the British, an embarrassing famine occurred in 1931 in Kontagora Division of Niger Province. Famine broke out in Rijau and Kumbashi in June 1931, lasting through November, killing over a hundred people, and sending some starving survivors wandering through the bushes for wild food. Some roamed the countryside in search of work while others migrated to Auna, Yelwa, and areas as far as Birnin Kebbi.[62] The "emaciated and weak" who did remain, could not obtain seed for planting. The area had suffered from acute food shortages in 1930, and the devastation caused by locusts aggravated the situation into a full-blown famine.

The collection of taxes, which depleted reserves and left little or no cash in farmers' hands, also contributed to the famine, a fact recognized by the resident of Niger Province, who reported the outbreak. In his first report on the famine, he advised a refund of farmers' taxes or at least a tax break. [63] The tax situation, even if not the trigger, helped create the remote circumstances that made famine possible. The food problem illustrated what Michael Watts calls "the critical role of tax in the cycle of peasant reproduction."[64] The "conjunction of high tax" and low produce prices sustained farmers' indebtedness to an impoverishing cash-advance system of produce buying. This convergence of causes removed the financial safety net instrumental to local economic resilience in pre-Depression times. For as Amartya Sen has posited, famine results not from the nonavailability of food but from the lack of the wherewithal to secure access to it.[65] As farmers traded cash reserves for food and food reserves for cash, food crisis became all but inevitable.

The revelation of the 1931 famine embarrassed Northern Nigerian colonial authorities, who had all along minimized the extent of rural misery and had either praised the adequacy of relief measures or claimed that local support systems would suffice. However, while Northern Nigerian colonial officialdom considered the loss of more than a hundred colonial subjects to starvation "a very grave reflection on our administration," it believed that the absence of international scrutiny "such as would be present in a Mandated Territory" mitigated the situation.[66] Although Northern Nigeria was not a mandated territory, the fear of negative international publicity forced officials into a mindset of strategic blame distribution, in which subordinate officials in the colonial hierarchy with jurisdiction in the affected areas were saddled with the burden of crafting satisfactory explanations for the famine. To portray the famine as a result of bad judgment and decisions of individual officials rather than a product of the vigorous implementation of the government's economic recovery policy, the authorities in Kaduna blamed the resident of Niger Province and the DO of Kontagora for not reporting the incident early and for not taking adequate measures for dealing with food shortage in the district.

In his defense, the resident noted that when he first reported acute food shortages in the province, he alerted authorities to the imminence of famine. He recommended the acquisition of three hundred tons of grain from across the region. Authorities responded that the "shortages should be met . . . from internal [Provincial] resources." Consequently, he managed to secure only two hundred tons from within the province, and ordered the balance of one hundred tons of maize from Cape Town, South Africa. The Cape Town order arrived too late to save the victims.[67] When the South African maize arrived, officials distributed it, according to the resident, on credit against the peasants' next harvest, because "as a result of enquiries in Rijau District it was found that there was a fair proportion of the population whose purchasing power was virtually nil."[68]

Unwilling to directly criticize the government, the resident touted the adequacy of relief measures put in place before the famine and instead blamed the locust invasions in May, June, and July for undermining the policies. The famine therefore did not result from a failure of British relief response mechanisms; it represented an inevitable outcome of nature's troubles. Additionally, officials could not easily ascertain the imminence of famine because "the Pagan Dukawa" are "very primitive, shy of the British," and "are very difficult to get in touch with."[69]

The resident, in his defensive discourse, fell back on the familiar and convenient alibi of "native" attitudes as explanations for colonial failure. He argued that the severity of the famine stemmed from relatives who abandoned each other and from those with reserves of food who refused to share or sell to neighbors and relatives. The failure of the familial support system and what he considered lethargic resignation on the part of the victims, more than the actual circumstances of the famine, culminated in the embarrassing deaths. The most remarkable element of the famine, the resident noted, was "the callousness with which Pagan regarded Pagan" as well as "the resignation of these Pagans to their fate and their lack of will to survive when faced with famine."[70]

This invocation of nativist causation—in the form of primitive self-preservation and a lack of altruism—contradicts earlier British valorization of "native" cooperation and altruism as bulwarks against economic crisis. Here, the "paganism" of the Wana people allowed officials to remove them from this normative African culture of altruism and communalism and to advance their alleged selfishness as the cause of the deadly famine. Such diversionary arguments did not, however, stop the resident from indicting the acute manpower shortage caused by retrenchment exercises of the Depression period. He argued that more officers, had they been available, should have visited the district to investigate the extent of the problem.[71] He also acknowledged that the most important measure that would have prevented deaths was "the expenditure of much larger sums by the Native Administration in purchase of grain," noting that "to have ensured that no deaths occurred would have necessitated a much greater expenditure."[72] Such moments of realistic self-appraisal were not uncommon during this difficult crisis.

CHIEFS, TAXES, AND THE LIMITS OF INDIRECT RULE

The superficial strengthening of the system of indirect rule through the empowerment of chiefs and the subsequent subversion of that same power by a direct scrutiny of local colonial agents was one of the cardinal underpinnings of the new regime of aggressive revenue generation. As chiefs answered the mandate to collect taxes more determinedly—even ruthlessly—it became difficult to keep this group of colonial agents from exploiting their new positions of power. Some used their standing for personal pecuniary benefits and for the settling of personal economic or political scores.

The demands of the colonial state on chiefs during the Depression increased the range of dilemmas that confronted the chieftaincy institution; if chiefs moved too aggressively on the collection of taxes, fines, and fees in the midst of such poverty, they risked losing their legitimacy in local eyes or provoking protests and violence against their power. Disgruntled subjects could seek escape from domains where rulers too harshly implemented revenue collection. Escapes and elopements ultimately depleted the population and revenue mobilization capacity of such towns and villages and rendered chiefs vulnerable to British charges of incompetence, fraud, or both. If, on the other hand, chiefs remained sympathetic to locals, allowing them time and space to maneuver out of the revenue nodes of the state, they faced deposition by the state, prosecution, or ridicule by superintending colonial officials. As intermediaries in the colonial encounter, they occupied a crucial position; they could by their actions and allegiances make or mar the economic recovery order.

The troubled relationship between chiefs and the state on the one hand, and between chiefs and locals on the other, produced its own drama that played out in interesting ways in different districts. As chiefs struggled to balance the sentiments of their impoverished subjects against the demands of a distant but powerful colonial state, the process of negotiating these tensions and retaining their positions was fraught with difficulties, provocation, and considerable personal loss. Some chiefs sought to meet the emergency fiscal demands of the state by maintaining the size of their domain's population and, if possible, increasing it by sheltering immigrants. They aimed to bolster taxpaying capacity—still the most important way for chiefs to ingratiate themselves with the colonial authorities. This created tension between chiefs of contiguous communities as each sought to prevent people from escaping from its territory to take refuge in another.

This tension erupted into full-blown disputes occasionally. Saddled with a greater-than-usual tax demand, local rulers began to fault each other for failures or expected failures to raise enough taxes to meet British expectation. As the British stressed the need for self-sustainability and the importance of contributing to British metropolitan recovery, chiefs increasingly came to bear the burden of imperial economic recovery. The intense tax drive put enormous strain on local rulers, who, as chief accounting officers of their districts, bore the responsibility for collecting as well as the blame for failure to collect the assessed taxes for their districts. Each chief sought to keep as many people as possible domiciled in his area of jurisdiction as a way of guaranteeing or increasing revenue generation. This fueled tensions and boundary disputes between communities and chiefs. Early in 1934 the paramount ruler of Koton Karifi District wrote a petition to the district officer protesting what he saw as an encroachment on his tax domain by the paramount ruler of a neighboring district, the Olu Aworo.

> After due respect, this is to intimate to you that the Olu Aworo [traditional ruler of Aworo] Musa, Chief of Abgaja, sent his messenger and policeman to the other side of the Kwara River. They came to this land and arrested a man who was staying here, by the name of Igbonu Igbera Rere. He was taken to the other side of the River, assessed [for tax] and given a receipt. I have remitted my taxes. When they came for him I, Ohimege Igu, was not at home, having gone to Hausaland. So the king of Agbaja sent people to arrest Igbonu Igbera who lives in Rere as I stated earlier. Olu Aworo has not dealt fairly with this issue and has not given a truthful testimony. He came and arrested them and tax-assessed them by force. That is why I am petitioning him to you. I want to inform you that my deputy had already assessed them on the 28th of May 1934, two men and four women. Also, the king of Agbaja assessed them by force. Igbonu Igbera himself told Olu Aworo that he preferred to pay his taxes to Koton Karifi, and that he was opposed to paying under Agbaja. So, Olu Aworo just wants trouble and confusion between us. This is all I have to say. Peace.[73]

Apart from portraying himself as a serious colonial agent by invoking his past diligence in meeting his community's tax obligations to the British, Ohimege Igu, the writer of the petition, also provided excuses up front for an expected failure to meet the tax target set for him. In a period when the British promptly attributed failure to remit complete tax amounts to local corruption, he may have strategically sensationalized any incident that seemed capable of reducing the amount of taxes collected. The actual reason why Ohimege may have feared a shortfall in the tax season lay in causes other than the trespasses of an aggressive, tactless rival. Not only did widespread and unprecedented resistance to tax payment exist in this period, but in Koton Karifi (as in other parts of Northern Nigeria), peasants and artisans chose to lead somewhat nomadic lives in order to escape taxes. Transience became a rampant tax-evading strategy. The fact that Igbonu Igbera was "staying" rather than living in Koton Karifi lends credence to the possibility that he too had become a transient who hoped to escape taxation altogether. He probably had no intent of demonstrating a preference for paying tax in Koton Karifi, as alleged by the petitioner. A report of the assistant district officer of Kabba Division supports the idea that Igbonu

Igbere may have chosen to become a strategic nomad. The ADO suspected that Igbonu Igbera and the other subjects of the petition engaged in constant transition to avoid paying taxes and "warned them against living from place to place and paying taxes in none."[74]

Other chiefs sought to annex outright adjourning communities to boost their tax collection. In 1930 the emir of Zaria began to pursue his claims for the taxes of the Achakka farming communities, which were clearly situated in Plateau Province and therefore outside the jurisdiction of his province. This fact did not matter to the emir, who persisted in requesting tax from the area until 1932.[75] In February 1932 the people of Achakka had had enough. They attacked and beat a tax collector sent by the emir of Zaria and only the intervention of the colonial authorities quelled the tension that resulted. This exemplified the urgency with which chiefs pursued avenues that could potentially boost their tax collection potential. The emir of Zaria may have found Achakka particularly interesting because authorities had not assessed it as part of Zaria Province. Exploring it as an extra tax domain would make up for shortfalls, surpass Zaria's target to the delight of the British, or improve the emir's personal economy.

Rarely did chiefs get commended for their participation in tax collection during the Depression. On the contrary, they came under intense and unprecedented state scrutiny and criticism. Authorities removed and punished many chiefs for financial offenses and incompetence. In all the recorded cases of chiefs' removal in the early 1930s, officials justified the action with a recurring charge of embezzling tax money, though little documentary evidence exists to support the accusation. The British were quick to attribute any shortfall in the estimated tax chiefly to embezzlement. Delays in collecting and failure to collect estimated taxes also elicited charges of corruption. This pressure represented one of the most difficult dilemmas for chiefs charged with the impossible task of wringing tax from impoverished peasants.

The realization that the noncompletion of tax collection could earn them a dismissal or the accusation of fraud prompted chiefs to resort to drastic measures to fulfill their tax obligations. These measures sometimes elicited unsavory repercussions from their subjects. But the alternative was often deposition by the British. The British did not bluff on tax matters; they considered tax embezzlement a serious colonial fiscal infraction. In 1931 they deposed a "well-known" district head in Dikwa Division of Bornu Province for "malpractices and shortages in the tax."[76] In 1932 two district heads—the Ajia of Owode and Jima of Oloru in Ilorin Province—lost their offices over charges of embezzlement.[77] In 1935 the British found two key officials in Igbirra Division guilty of misappropriating tax money and of extortion. They discovered a scribe who was "embezzling small sums of tax"; another was "found . . . to be embezzling court fees"; yet another had extorted money from itinerant traders, using the authority of the state.[78] Similar fates befell chiefs throughout the Northern Provinces. A colonial official implicitly communicated the prevalence of this phenomenon in his remark on tax collection in Kano in the 1931–32 tax season: "General tax began to be collected at the beginning of November and was entirely finished at the beginning of April, 1932. . . . We should be glad to hear this, as it means that every official is able to retain his office, for we know that failure in the collection of taxes often results in retrenchment of officials."[79]

In Zaria Province alone, authorities sacked forty-four village heads for their inability to meet colonial tax obligations in 1931.[80] The magnitude of the spate of depositions may have led chiefs to unethical means of meeting tax obligations and maintaining their privileges, privileges that had been curtailed by the pay cuts of 1930. The ways in which chiefs tried to maintain their carefully cultivated lifestyles and privileges in the face of pay cuts and a cash crunch underlines the problem of chiefly extortion and rural exaction. Extortion and embezzlement reportedly occurred occasionally before the Depression.[81] The onset of the Depression, however, made it a major violation of colonial fiscal ethic because of the new commitment to revenue generation and the simultaneous fear of the political and social repercussions of overexaction. Embezzlement became both a Depression-era reality and a trope for explaining the increasingly impossible task of squeezing taxes and fees from depressed household economies. Chiefs seeking to maintain their lifestyles amid dwindling incomes had to make a choice between extortion of subjects and the embezzlement of tax money, and some daring and crafty ones devised innovative ways of doing the latter. However, as a trope, once the concept of embezzlement had entered the political communication of colonial officials, they continually invoked it to indict chiefs who merely "proved unequal to the responsibilities of tax collection."[82] If embezzlement had become an indeterminate phenomenon, extortion had become less ambiguous.

Empowering chiefs and other local colonial agents to collect taxes vigorously meant that these officials were tempted to go beyond their official mandates to enrich themselves. After all they too suffered from the cash crunch associated with the economic crisis. Having created these rural autocracies in the name of revenue generation, and having authorized them to carry out what amounted to emergency state-backed extortion, the state's efforts to limit their extortionist predilections demonstrated as much hypocrisy as futility. The magnitude of the problem of rural extortion by local colonial agents increased with the Depression for two reasons. First, the prestige and personal economies of chiefs and other colonial agents were at stake and, second, chiefs felt emboldened and relegitimized in their extortionist activities by the emergency economic declarations of the government. That colonial officials chose to deal with cases of extortion during the Depression underscored both the magnitude of the problem and their own fears about rural instability resulting from excessive exaction.

Chiefs became targets of colonial officials' frustrations in a period when impoverishment and dwindling administrative expenditure, not to mention the dearth of staff, made tax collection extremely difficult, complicating the goals of British emergency economic measures. Chiefs also became targets of the anger of local peasants, who felt that their dwindling income entitled them to a tax break or a reduction of tax rates. Many chiefs found themselves in this position; frustration from the colonizer and the colonized converged on the local chief or his agent. Sometimes these frustrations erupted into violence. Take the case of the district head of Zinna District in Muri Division of Adamawa Province who was murdered by his kinsmen while on a tax collection tour in his domain. The murder resulted from the insistence of the district head to press on with tax collection when peasants in his domain, whose income had been eroded by falling prices and by a locust invasion in 1931, did not intend to pay. While official reports disguised the protest, the intelligence report on the incident admitted the connection between tax resistance and the murder. "The murder," the report noted, "was due to the intention of the people to resist payment of tax this year as well as last." The report held that the murder had nothing to do with any "animus against the District Head who was personally popular." The district had also "suffered somewhat heavily from the locust invasion"[83] A similar incident occurred in the village of Jok in the Pankshin Division of Plateau Province in 1932, where angry villagers murdered a district scribe and a native authority policeman who were on a tax collection tour.[84]

Some incidents turned into full-blown riots in which local colonial agents and village heads who served as tax scribes struck back at the establishment that waited eagerly to accuse them of embezzlement. In some instances such colonial scribes merely allowed peasants room for maneuver in their tax jurisdictions, thus undermining official tax collection projections. That may explain why their communities mobilized to take on the perceived local representatives of the colonial status quo—the chiefs. That seems to have happened in the case of Odogo, the village head of Gabiji, who led a gang of peasant militants from his village to attack a neighboring district that had administrative and taxation jurisdiction over his village.

In early June 1931, Odogo led an armed mob composed of men from his own village and twelve other villages—two hundred men in all—to the village of Adenye, where the district head of Bassa Komo in Igala Division had gone to "hasten the tax collection."[85] In a swift and fiercely executed move, the mob swooped on Adenye, attacking the royal residence and setting fire to houses indiscriminately. At the end of the raid the district head of Bassa Komo and a few of his aides lay dead while £85 10s. out of £133 18s. that officials had collected as taxes from Adenye and some neighboring villages had been carted away. During subsequent hearings, the commission of inquiry set up to probe the incident questioned British officials about possible causes of the anticolonial outburst. The officers answered that neither the Depression nor its consequences (including the government's economic recovery measures) had anything to do with the uprising.[86]

In the effort to manage the fallouts of and African reactions to its economic recovery measures, the state confronted two debilitating dilemmas: how could the authorities consider the colonial system *colonial* in the positive sense authorized by British rhetoric when its avowed benefits could no longer be seen by Northern Nigerians? How could the state sustain a program of systematic fiscal exaction amid economic distress without destroying the productive and reproductive basis of Northern Nigerian societies—on which the future viability of British colonialism depended?

The Northern Nigerian colonial authorities made two crucial choices. They chose to extract as much revenue from impoverished rural sectors as they could, contracting an already troubled rural productive base, making colonial exploitation virtually impossible, and compelling rural peoples to adopt a myriad of practices to escape from colonial institutions of economic management. To assuage its fiscal anxieties, the colonial bureaucracy bestowed new powers on chiefs to enable them to extract much-needed revenue from farmers. In doing so, however, it undermined that same power and, by extension, the logic of indirect rule. The obsession with revenue generation intensified British officials' scrutiny of chiefs and increased the frequency of their direct involvement in tax collection and other practices of British colonial rule. As chiefs proved incapable of repairing and stabilizing a colonial situation made volatile by counterproductive extractive practices, British officials stepped in to engineer financial and socioeconomic order. Indirect rule acquired a more direct character.

These retreats from indirect rule and the embrace of direct rule reflected the colonial anxieties of a difficult economic moment more than they did a failure of indirect rule as a policy. Nonetheless, this precedent, along with numerous other violations of the rhetoric of ruling by proxy, serves to illustrate the convoluted trajectory of British power in Northern Nigeria and of the unstable character of colonial power formations generally.

3 ⤳ Social Transformations and Unintended Consequences in a Depressed Economy

THE UNINTENDED consequences of colonial economic recovery policy as well as local reactions to, and innovation in the face of, rising prices of imports and falling prices of domestic products confounded colonial efforts to draw more Northern Nigerians into the export economy through colonial economic institutions. As I have shown, colonial officials desired increased, not decreased, African participation in, and dependence on, the imperial marketplace as a strategy of economic recovery. The unintended consequences and local reactions analyzed in this chapter served to remove many Northern Nigerians from imperial markets and colonial economic practices and institutions. They also dissuaded others who may have considered the export crop market as a means of escaping further impoverishment.

Despite the modest success of the British effort to boost local export agriculture and to engage more Northern Nigerians, the loss of confidence in the world market and in colonial economic practices and institutions compelled many Northern Nigerians to seek more predictable, locally embedded economic vocations. As more Northern Nigerians took their economic fates into their own hands, using both legal and illegal means, the uncompleted colonial project of integrating them into the colonial economy—which the Depression had disrupted—suffered further reversals. Anticolonial and self-help criminality became a veritable weapon in the hands of Northern Nigerians for coping with the crisis.

As economic hardship and the state's economic recovery effort intensified through retrenchment, vigorous tax collection, and pay cuts, Northern Nigerians sought to both cushion themselves from financial peril and escape the unsavory effects of the government's economic recovery schemes. Retrenched tin mine workers resorted to petty theft; retrenched railway workers stole railway track components and sabotaged the lines; women cloth makers expanded production to meet a growing demand for local cloth, as imported cloth became too expensive for most people; gold prospectors fanned out in the hope of finding mineral wealth as a way out of poverty; and currency counterfeiters expanded their underground industry to fill the monetary niche created by the prevailing cash crunch. All these efforts, as well as criminal and non-criminal self-help, carried the same objective of escaping the troubled formal, state-regulated economy and exploring ways of avoiding the intended and unintended consequences of state economic recovery.

The noncriminalized strategies of economic survival and self-preservation helped reduce pressures for state-provided economic relief, to the delight of British officials. But, along with the criminalized acts, they also undercut the formal economy and its many nodes, hurting state control and ability to collect revenue, regulate economic flows and behavior, and maintain law and order in a difficult period. In the end, state reactions to these strategies; the failures of state interventions; the social troubles on mines and railways and in urban centers; and the entrepreneurial innovations of women, gold prospectors, and other groups all underlined the economic and political insecurity faced by Northern Nigerians. They also increasingly stripped the state of its legitimizing claims.

LABOR TROUBLES

The responses of Northern Nigerian colonial authorities to the Depression not only took their toll on peasants and chiefs, they also impoverished laborers—both casual and permanent—as well as those who were laid off as part of the government's economic recovery policy. Bill Freund has documented one of the major legacies of the Depression on Northern Nigeria—the collapse of the tin industry.[1] Most studies have focused almost exclusively on how the tin bust affected the fortunes of the mining companies and mine laborers. Freund shows, among other things, how the Depression intensified the struggle between capital and labor on the mines. An often-neglected part of the story of that industrial collapse are the economic and social problems that accompanied the wave of mine closures of the early 1930s, problems that reverberated through the Jos Plateau and beyond.

Evidence from colonial intelligence reports reveals that, in addition to its immediate and predictable outcome—namely the closure of mines and the resulting layoff of workers—the tin bust resulted in an enormous dislocation of normal socioeconomic patterns on and around the mines. With one of the major employers of wage labor in Northern Nigeria beleaguered, only one other major employer of labor in Northern Nigeria, the re-laying of the Kaduna-

Minna railway, remained. It employed about twenty thousand laborers between 1930 and 1931.[2] A large number of laborers and artisans also worked on the construction of the Benue bridge, which connected Northern Nigeria to the South. This surviving center of employment provided economic relief for a few Northern Nigerians—for a while. In December 1931 the new regime of thrift drastically cut the number of workers.[3] In 1932 the completion of the bridge rendered still more workers unemployed. The wave of retrenchment that swept through the colonial civil service created a class of unemployed, semieducated, and partially urbanized Northern Nigerians, already attracting attention from the colonial authorities because of their disaffection.

On the mines only a few companies continued to operate to meet the production quota allocated to Nigeria under the international tin agreement, which cut tin output as a way of shoring up its price.[4] These companies were too few to absorb a significant number of workers. Most of them retained what colonial officials referred to as "skeleton staff," leaving "large numbers of unemployed artisans looking for work."[5] Those they retained became the victims of a distinctly novel regime of acute wage squeeze crafted by the mining companies to sustain operations in the face of falling tin prices. The mining companies paid wages that secret colonial reports recognized as a "starvation point." This continued even into late 1931, when the price of tin recovered slightly, boosting mine revenue.[6] Most noticeably, this state of affairs meant that the majority of African laborers and artisans suddenly found themselves without jobs, trapped on the mines, and compelled to adopt different strategies and antics, legal and illegal, in order to survive. Many of the European workers also lost their jobs. A 1930 report spoke of how "the slump in tin" had swelled the number of the unemployed. Conditions affected Europeans workers so badly that they "would gladly accept £10 if they could obtain work."[7]

The grim employment situation in the region mirrored the general economic situation in the country. As the government cut funding to public-works projects, restricted railway construction on the economically important Kaduna-Minna line and the Benue railway bridge, and as the mining industry became depressed, a disturbing, unanticipated unemployment situation emerged to compound the pains of locals and the anxiety of the government. An intelligence report in January 1930 summarized the situation succinctly: "The curtailment of Public Works, the closing down of Railway construction, the Depression of the Mining Industry and of trade generally have all contributed to throw many persons out of employment. At the present moment there are a considerable number of unemployed at Zaria and Kaduna . . . of the clerk and artisan class. Everyday public works offices have been besieged by applicants."[8] H. P. Elliot, who arrived in Nigeria for colonial service in 1933 (the worst year of the Depression), tellingly captured the situation as well. On arrival in

Nigeria, Elliot was "met by a district officer who steered me through customs and into a mob of applicants seeking jobs as cooks or stewards to newcomers. It was my first shock to realize the poverty and unemployment caused by staff reductions. Nigeria had been greatly affected by the world slump. The 'boys' (as I was told they were called) pushed and shoved and waved their testimonials in our faces."[9] Estimates put the number of unemployed on the tin mines at nine thousand in 1931,[10] more than half the mine workforce before the Depression. The sheer number of these economically ravaged young men worried colonial officials, who expressed anxieties about the "difficulty of dealing with the unemployment question." The tendency of mining companies to encourage retrenched workers to remain on the mines "even though they [could] not hold out any prospect of employment" complicated matters.[11] Some of the mining companies provided land to the unemployed miners to cultivate and sustain themselves, but it remains unclear whether the former miners actually took to farming. It seems from the evidence that farming by the unemployed miners, if any, occurred on a limited scale. Besides, "the number of applicants [for farming plots] far exceeded the number of plots available."[12]

The unemployed set up temporary abodes in major sectors of employment and in major economic nerve centers of Northern Nigeria. They set up camps at different railway stations, where they engaged in criminal and semicriminal activities. One such railway town, Funtua, proved "a source of anxiety owing to the influx of the unemployed."[13] In 1931 someone reported the theft of £100 belonging to the British Cotton Growers' Association. The crime was attributed to the unemployed railway laborers.[14] But that illustrated only part of a bigger social problem that completely overwhelmed British vigilance and disrupted whatever social order they had managed to install in pre-Depression Northern Nigeria. In fact, the labor problem during the Depression went beyond the unemployment question; it included the seething discontent of those who managed to keep their jobs. For not only had their wages drastically decreased, as they had elsewhere in British Africa, where labor had become similarly abundant and cheap,[15] but the opportunity for paid employment became little more than a quest for survival. As a result, as will be shown shortly, the abundance of labor enabled British employers in Northern Nigeria, especially labor contractors, to shortchange workers.

The British found themselves dealing with a labor crisis that manifested on two levels: first, labor riots that pitched employees against employers, a crisis in which the government could only arbitrate; second, crime and violence, which sought to undermine the government's increasingly fragile rule. The authorities had to keep an eye on both the tin mines and the railway, both of which became hubs of crime and subversive activity. As a secret report pointed out in 1931, the provinces of Benue, Zaria, and Plateau — Northern Nigeria's railway and mining centers—harbored most of the unemployed and thus were the centers of potential trouble.[16]

HARDSHIP AND CRIME IN THE DEPRESSION EXPERIENCE

An upsurge in both the prevalence and diversity of crimes demonstrated one of the gravest consequences of the Depression and the government's retrenchment exercise. Some of these crimes bordered on perverse ingenuity on the part of Northern Nigerians and some amounted to the venting of raw anger and desperation in the face of hardship. Whatever their motivations and the forms they took, the crimes troubled a colonial state smarting from the imposition of much-dreaded reforms in the revenue and expenditure domains.

As crimes began to manifest throughout Northern Nigeria in unprecedented forms and cruelty, officials quickly made the connection between the new trend in crime and the Depression, albeit secretly. Publicly, the mantra tended to focus on the degenerate nature of "native" character. Secretly, in the intelligence reports, however, officials recognized the novel crime wave as having origins in the hardship imposed by the Depression and the ensuing economic recovery policies. A report in March 1931 spoke of an "increase in crime caused by the Depression in trade and in the tin industry" in and around Plateau Province.[17] The report considered the situation under control and noted that the "infliction of exemplary sentences" was "frightening away some of the worst characters."[18] This illustrates an official attempt to put a brave face on a bad situation, but later reports indicated a worsening of the situation. Earlier, in June 1930, the intelligence reports had unequivocally linked the rising crime rates on the Jos Plateau to the Depression: "the continued fall in the price of tin has resulted in increased unemployment on the Minesfield and consequently in an increase of crime as well."[19] In the same year, reports of criminal activities proliferated, activities that colonial officials "attributed to the unemployment caused by reduction of labour by the mining companies." The report further noted that "the unemployment problem amongst the native artisan class [was] still acute and . . . no doubt, account[ed] for the many cases of thefts and burglaries."[20]

The situation quickly took on a more disturbing magnitude both in variety and intensity. Highway robberies became common, the robbers sparing no one, including native authority policemen.[21] The geographical scope of the criminal activities also widened. In fact the entire Plateau Province became the vortex of a constantly expanding crime corridor. The theft of foodstuffs soon swelled the criminal repertoire of unemployed and desperate young men, most of them former miners and railway workers. Young men would traverse the areas around the minefields stealing "seed yams or seed rogo [cassava] from farms soon after they have been planted."[22] This caused enormous concern to colonial officials at a time of acute food shortages, locust invasion, and general food crisis. They feared that this crime could "endanger the future of food supply at a time when food may be scarce." Even more disturbing, during two such thefts, the criminals murdered the farm owners.[23]

As the colonial police increasingly clamped down on theft on the Jos Plateau, suspect after suspect invoked hunger, lack, or tax payment as the motive for engaging in crime. An examination of the record of the magistrate court of Jos reveals the extent to which, whether as exculpatory rhetoric or as a reality, or both, the plea of hunger and poverty had become central to most criminal proceedings for thefts during the Depression. Between 1931 and 1934 the hunger element featured prominently in these criminal proceedings. The trial of one Sashi, accused of stealing clothes, descended into a quagmire because "the accused says he has nothing to say—he was hungry."[24] Another accused, Habu of Jeidigi, accused of stealing "a quantity of cassava flour," a local staple, also "says he stole because he was hungry." The refrain "accused says he was hungry" dominates the records of criminal proceedings in the Jos judicial district of the early to mid-1930s.[25] Others accused of theft defended themselves by citing the pressure from impoverished kinsmen who relied on them for tax money. The economic downturn had made it difficult for them to remit money to their families for the purpose of tax payment as employers laid off workers or cut pay. One suspect, Adam, told the magistrate court that he stole some clothes because he had not received his salary from his employer, that "he wanted money to pay tax, [and that] they [his kin] had sent to him for it [tax money]."[26] He elicited some measure of sympathy from prosecuting court officials. Although the court found Adam guilty and sentenced him to three months with hard labor, the British district officer who presided over his case reported that "it may be quite true that his people were pressuring him for tax money," but he argued that "that does not excuse his stealing."[27] Judicial empathy, though it did little to mitigate the punishment meted out to convicts, also inhered in British officials' constant reference to the fact that accused persons were "out of work." This delineated a subtle legal acknowledgment of unemployment and retrenchment as a moral, if not legal, mitigation in the growing problem of theft.

The crime situation presented yet another problem for colonial authorities. Though heinous, these crimes appeared motivated by necessity. For, as one report put it, "the motive generally given is hunger due to unemployment or a decrease in wages and increase in the cost of living."[28] The challenge, for colonial officials, was acknowledging the economic motivation for the crimes without either appearing to endorse them or letting them undermine the already precarious food situation and the volatile social order. Further, colonial officials appeared unconvinced that resorting to brutal security measures without the removal or reduction of the prevailing hardship would solve the problem. They understood that some of the criminals might have taken advantage of the hardship to commit crimes, but they lacked an objective means of determining motives. As a result, even though officials talked tough about imposing "exemplary sentences," in practice they tempered any such resolve with an acknowledgment of an underlying problem they had yet to solve.

Implicated in this crime wave was a new class of unemployed young men, both uneducated and semieducated, who had become accustomed to urban life and paid work. They had no intention of reentering the agricultural domain from where they had come to serve the labor needs of colonial capitalism. Clearly, hunger complicated the situation. On the tin mines the Depression had virtually put an end to the trade in foodstuffs from the agricultural belt of Benue and Kabba provinces to the mining community. Without a profitable market, that trade dwindled and collapsed altogether, upsetting the food supply equilibrium in the plateau area.[29]

The social cost of economic recovery, especially retrenchment, continued to mount over the next months and years; so too did the anxiety of British officials. For instance, as reported in September 1932, an "increase in the number of thefts of foodstuffs and farm produce in the Jos and Pankshin Divisions" reportedly resulted from the growing "unemployment on the Plateau."[30] Authorities worried that "thieves and other undesirables are finding homes and centres from which to exercise their criminal activities in the large number of abandoned mining camps."[31] These concerns had merit; retrenched miners had begun staying in large numbers in abandoned mine compounds. With no visible means of livelihood, officials naturally assumed them to be the perpetrators of the crimes in the plateau area. Still, colonial officials, while making "arrangements" for "systematic surprise raids" on the camps, subtly admitted that the problem was beyond law enforcement. Consequently, authorities mandated that the resident of Plateau Province "differentiate between thefts committed as a result of genuine hunger and hardship and those committed by persons who are merely taking advantage of present conditions and have made no attempt to cultivate their own food supply."[32] They did not, however, provide modalities for making this distinction. Officials gradually came to terms with the refusal of the newly unemployed to accept their newly assigned official status as farmers and with their subsequent effort to maintain their minefield lifestyles through crime. But this official understanding did not seem to lead to a corresponding solution that would tackle the problem from its origins. Instead, knee-jerk reactions and judicial violence continued to characterize the British fight against crime. It therefore came as no surprise that crime merely became more disruptive.

In one example of the British colonial self-congratulatory ethos, officials prided themselves as the great liberators of slaves and the destroyers of an outdated domestic and plantation slave system in Northern Nigeria. Paul Lovejoy, Jan Hogendorn, Frederick Cooper, and other contemporary scholars have challenged this exaggerated claim and have sought to situate the so-called abolition of plantation slavery in more dynamic circumstances.[33] Yet they also insist that colonial conquest set in motion several dynamics that quickly spun out of British control and ultimately led to the demise of the system of plantation and domestic slavery in the first decade of the twentieth century. By 1910 the Sokoto Caliphate, backed by British colonists, had outlawed the legal status of domestic and plantation slavery and the transfer and sale of slaves. Similarly, records show that by about the same time the illicit traffic in humans in nonemirate Northern Nigeria,[34] where most slaves originated, had drastically decreased.[35]

During the Depression, however, officials reported that slavery had resurfaced. Impoverished and desperate locals, it seemed, sold "slaves" to opportunistic "dealers," who supplied them to relatively wealthy Fulani cattle owners and cocoa planters. For British officials, the emergence of a practice designated by them as slave dealing and human trafficking marked an escalation of the economic crisis and the "crimes" associated with it. From 1930 reports surfaced of interceptions of truckloads of child laborers contracted or pawned away by their parents. In Plateau Province desperate, unemployed young men forcefully captured some of the child laborers and then sold them to "Fulani herders who used the slaves to look after their flocks."[36] More reports on the disturbing practice continued to filter in, becoming increasingly alarming. It seems that the thin presence of colonial officials in rural areas (a result of the reduction of colonial staff as part of the government's austerity measures) only encouraged this new generation of "slave" brokers. In 1932 ninety-two persons were convicted "in connection with the traffic in children" in two districts alone in Plateau Province.[37] Even more disturbing, at their trial, all the "traffickers" in children, including those arrested for "selling" their own children, cited the shortage of food as the motivation, a defense that colonial officials had found "justified" only in the cases recorded in 1930 and 1931.[38] The admission that 1930 was economically worse than 1932 and that the shortage of food in those years mitigated the practice of child sale was counterproductive as an official explanation of the phenomenon. By invoking the connection between famine and human trafficking, officials yielded ground on the discursive level to Africans who insisted to colonial courts and investigators that hardship, not laziness or moral debasement, had pushed them into crime. Officials now acknowledged that times were hard, a fact some colonial commentators had denied or deflected. Although this admission appeared only in secret reports meant for select audiences, the fact that it became a valid explanation for the resurgence of an abhorrent practice suggests that the prevailing situation may have posed a difficult trial of conscience for officials.

Instructive, not to say puzzling, was the simultaneous and contradictory insistence of colonial officials to consider the validity of the hunger and hardship claims of the arrested culprits and their propensity for describing the new phenomenon within the framework of "traditional" African slavery with all its idioms—capture, sale, transfer. It takes a leap to interpret this harking back to a notion of African slavery as an attempt to untangle the problem of child labor and pawning from the economic crisis. Instead, I would argue that this invocation of African antiquity supported a preferred official explanation for a disruptive social phenomenon. This official explanation mirrors the bewilderment of the colonial bureaucracy and the tension between the public and private scripts of officials, who wavered awkwardly between officious aloofness and human empathy in their engagement with local hardship. Officials' attitude toward the new wave of crime remained tentative, vacillating between denial and affirmation of the economic hardship factor.[39]

The renewed practice of child pawning and child labor (described by colonial officials as child sale and slavery) occurred outside Plateau Province as well. In July 1932 the native authority police in Idoma Division of Benue Province intercepted a gang of "slave dealers." They arrested eleven of the criminals and detained three truckloads of children destined for the cocoa groves of Western Nigeria. Here, as in Plateau Province, the defendants invoked food shortage and taxation as motives. But unlike in Plateau Province, the illicit "trade," according to the colonial sources, took place with the "connivance and support of prominent people in the Idoma Division and the Ankpa Districts."[40] These were community affairs, it seemed, not just the isolated criminal behavior of individuals.

Many factors influenced and sustained child trafficking in Idoma Division, a situation my own ethnographic research has reaffirmed and that may help explain why such activity received the approval of traditional chiefs. Brokers offered the child laborers, unlike their Plateau Province counterparts, for work in the cocoa-producing Western Region of Nigeria as farmhands on cocoa plantations and as domestic servants. That difference, and the communal support that the "trade" enjoyed in Idoma Division, indicate that this practice was, far from slavery, a well-organized system of migrant child labor. Significantly, despite involving shady dealings, trickery, exploitation, and servile subordination, the practice partly contributed to whatever solvency existed in the Idoma economy during the Depression (see chapter 5).

The description of the phenomenon as a reemergence of slave trading reflected the anxieties and prejudices of colonial officials more than it did the on-ground situations that produced child labor pawning and child labor contracts. Informants in Idoma Division told me that until the 1960s child pawning and, sometimes, outright sale, remained an acceptable way of dealing with economic distress and debt.[41] As colonial officials frowned on pawning, locals did not attempt to make them understand the meshing of economic necessity with the cultural tolerance of the practice. To the British, then, this new phenomenon represented a resurfacing of slave dealing brought on by financial distress and opportunism.

LABOR CRISIS AND CRIME ON THE RAILWAY

The railway system in Northern Nigeria proved a site of diverse crimes during the Depression, for reasons not far-fetched. In the wake of the fiscal problems of 1930, the retrenched railway workers, like the miners of the Jos Plateau, remained in the railway towns and most of them still lived on railway property. Furthermore, the railway provided unemployed transients with a cheap means of transportation—a means to evade tax and escape colonial security surveillance. Also, as stated earlier, the re-laying of the Kaduna-Minna railway employed as many as twenty thousand people. Small camps quickly developed along the rail routes, peopled at first by workers and later by transients, part-time laborers, and prostitutes. One intelligence report on the railway town of Kuta observed, "criminals of all descriptions are attracted by the relaying work and congregate in the neighborhood of Sarkin Pawa." The Benue railway bridge emerged as another major employer of labor in Northern Nigeria during the Depression. Before completion in 1932 it was host to a series of labor disturbances and thefts.

The railway thus provided one significant source of anxiety for the colonial government, not least because the transience of life in the railway camps encouraged subversion, labor activism, and crime. The cheapness of the railway and the communication network it created brought with it the potential to facilitate sociopolitical agitation. Officials therefore dissipated much ink and many resources reporting on and dealing with the labor problems and crimes on the railway. The Depression worsened an already combustible theater of crime and labor trouble.[42] The volatility of the railway situation rested in part on the fact that, for most of those employed within the railway infrastructure at this time, their families in rural districts depended on menial railway work as their only source of cash.

Households and clans sent these laborers with specific instructions to earn cash on behalf of the family and to return with a haul of cash for tax and other purposes.[43] Understandably then, as labor conditions deteriorated and as contractors reneged on their promises and labor contracts, a pall of frustration descended on the railway. Transients—some economic refugees from the Jos Plateau, others retrenched from the railway and the colonial civil service—also became a menace on the railway. These groups set up gambling, money lending, and other not-so-legal businesses in the vicinity of the Kaduna-Minna railway, fleecing laborers of their earnings and engaging in petty thievery.

A new genre of crime surfaced in 1930, catching Northern Nigerian colonial officials unawares. Thieves stole railway track components made of copper (known in British colonial railway parlance as keys) and sold them to local blacksmiths, who melted them down to make agricultural tools and household items.[44] Widely reported along the entire Northern Nigerian railway network, especially in Benue, Plateau, and Niger provinces, the situation forced authorities to begin treating the practice as a serious crime. Unsurprisingly, the persistence of the practice forced colonial officials to adopt harsh punitive measures against culprits. In July 1931 members of a group of thieves stealing railway keys in the Lafia area were sentenced to prison terms of various lengths.[45] This did not deter desperate, cash-strapped young men with no sympathy for, or loyalty to, the railway system. In most cases, the thefts were committed by railway employees, former employees, or their associates. However, though they were familiar with the operations of the railway, especially the technical components of the tracks and the location of the keys, these thieves faced not only a high risk of getting caught but the even greater risk of certain death by an oncoming train. I would, therefore, argue that some of the thefts also represented acts of subversion and subtle protest by workers and former workers. Some railway transients remained angry at the layoffs, others seethed with the decline in pay, and still others resented the squalor that had come to characterize railway work.[46]

Still, available evidence shows economics as a very strong motive for crime. Hardship made the thieves criminally innovative. In several cases, thieves skillfully removed keys without compromising the safety of the line; a thief bent solely on sabotage would not have been so careful. Another indication of an economic motive is that the theft of railway keys was not the only economically desperate act of survival that retrenched workers engaged in. The evidence indicates that railway workers took up farming to make up for loss of income and even paid locals to do the actual work for them. As one reported stated, "the thefts are committed with the knowledge of railway employees, whose practice of paying local natives to make farm for them may well be responsible for some of the key stealing."[47] The theft and sale of railway keys to earn money with which to cultivate an agricultural plot was part of a retrenched railway worker's desperate fight against destitution.

The 1931 prison sentences did little to stem the tide of railway key thefts. Late in that year an intelligence report stated that the "stealing of Railway Keys continues in the Benue Province." In 1932 the thefts intensified, necessitating the replacement of copper keys with steel keys. But the pace of replacement could not match the pace of the theft. As replacements arrived for one section, an "inspection of another section revealed that many keys were missing, many being so loose that they could be removed by hand and others lying at the side of the line."[48] More brazen and ambitious thefts on the railway raised the stakes. Targeting railway station safes, some thieves operated on the Minna-Baro section of the railway. Though authorities made several arrests between 1930 and 1932, it remains unclear if that terminated the thefts.

Despite the rampant theft of railway keys, colonial officials' attention focused more on the labor camps and on towns along the railway than it did on the railway itself; the camps and towns had become hubs of crime as economic refugees, criminals, and opportunists converged on them. Officials feared that riots would break out and that frustrated laborers would invade the farms of local farmers and cause a crisis that might consume both the railway work and the fragile peace existing on the railway. Circumstances soon confirmed these fears.

Officials attributed common petty theft to the unemployment situation. In Benue Province "there were large numbers of Ibo and other Southern unemployed in towns on the railway, and petty crime [was] prevalent."[49] As Southern Nigerian artisans, technicians, and clerks lost their jobs on the plateau, on the railway, and in the colonial civil service, they tended to move closer to South Nigeria. They settled in any of the railway towns in Benue Province, from where they could easily get to the South. Some secured temporary menial jobs on the railway while others relied on their wits for survival. Often poor and leading miserable lives, they knew these towns offered limited opportunities and grim economic prospects. Railway work gangs were reportedly sullen, with "sour looks" indicating suffering and frustration. Some colonial officials felt that the deplorable situation arose "apparently due to reductions both in pay and the number of men unemployed." For these self-critical officials the situation clearly resulted from the excessive austerity policies of the government, and they declared that "government and its officials are [to be] held responsible."[50] The angst generated by the government's economic recovery measures demonstrated the extent to which they impoverished and radicalized workers, compelling officials to include some degree of self-blame within the secrecy of intelligence reports, as illustrated by the quotation above.

Official anxiety stemmed partly from the fact that many Southern Nigerians mingled freely with both the railway labor gangs and the unemployed. Southerners gradually became associated with agitation, as they were seen to embody the unwanted effects of Western education. Officials considered Southerners, the more educated group of laborers, capable of a radical appreciation and interpretation of the prevailing conditions of the economy. For this suspicion, they became subjects of British disdain. A colonial official working on the railway observed, "Originally an enthusiast for education for Africans, [I] was left with an uncomfortable feeling about the products of the schools in the South."[51] Reports focused sharply on the unemployed Southerners. Officials complained about the "natives of the Southern Provinces [who] have found themselves without work." They regarded the Southerners with suspicion—as much for what was seen as their troublemaking capacity or perceived criminal tendencies as for their perceived radicalism and the influence it might bring to their Northern colleagues and associates. In late 1931, as work on the Benue railway bridge neared completion and a reduction in the number of workers took effect, officials' fear focused on the "unemployed Ibos in the vicinity of Railway Stations, where petty stealing is prevalent."[52]

The causal relationship between crime and unemployment among young Igbo men, itself a construct of British frustration, had become entrenched in the British administrative imagination in Northern Nigeria. Needless to say, it engendered great concern among colonial officials. They viewed young Igbo men as completely removed from traditional life, a floating population that threatened social and economic order in Northern Nigeria. A colonial official remarked, "the [Igbo] labourers themselves left me in no doubt about the effects of detribalization, that is to say of giving up village life and its discipline."[53] British officials, on the other hand, perceived Northern laborers as still having a connection to rural life.

By far, conditions in railway labor camps and stations, especially (but not exclusively) on the Kaduna-Minna route, provided the most serious sources of concern for authorities. The camps had become notorious for their poor working conditions. Contractors on both the Kaduna-Minna railway and the Benue bridge took advantage of the illiteracy of laborers and the abundance of labor during the Depression to shortchange workers. This practice had already become egregious by mid-1930, leading to labor agitation and inchoate organizing. In May 1930, for instance, contractors dismissed six employees from the Benue bridge project for trying to start a strike to protest arbitrary cuts in pay, nonpayment, and neglect of overtime payments.[54] This incident was the first in a series of labor troubles on the railway during the Depression. The Kaduna-Minna railway became a center of trouble, sometimes threatening the peace of a wide swath of territory within Northern Nigeria.

The major source of grievance appears to have been delays or nonpayment of laborers' allowances. It seems that both Nigerian contractors and their expatriate counterparts participated in this practice. They consciously used the economic situation as an excuse to deny workers their entitlement in a period in which the abundance of labor all but eroded the bargaining power of workers. The system of delayed payment not only gradually made railway work unpopular, it emerged as a ploy by contractors, especially the Italians, to avoid payment altogether. As one discerning British official observed, "in many cases labourers who, perhaps, do a fortnight's work and are told to come back in two or three weeks' time for their pay prefer to sacrifice it."[55] In early 1932 the "tardiness of contractors in paying wages" became a recurring concern.

The problem proved more serious than a mere "tardiness," as shown by the testimony of W. R. Crocker, a colonial official in charge of security on the Kaduna-Minna railway project in 1931. His investigation revealed that Nigerian and expatriate contractors (the former were employed by the latter) connived to shortchange laborers. He spoke of the "grosser thieveries of the contractors, mostly Ibos." He also unveiled a contractor who "had squandered much of his income in trying to live like a Chief, [and] and became unable to pay his laborers."[56] But he also indicted European engineers who, secured in the knowledge that cash-poor laborers could be exploited without protest, refused to pay laborers or their contractors. Two of them were particularly notorious in laborers' complaints and featured prominently in Crocker's report. This revelation provides insight into the true nature and hierarchy of labor exploitation that railway laborers confronted during the Depression. It seems that everyone in a position to employ labor invoked the Depression to justify shady dealings that went against the interest of laborers. Contractors and engineers persisted in trying to anchor their personal financial recovery on the backs of laborers.

Crocker's investigation into the activities of an engineer named Jameison, one of the European engineers, "made it clear that he had been cheating his labourers by paying them only a portion of what was due to them, but they had been putting thumbmark receipts against the amount due to them. The labourers being illiterate, had no idea what figure they were putting their thumbmark against."[57] Another European contractor, nicknamed White Cargo, had also made a habit of not paying his laborers. Crocker recalls how he had visited the contractor while the latter was terminally sick from blackwater fever. According to Crocker, the frustrated, unpaid laborers confronted the contractor for their money on his deathbed: "Scores of labourers were sitting around the hut waiting, clamouring, for their pay, and, prior to my arrival, every now and then one, bolder than the rest, would push his way past the concubine [an African female companion] and enter the hut to importune with, or even threaten, the dying man."[58] The government seemed to have acquiesced in the practices of employers and engineers by tacitly conceding to them an operational freedom, and it seemed bent on treating the labor problem on the railway only as a law-and-order issue. Even after unearthing the shady practices of Jameison, Crocker found his attempt to bring the European to justice rebuffed: "The Legal Branch, to my fury, advised me that the case against him would not hold in law." This attitude of government increased discontent among the populace; it advertised, for good or ill, the government's failure to act against those taking advantage of the prevailing conditions to shortchange desperate laborers.

The failure of the government to protect workers against the exploitative practices of Europeans proved socially costly, as did its failure to check the activities of European produce-buying firms (see chapter 2). This latter phenomenon, though, often resulted in violent repercussions. Between 1930 and 1932 several riots broke out in the railway labor camps. In July 1931 a particularly violent one erupted at Sarkin Pawa, on the Kaduna-Minna railway project, in which laborers attacked some Nigerian subcontractors who failed to pay them appropriately. The contractors in turn blamed the European contractors, especially the notorious Jameison, for withholding the monies.[59] In August 1932 another riot in Gwada, also on the Kaduna-Minna project, required a police detachment to restore peace. The riots became so incessant that colonial authorities sent W. R. Crocker to maintain law and order on the railway. Crocker "was sent in hurry because there had been riots," underscoring the urgency of the labor problem on the railway. Crocker claims to have halted the spate of riots but he remained curiously silent as to how he accomplished the task.

The most disturbing of the labor troubles pitched laborers against the Gbagyi villages through which the railway line ran. Impoverished, unpaid, or underpaid laborers trying to save their earnings to meet demands in their home areas often invaded the farms of the local Gbagyi people for fruit and other food. The Gbagyi would fight back, attacking the laborers with arrows and sometimes pursuing them to the labor camps. Crocker's job was to "discourage" the aggressive response of the Gbagyi, "for they were accurate bowmen."[60] Once again, the colonial state considered this crisis a law enforcement issue. From late 1932 the aftereffect of labor frustration began to hurt the contractors and engineers. The pool of labor continued to decrease as workers simply stayed away from the poor labor conditions on the railway. As a 1932 report noted, "if it were not for [the nonpayment, underpayment, and late payment of laborers' wages] much more labour would be available."[61]

LOCAL RESPONSES AND UNINTENDED CONSEQUENCES

Northern Nigerian peasants, artisans, and skilled and unskilled laborers—all affected to varying degrees by the Depression and by British economic recovery measures—refused to remain passive and helpless participants in the economic configuration of the Depression. Where possible, they maneuvered their way into positions of relative economic ease. They used the little space left unregulated by the emergency economic regime to either boost their economic resilience in the face of hardship or to seek escape from the institutions that facilitated or accentuated their vulnerability to economic adversity.

As locals sought cheaper local alternatives to expensive European imports, the market for local crafts and products expanded in what became an unintended consequence of the depressed economy and of imperial preference. This new consumption pattern favored local craftsmen, who rose to meet the demand for local substitutes for European manufactured products. In Northern Nigeria the women cloth makers of Kabba and Igbirra were the most visible of such groups of artisans. The Igbirra cloth makers showed particular innovation while adapting to this new economic opportunity, as evidenced by colonial records and oral accounts. Some of the first documentation of the Depression-era expansion in the production of handwoven cloth in Igbirra Division came in the division's 1932–33 annual report. The report spoke of the "sound lines" on which the people of Igbirra were "able to weather the economic storm with less discomfort." It went on to state that "the reduction in purchasing power has led to a return to this local Igbirra . . . cloth and has at the same time stimulated the export market for this material."[62] The government encouraged the development of local craft and clearly seemed resolved to promote this Depression-induced expansion in spite of its commitment to the promotion of British imports.

Not a matter of either legislation or compulsion, consumption, the government realized, was a product of rational economic judgment, especially in a time of economic crisis. Moreover, the government at times seemed at ease with developments like the Igbirra cloth boom because they enabled locals to meet their financial obligations to the state. At such times they seemed less concerned that such isolated booms threatened the state's promotion of British imports. The geographically limited artisanal boom had the added advantage of reducing the economic and political troubles of colonial subjects in those areas. This consideration justified the government's support for the revival of local craft, a support that led it to exaggerate the extent of the revival of local cottage industries and the potential volume of local cloth production. The government's unrealistic projections for this burgeoning industry reflected its own self-interested economic and political goals and perhaps its almost obsessive aversion to the influx of cheap Japanese textiles.

These colonial aspirations and anxieties differed markedly from the goals that women textile entrepreneurs set for themselves. The expansion clearly came from the new demand for local textile products. Oral sources have dated the development of key production centers, such as the ones in Ogaminana and Okene, to the early 1930s.[63] Many of these centers have survived and, with the installation of machines, have become fairly modernized. Some have even become training centers.[64] Though this expansion of local textile production did not meet the government's projections, it created a momentary oasis of prosperity in a desert of economic despair. Additionally, it represented one of few cases in which the prevailing economic adversity economically empowered local groups.

The feminization of local economic recovery, bolstered by the commercialization of the age-old craft of women's cloth making, remains one of the most significant products of the Depression. Women entrepreneurs in the Okene-Kabba axis stepped strategically into a niche that opened up as a result of the rising price of textile products from the British Empire. The economic crisis expanded and consolidated women's domination of the textile sector. It also empowered them in their domestic and social relational arrangements by turning many of them into economic providers for their families and kinship units.

Economically distressed Northern Nigerians also sought financial relief from the Depression by prospecting for precious metals. Looking to weather the economic downturn, many took to prospecting for gold. A gold rush of sorts ensued. Many individuals who sought both an economic cushion against the Depression and personal fortunes gravitated toward the potential centers of gold mining. Logically, the development of gold mining in the early 1930s in Northern Nigeria had an international component. During the Depression people across the globe recognized the stability of gold prices and the value of that stability. This awareness did not escape Northern Nigerians and seemed to have spread as the crisis deepened. As a result the possession of, or access to, gold gradually came to be regarded as a means to financial security.

Gold exploration started in Sokoto and Ilorin in about 1930. Looking to make a fortune in the colony, European entrepreneurs led the initial efforts, which relied on crude methods. Opportunism may have fueled the gold-prospecting efforts of European entrepreneurial mavericks, but their indigenous laborers and allies took to the risky and uncertain vocation of gold exploration as a last ditch effort to escape the prevailing hardship. Citing colonial records from Plateau Province, Zakariah Goshit has posited that more than three thousand semiskilled Hausa laborers on the tin mines migrated to the Sokoto and Ilorin alluvial gold mines after the tin mines fell on bad times and laborers were laid off.[65] Similarly, reports in 1932 spoke of how the "high price of gold" was beginning to "attract miners and prospectors to the east of Sokoto Province, and to Rimi, in Kano Province."[66] The transfer of skills and labor from the tin mines to the gold mines exemplified one of many such migrations to areas of potential or existing gold mining during the Depression. Many scattered, unorganized small-scale gold exploration operations were not documented. Nonetheless records show that they attracted young men from across Northern Nigeria who were willing and ready to take risks and get into uncharted vocations in the desperate quest for economic survival.

The Ilorin and Sokoto mining works pioneered what blossomed into a viable, albeit loosely organized, activity in the creation of value through gold mining. In 1932 gold prospecting in the Molendo River region of Kuta Division, which had started in 1930, intensified.[67] In March 1934 a European gold prospector—whose agent, known simply as Umaru, prospected for gold in the Abuja area of Niger Province—undertook a major endeavor. Umaru struck gold almost immediately and obtained the approval of the emir to embark on mining in the area.[68] He returned with his European backer, laborers, and tools in the rainy season to begin what would develop into a multicamp gold-mining field in the Abuja area, buying up farms from locals on which to establish the mine pits.[69] The mines flourished and attracted many more Europeans and enterprising Southern Nigerians. This became not just a new opening for laborers starved for work opportunities but also a platform of potential economic recovery for produce-buying middlemen, failed traders, artisans, and laid-off civil servants. One indigene of Tapa, the village in which most of the mining took place, recorded the unprecedented economic activity in the Tapa area: "Before long, the mining work had really intensified. European visitors from Britain, France, Germany and people from Kwara [Province] all came to look for wealth. Even some well-to-do Southern Nigerians came with laborers and work tools. There are now ten camps, the biggest of which is Barikin Rimi. It was set up by Mr. Heath. . . . There are four companies there. . . . Every company has about 200 laborers. This camp is the most prosperous of all the camps because there have been more gold finds."[70]

The regionwide gold-mining effort intensified in the early to mid-1930s, enriching some participants and raising the prospect of alternative means of wealth creation in Northern Nigeria. It remains unclear whether the government regulated this wave of mineral exploration and, if so, how much of it they could actually document and tax. It seems that due to its ad hoc nature, the exploration went on outside the mechanisms of government controls and regulations. However, the government recognized the Depression-era surge in mineral exploration and the benefits it presented or portended for the depressed Northern Nigerian economy. An editorial in the government-published *Jarida Nijeria ta Arewa/Northern Provinces News*, the official news organ in Northern Nigeria, seems to suggest that this was the case: "The mining industry fortunately is in better shape and the high value of gold is attracting much interest in this metal; our readers will be interested to hear that in one month recently the amount of gold mined in Nigeria approached very closely the mining for the record for the [record] year of 1915."[71] The gold boom of the 1930s enriched some of the Europeans who participated in it, including Jameison, the notorious engineer on the Kaduna-Minna railway. Harassed by laborers and haunted by his sharp practices on the railway, Jameison abandoned his job as a government contractor and went into gold prospecting. It paid off: "He struck gold in the 1933–34 boom and retired to Europe, apparently well off."[72] For Africans, gold exploration provided financial stability in a time of distress; it demonstrated that real wealth came not in coins or paper money; and it proved that wealth abounded latently in the country. One astounded observer noted that the prevalence of gold mining "indicates that Nigeria is blessed with enormous wealth."[73] If nothing else, the gold exploration activities supplied psychological succor for those close to the centers of gold mining and for those who participated in it. More important, this new belief in the local origins of wealth and in the abundance of latent wealth signaled an intersection of local strategies of economic recovery with the state's rhetoric of self-help. Both sought to locate the impetus for economic recovery within the region, specifically in local entrepreneurial initiative. This fortuitous convergence illustrated the different reasons government and the gold prospectors embraced the boom. African gold prospectors saw it as a means of survival, while colonial officials considered it a strategy to deflect attention from governmental relief. The gold rush and its potential to redirect local thinking about the Depression and recovery understandably made the government more receptive to it.

The gold boom raised enormous expectations; perhaps the government encouraged that as a way to foster hope in a despairing population. The mineral boom in general did inspire hope for recovery and for prosperity in some Northern Nigerians. One observer's remarks typify this group of optimists: "presently, gold mining is expanding; recently a precious stone called diamond was discovered; it is a stone with much value, much more than gold."[74] The discovery of diamonds in Niger Province added to the sense of hope. But, more important, it convinced some Northern Nigerians that the way out of the Depression involved taking one's economic destiny into one's hands by exploiting the latent resources of the land. This sense of local initiative spread quickly and soon communities began to initiate and lead mineral-prospecting efforts. For instance, in 1935 the young men of Yagba District, in Kabba Division, organized themselves and started prospecting for gold in their district. They succeeded and by 1937 "there had been a considerable development of gold mining activity," resulting in the extraction of over two hundred ounces of gold a month by about six hundred local laborers.[75]

Gold mining never became the regional economic lifeline that Northern Nigerian colonial officials would have wished it to be. Other than helping prospectors, villagers, and communities near gold-prospecting sites ride out economic difficulties, it did not significantly affect the long-term economic planning or goals of the colonial administration. The industry, born as it was of economic crisis, fizzled out gradually after Nigeria recovered from the Depression.

MIGRATION AS A STRATEGY FOR ESCAPE AND RELIEF

As the Depression took its toll on individuals and families and as the government enforced taxation with unprecedented vigor, desperate measures—such as flight and cash-earning migratory adventures—suggested themselves to young men and women. Desperate young men began to act on their adventurous desires for economic relief. Considerable human mobility and demographic shifts emerged in Depression-era Northern Nigeria, including the migration of labor to gold-prospecting sites. Many patterns of migration within and away from Northern Nigeria evolved during the Depression as its use as a hardship-cushioning strategy became increasingly popular. Retrenched young men responded to the economic downturn in several migratory ways. Some returned to their hometowns and either became a burden on their families or participated in local agriculture; others wandered from town to town, village to village in search of work and to escape taxation. Still others, desperate for cash and eager to help shore up their families' economy, began to look outside Northern Nigeria for cash-earning opportunities. Some went to Lagos to work in the seaports while others went to the cocoa belt in southwestern Nigeria.

Kabba Province provides a good setting for examining the migration to Lagos, the internal strategic movements of people within Northern Nigeria, and the hometown-bound migrations of young men from the tin mines and other distressed centers of employment. Colonial officials noticed the strategic use of such migrations for defeating colonial taxation and economic control. At the same time, officials realized the economic benefits of transregional, labor-oriented migrations. This dual awareness shaped colonial responses to the demographic shifts of the early 1930s.

The new migratory patterns worried colonial officials because they had implications for colonial tax measures and for social control. Anxieties about transience and the difficulties it posed to tax assessment and collection were rife. The 1933 annual report for Kabba Province noted that "in Kabba and Koton Karifi Divisions the economic difficulties have driven a number of people to seek their means of livelihood further afield." It noted that "the high tax had caused emigration to neighboring Divisions where the incidence of tax was lower."[76] This rural population drift involved mostly peasants and artisans. But it had its urban analogue. To maintain urban order and to protect the interest of a local class of landlords, the colonial authorities allowed them "a certain amount of latitude" in increasing house rents, ostensibly to meet tax obligations and liabilities.[77] However, not only did high rent compel many urban dwellers to migrate, the liberties exercised by the landholders hardly insulated them from the prevailing economic difficulties, although they arguably enjoyed a better economic deal in general. One report underscored the fact that even landholders had to seek economic relief outside their land-holding. "Poor trade and the shortage of cash compelled many plot holders to go far afield in search of work, [and] some of them have been absent for the greater part of the year leaving their dependents a mere pittance for their subsistence."[78] The dislocation of families and communal cohesion through migration continued despite the concern of British officials. Since migration itself had always been a common part of rural life, and they lacked an articulated legal code for dealing with it, British officials could only complain about it, which they did throughout the Depression.

Women bore most of the economic burden of these strategic migrations and of the return of retrenched and destitute young men to rural areas. In the face of the economic emasculation of husbands and male household heads, many women took on the responsibility of economically sustaining the family. Having taken control of rural domains of production and reproduction as men's mobility became central to their economic self-preservation and to their ability to escape colonial justice for nonpayment of taxes, wives, mothers, and sisters often used their savings to finance the expensive male migrations to Lagos and other centers of commerce.

Migration was not the only demographic response of Northern Nigerian colonial subjects to the Depression difficulties, nor was it the only threat to the attempt of the British to demographically map Kabba Province for tax purposes. Complaints that tax censuses and assessments were being sabotaged by cases of "concealment of children" ran rampant. Because the government based tax assessments on the size of a household, concealment of children became a rational, albeit novel, way of reducing the household tax. Women played a central role in the creative trickery of escaping taxes, since the Victorian orientation of colonial officials conceded little creative agency to African women and thus reduced their visibility to officials' suspicions of African deception. Often, women also had to creatively hide remittances from migrated husbands and relatives from colonial tax gatherers, in addition to working the fields, maintaining what was left of the family's wealth, and reducing the family's tax obligations through child concealment.

The concealment of children, husbands, and other male relatives by ingenious women challenged colonial efforts to boost revenue. Migration, however, remained the biggest worry of colonial officials. But migration by itself did not present a problem. The British did not formulate a definitive policy against migration, nor did they appear to have opposed all migratory activities. But the purpose and nature of such migration as well as its propensity to produce vagrants and transients (in rural areas) and a "floating population" (in urban centers) frightened officials. Colonial officials in Kabba Province appeared at ease with purposeful labor migration. They acknowledged that with the onset of the Depression, young men had begun to leave the province, especially from the West Yagba area, to go to industrial centers like Lagos. These young men soon began to remit money to their relatives, thus increasing cash flow into the province and potentially making tax payment easier. A 1938 report noted "the big West Yagba connection in Lagos," stating that "it is probable that a certain amount of money passes from people employed there to their families in Yagba."[79] Although the Yagba, obviously trying to escape higher tax assessments, failed to declare the monetary remittances, colonial officials knew that this Lagos-bound migration benefited both the division and Kabba Province as a whole. Migration did not present a problem but its use as an escape from tax assessment and payment did.

This concern also underlined the colonial anxiety about vagrancy and the unemployed, floating population of educated and semieducated youths who had lost their jobs in the wave of retrenchment that followed the Depression. A 1934 report from Kabba Division alerted the resident of Kabba Province to the "considerable number of retrenched clerks, artisans, shopboys, and the like" that were "returning to their homes from far afield." The report complained that these returnees were "living on their wits" and that they had become a source of embarrassment to their parents and kinsmen, who had become saddled with the responsibility of providing them with the "necessities of life."[80] The divisional officer of Kabba Division, author of the report, viewed this group of retrenched skilled and semiskilled young men as a social and economic problem, especially since they refused to go back to farming. While workers laid off during the Depression mostly remained in industrial and commercial centers, constituting an urban floating population and straddling the boundary of rural peasant life and urban working life,[81] this group of Kabba workers chose to return to Kabba Division. There they reconnected with their rural roots but refused to take up farming and thereby strained the finances of relatives, making tax payment more difficult. The divisional officer suggested closing the "food bins" to these young men so that they "would not be too proud to farm."[82]

Many retrenched young men, accustomed to life outside their home areas, did not return to their hometowns or, if they returned, did so temporarily. Many went to the cocoa belt to work on cocoa plantations, as did many others with no migratory experience but who desperately needed the cash. Sara Berry captures the attraction of the cocoa belt in her compelling analysis of relative cocoa prosperity and increased cocoa production in the Depression.[83] According to her, "people began to migrate into the cocoa belt from other parts of Nigeria in search of work" in the 1930s, and this migration was both a cause and a product of the cocoa boom of the Depression.[84] A significant number of the migrants came from the Idoma, Igala, and Igbirra areas of Northern Nigeria. Oral sources date the beginning of this migration to around 1937,[85] but it might have begun much earlier.[86]

RESORTING TO COUNTERFEIT COINS

The currency policy of the British during the Depression consisted of a sustained withdrawal of funds from the Nigerian economy. The policy of withdrawing silver coins from the Nigerian economy started in 1920 with the introduction of new alloy coins. When the Depression hit, the withdrawal of silver coins was intensified as the British economy needed gold and silver as instruments of financial stability. Officials sent the withdrawn coins to Britain to be melted and stored as part of the strategic gold and silver reserves. By the 1931–32 fiscal year, officials had removed £6,184,000 in silver coins from circulation in Nigeria.[87] Between 1931 and 1933, in the very difficult years of the Depression when the scarcity of cash hit the hardest, they withdrew £204,000 in silver coins. The spate of currency withdrawals caught Nigerians unawares; they had accumulated little or no reserves. The "lack of money reserves among natives" presented a problem that even some organs of the colonial establishment acknowledged.[88]

To replace the withdrawn silver coins, state officials injected some alloy coins into the economy. This aggravated the complexity of the currency situation as multiple currencies circulated. Monetary fluidity and diversity was a feature of the pre-Depression Northern Nigerian economy. However, the new policy of intensified money withdrawal and the introduction of yet another coinage (alloy) compounded the monetary confusion. As with every other British economic recovery policy, the people of Northern Nigeria responded to this new policy in ways that presented colonial officials with new challenges in the management of the region's increasingly volatile economy.

As colonial coinage became scarce—as a result of the decline in the volume of money in circulation—the peasants of Northern Nigeria reverted to a barter system. They also returned to the use of brass rods, a precolonial currency that enjoyed wide circulation in the Benue valley and in the area of the Niger-Benue confluence.[89] Colonial officials thought they had eliminated them in the first few years of colonial rule as they tried to monetize the economy. Instead, they discovered that the rods "had been hoarded for years, are being dug up, and can be seen in all markets."[90] The reemergence of precolonial currencies complicated British taxation and economic activities, where this reemergence happened with the most intensity. It reflected the tactical, though incomplete, withdrawal of Northern Nigerians from certain nodes of the colonial economy. It also threatened taxation, because the government could accept only colonial currencies for tax payment. More important, it marked the emergence of a parallel monetary domain engineered by locals residing on the fringes of the colonial economy, whose access to the colonial currency all but fizzled out during the Depression.

Peasants also responded to the new monetary policy by refusing to adopt the cheap-alloy coins introduced in place of silver coins.[91] As a result, the monetary basis of the colonial economy lost some of its appeal, causing confusion among locals and undermining local trade. Like other measures designed to transfer wealth from colony to metropole to help British economic recovery, monetary withdrawal and the introduction of substitute currency (alloy) generated their own dynamics at the colonial grass roots.

By far the most brazen and organized response of the people of Northern Nigeria to the new monetary regime came from local opportunists, in the form of counterfeiting. The scarcity of cash created by the silver withdrawal and the unpopularity of alloy coins spurred a coalition of regional (Northern Nigerian) and national actors to meet the cash needs of the period in a different way. This new vocation of counterfeit coinage must be understood as part of a growing trend during the Depression: different groups of people took advantage of different fallouts from the government's economic recovery program to make a living or to profiteer. As Ayodeji Olukoju argues, "the 1930s witnessed great intensification of counterfeiting and prompted calls for a new coinage to replace the alloy that was easy to forge."[92] His accurate observation fails to highlight the causal relationship between the currency shortage and the prevailing hardship, and the spread of counterfeiting. While this activity (unlike some others) had a distinctively criminal character, it thrived because it was sustained by the same forces of local desperation and need that provided local produce buyers and moneylenders a niche to make money. Counterfeiting became one of the biggest problems of the Depression in Northern Nigeria. It also became one of the biggest niches created inadvertently by the fiscal priorities of the depressed colonial state. This niche not only threatened the formal economic and monetary fabric of the region, it created a liminal economic space whose terms were dictated by local actors. It also opened a whole new informal zone of economic life that created opportunities for participants.

Widespread counterfeiting and the elusiveness of the cottage coin industry became a source of British anxiety. Counterfeiting had become so widespread and so disruptive of economic harmony in Northern Nigeria that it attracted more commentary in the intelligence reports than any other issue. As early as 1930 colonial intelligence reports began to describe the operation of what they called counterfeiting gangs all over Northern Nigeria, especially in the areas traversed by the railway. Reports spoke of the arrival in Kano of large numbers of "various coins known as chinku (usually five franc pieces) . . . being imported from Marseilles by Syrians through the Gold Coast."[93] Officials identified some of the coins as having Swiss, Peruvian, Sardinian, and Czechoslovakian origin and suspected that a trade in the "chinku" silver coins had developed between Europe and Kano.[94] The local interest in silver coins had deep and cultural origins. In Kano, for instance, residents paid dowry in silver coins.[95] It seems that colonial officials became aware of these cultural associations (as well as the use of silver coins in transborder trade between Northern Nigerian traders and traders from neighboring territories in West Africa) only after they realized the prevalence of the unofficial coins. The attempt by Northern Nigerians to go back to the old silver coinage in the far northwestern provinces, and the return to precolonial currencies as well as the embrace of counterfeited alloy coins in the north-central provinces, all derived from the same phenomenon. Locals were exploring alternative monetary affiliations as the monetary system in Northern Nigeria became more problematic and constricted.

Commentary on the problem of counterfeit coinage continued with numerous reports in the following years. These reports portray the activity as having a transregional character, with actors using Southern Nigeria as the manufacturing center and Northern Nigeria as the distribution zone. A March 1930 report spoke of a surveillance on a "suspected coining gang" operating from Ijebu Ode, in Southern Nigeria.[96] A subsequent report lent credence to the group's transregional operation when officials arrested a gang of counterfeiters at Gusau, in Sokoto Province, and discovered their base to be Ijebu Ode. Discoveries of this nature pointed to a much deeper root for the emergence of the coin-counterfeiting industry; officials began to view the problem in a national context, stopping short only of tying it to the national policy of withdrawing silver coins from circulation. Although "the majority of counterfeit coins [were] manufactured in the Southern Provinces," officials feared that Bida, in Niger Province, could become a manufacturing center in the North. Similarly, areas along the railway, which "offer[ed] facilities for distribution and . . . a certain amount of safety from detection," began to feature prominently in reports on counterfeiting.[97] A distribution network supposedly operating in Northern Nigeria transported its merchandise to "remote country districts" to "dispose [of] their stock among the unsophisticated peasants."[98]

The impression that counterfeit coins thrived only in rural areas and were accepted by naive peasants was at best only partly true. While it was easier for counterfeiters to escape detection in rural areas, due to higher reception levels and the thin and intermittent presence of colonial infrastructures and personnel there, the issue involved was beyond the simple dichotomy of sophistication and naiveté. Evidence exists that in urban areas like Kano City, counterfeiters enjoyed a good circulation for their coins.[99] The most important issue remained the cash shortage. Since the cash scarcity manifested more patently in rural districts, and since peasants suffered the most, rural areas and their peasant inhabitants, understandably, became the biggest patrons of counterfeit coins. This reality embodied the dynamic of demand and supply, albeit perversely. Counterfeit coins continued to circulate in the provinces of Sokoto (Yauri and Zuru), Niger (Baro), Kabba (Igbirra), and Ilorin (Borgu) despite the best efforts of colonial officials to stop their circulation and reaffirm their illegality.[100]

Currency counterfeiting severely disrupted taxation. As peasants began paying their taxes with counterfeit coins, causing shortages in British tax projections (since fake coins had to be discarded), officials began to respond more vigorously to the problem. The tax system witnessed the most articulate response to the counterfeiting problem. If officials could not stop the circulation of fake coins or destroy the centers of their manufacture, they would prevent the coins from entering official state funds. The government mandated the Bank of British West Africa (BBWA) to undertake the task of detecting and isolating fake coins from the bags of tax money deposited with it. But as the volume of counterfeit money paid as tax increased, the bank became overwhelmed. In 1933 it increased the commission it charged the government for acting as its official banker.[101] In a memo to the division officer of the Daura native authority in January 1935, the bank cited as one of its reasons the "heavy cash work connected with the work of checking of tax money which has recently been rendered more onerous by the prevalence of counterfeit coin and the subsequent need for increased vigilance."[102] That the government not only experienced shortages but was also charged a fee by the bank for sorting the coins brought in by tax collectors seemed to reinforce the determination of the authorities to move more decisively against the prevalence of fake coins in tax money. However, this determination to tackle the problem encountered problems of its own.

Even before the action of the BBWA, officials worried enough to begin formulating the outlines of what would become the government policy regarding counterfeit coinage. In 1931 the Secretariat of the Northern Provinces issued the first set of directives to colonial officials on tax shortages resulting from payment with counterfeit coins. The directive firmly placed responsibility for counterfeit tax money on African colonial tax collectors who failed to detect them: "Native Administration officials who accept counterfeit coins in the course of official business will be held personally responsible, but each case will be considered on its merits, and the loss will be written off if the spurious coins are of such exceptionally good workmanship and the proportion of counterfeit to good coin is reasonably small."[103] In the subsequent refinement of this policy, tax collectors who failed to detect fake coins would have advance salary accounts created for them, from which they would have to make up for the amount of counterfeit coins in their tax collection. The policy further directed officials to deface detected counterfeit coins, making them unusable, before returning them to the taxpayer.

Authorities employed this policy for a few years. Reports spoke of how "native treasury staff, district and village heads" exercised "the greatest care to detect counterfeit coinage tendered in payment of tax" because they "expect[ed] to be held financially responsible for counterfeit coinage detected in their remittances."[104] The state considered at this point that lessening the financial responsibility on tax-collecting officials would make them relax their vigilance. But that position raised new issues. First, placing responsibility for fake coins on officials meant that they could seek to make up for the loss either by extorting money from innocent taxpayers or by overestimating the tax obligations of households. Second, the colonial authorities themselves acknowledged several mitigating realities: most of the coins were so well made that only banks could detect them; in most cases this represented the only money available to the taxpayer; and the taxpayer might not even recognize it as counterfeit money, having earned it from legitimate business transactions.

In fact, in February 1936 the government had to accept the flaws in the principle that informed its decisions. A test by the BBWA on some suspected counterfeit coins missed a significant number of counterfeits. Though described as an error, the test forced the authorities to reason that "the fact that a European banking official could make such an error . . . would make it seem inequitable to make natives bear a great deal of responsibility." Furthermore, officials realized the unfairness of dealing "too severely" with villagers who were "of a lower intelligence than that of the makers [of the coins]" and the bank that carried out the coinage detection exercise.[105] As the problems of government deepened and in the months and years that followed, some level of moderation entered the policy on counterfeit tax money. The state urged public enlightenment in place of punishment, warning native authorities that "imitations of the alloy currency so skillfully executed as to be very difficult to detect, are being introduced in increasing quantity." The state further encouraged the native authorities to demonstrate the difference between genuine coins and counterfeit coins before villagers in markets, and directed touring officers to give "useful advice" to the peasantry and point out the penalty for knowingly transacting with fake coins.[106]

With time the colonial authorities conceded more ground and came to terms with more problems. They acknowledged that it did not make sense for officials to simply refuse to collect the fake coins as tax since that would leave them in circulation and amounted, technically, to abetting the circulation of the bad coins.[107] Another problem involved the fairness of the policy to collect and destroy coins tendered for tax and then make taxpayers pay a second time.

The government auditor captured the problem succinctly: "to confiscate all suspect alloy, without even regarding it as a token of payment would (a) inflict unnecessary hardship on the population, by forcing them to collect their tax again and (b) possibly prejudice future attempts to apportion responsibility in an equitable manner, and (c) shake the confidence of the population in alloy currency, a result strenuously to be avoided, since the supply of nickel is short already."[108]

The unintended consequences of strict official intolerance of counterfeit coins, which the auditor underlined, must have convinced the authorities to relinquish a degree of strictness toward peasants and local tax officials. The Secretariat of the Northern Provinces, acting in line with the Nigerian government's new moderation in policy, directed that "financial responsibility of Native Administration officials who accept [counterfeit coins] should be limited."[109] It also recognized the impossibility of identifying those who paid their tax with counterfeit coins and of returning their coins to them in unusable form, since district heads often kept tax money in a "common cash tank." It further acknowledged that even if officials could identify the payers, it would be "difficult to force them to pay again, and possibly unwise."[110]

The counterfeit-money industry inadvertently created by the monetary policies of the government during the Depression did not end with recovery from the downturn. Unintended policy consequences and unwittingly created dynamics tend to take on a life of their own, perpetuating themselves in the polity much longer than the situation that gave rise to them. Thus, although by all accounts, and from the available evidence, one could say that Northern Nigeria had embarked on the path of economic recovery by 1936, counterfeit coinage continued to constitute a problem for the authorities until the 1940s.[111]

↬

As a result both of the government's policy of retrenching African workers from mining and railway employment and of pay cuts, the 1930s witnessed the reemergence of social disorder marked by vagrancy, thefts, and various illegal acts of survival. The attempt by the colonial authorities to criminalize and detach these acts from the economic recovery policies of government faltered because of palpably inescapable connections between the two.

British officials maintained a narrow perspective, constrained by their own rhetoric and doctrine of economic recovery. The phenomenon proved more significant and widespread than officials admitted: Northern Nigerians sought escape from the organs of colonial economic control and pursued comfort and recovery through self-help, both legal and criminal. From the criminal acts of survival by retrenched mine and railway workers, to the quasi-anticolonial acts of stealing and sabotaging railway equipment, to the self-cushioning innovations of local craftsmen and women, to the desperate innovation and enterprise of new gold prospectors, to the activities of currency counterfeiters, the theme remained the same. Northern Nigerians had begun rejecting and removing themselves from imperial markets and economic institutions that subjected their economic fates to global and imperial forces and policies. They chose to insulate themselves from the unintended consequences and collateral effects of economic recovery. These local strategies ran counter to the colonial economic recovery strategy of boosting export crop production by integrating more Africans into the export sector and increasing yield. They also undermined African consumption of British manufactures, a key source of solvency for the home economy and a key source of revenue (import duties) for the colonial government. But the strategies were tolerated to some degree because they took pressure off the state and suggested that Africans were responsible for and capable of engineering their own economic recovery.

4 ❧ Protests, Petitions, and Polemics on the Economic Crisis

THE 1930S illuminated colonial failures and the hollowness of colonial claims about economic paternalism with an unprecedented clarity. Members of Northern Nigeria's embryonic elite quickly picked up on the ways in which the Depression exacerbated and highlighted the failures and weaknesses of the colonial system. Most of them had become casualties of the state's cost-cutting retrenchments. They saw an opening to criticize state failures, using their individual plights and those of regular Northern Nigerian colonial subjects, who had no intellectual voice of their own.

Bundling their own personal and group financial crises with those of Northern Nigerian farmers, laborers, chiefs, traders, and women, a small group of Western-educated Northern Nigerian commentators, led by a former colonial auxiliary and ad hoc newspaper publisher, Samuel Cole-Edwards, assailed the failure of the Northern Nigerian colonial authorities. In strident newspaper commentaries and petitions to colonial authorities, they lamented their plight as unemployed and economically destitute colonial subjects and criticized the failure of the state to grant tax relief, financial help, or patronage to Northern Nigerians. They also inverted familiar colonial discourses of benevolence and paternalism to demand state intervention in the prevailing economic hardship. Cole-Edwards and his group of ad hoc, crisis-driven anticolonial critics demanded, unlike their postwar counterparts, more, not less, colonial paternalism.

In asking difficult questions and holding British colonialism accountable for its rhetorical promises of economic protection and prosperity, the critics sidestepped state claims of bankruptcy and financial distress and inaugurated a sphere of debate on the very essence and mission of British colonialism in

Northern Nigeria. Stung by these criticisms and their potential to resonate with the Northern Nigerian colonial public, officials established their own newspaper, through which they sought to blunt the populist appeal of the poignant analyses and criticisms of Cole-Edwards and his group. Publishing a variety of counterclaims and propaganda materials, colonial officials (and a few local sympathetic interlocutors) tried to exonerate the state from the economic crisis and thus from the responsibility of recovery. They also cast Cole-Edwards and his group as troublemakers and inciters, while persecuting, monitoring, and harassing them.

Cole-Edwards and other commentators proved unforgiving in their indictment of state responses—and lack of them—to the Depression. But their activism by no means mirrored the intent or rhetoric of anti-British nationalists' movement for independence. Many of them had served and continued to serve in the colonial system as employees, contractors, and clients. Their criticism therefore did not constitute a critique of colonial exploitation per se but rather a lamentation for its momentary cessation. They voiced their frustration at the dearth of the profits and surpluses that had made it possible for them to keep jobs, earn good salaries, and get patronage from colonial bureaucracies. They complained of the unsavory consequences of the cessation of the pre-Depression economic order.

FROM PERSONAL DISTRESS TO ANTICOLONIAL CRITIQUE

Samuel Cole-Edwards, a Sierra Leonean, had come to Northern Nigeria in the 1890s to serve as secretary to Frederick Lugard, the administrator of the Royal Niger Company. In October 1930 he penned a lengthy petition to the lieutenant governor of Northern Nigeria through the resident of Kabba Province. In the petition, Cole-Edwards railed against several practices of the colonial government and lamented that he had become a victim of suspicion, ridicule, and unfair treatment because he promoted the economic interests and aspirations of Northern Nigerians. Cole-Edwards, a trader, shipping middleman, and colonial contractor, also served as president of the Lokoja Traders' Association, an umbrella body of Northern Nigerians who participated in the trade of the Niger-Benue confluence, in the town of Lokoja. The increase in shipping and freight duties charged by British shipping conglomerates trying to cope with the Depression had eroded the economic viability of the local middlemen and traders at the onset of the Depression, in 1929. As Cole-Edwards put it, "The high rates of freights charged by the Niger Company now the United Africa Company [UAC] gave a death blow to traders mostly middlemen. . . . Traders became crippled and exceptionally few were able to combat with the existing condition of freight others had to retire and seek for employment."[1] Cole-Edwards found himself displaced by this new economic reality and thus wrote from a rich experiential repertoire. He centered his petition on the prevailing economic Depression, which he claimed had impoverished the people of Northern Nigeria. He appealed to the resident to use his office to reduce the burden of taxation on Northern Nigerians as a gesture of state empathy: "From your many years of experience in this country and in your position as a Resident you will be in a position to recommend reduction in taxation to meet the needs of the people in this world-wide Depression of trade."[2] He also wanted "women [to be] exempted from taxation" as part of the economic relief package he was recommending to the government. Cole-Edwards saw himself as an intercessor, helping to convey to the government the gravity of the situation, and as someone willing to tell the government what locals hesitated to say— that the state had an obligation to ease the economic uncertainty. He further considered himself an "honest, outspoken, and independent-minded" person, and found it "unfortunate" that the colonial bureaucracy had not matured to the point of developing a policy "by which the honest, outspoken person is encouraged instead of persecuted."[3] Cole-Edwards elaborated his indictment of the state for its intolerance for opposing views, especially criticisms of its management of the Depression: "The pity of the situation lies in the fact that even though there may be the conviction that such [critics] are on the right lines, yet as it is not human nature to endure opposition difficulty arises."[4] Here Cole-Edwards questioned the supposed intellectual supremacy of the state. His thesis, simple but powerful, berated the colonial state for regarding critics like himself as "obstructionists, trouble makers and haters of the white man's rule" rather than as allies and constructive critics.

In a subsequent petition sent directly to the lieutenant governor, Cole-Edwards bared the depth of his antigovernment grievances and elaborated on his earlier complaints. If his earlier petition was laced with altruistic rhetoric and he came across as a principled anticolonial activist, his second petition, written a year later, revealed that his grievances were as personal as they were nationalistic. It emerged from the second petition that Cole-Edwards, like other African clerks, merchants, contractors, and artisans had lost the economic patronage that he enjoyed from the government before the Depression. Although he had run afoul of colonial goodwill and etiquette, the Depression all but obliterated his chances of securing favors and contracts from the government. His insistence on these economic lifelines as instruments of personal economic relief, in disregard of the government's rhetoric of financial insolvency, brought him into direct confrontation with the state. Colonial officials saw Cole-Edwards as an irritating agitator tapping opportunistically into the veins of local hardship.

Cole-Edwards complained about losing a contract to supply foodstuffs to the prison in Lokoja, which he claimed he was qualified for, having earlier executed a similar contract.[5] He spoke of another foodstuff supply contract for the

African hospital in Lokoja, also denied him, he believed, as part of officials' effort to punish Africans who, like himself, were critical of the government's indifference to local suffering. He waxed personal again: "These, and some-things akin, are the difficulties and treatment of their worst kinds meted out to me, and in these days of Depression, as one is compelled to find outlets to obtain an honest living, when His Excellency would have gone into the merits of my case, and the parts I played in assisting the administration of the north, I trust he will assist me in one direction to bring about a better understanding between myself and administrative officers."[6] None of these perceived personal persecutions seemed to diminish Cole-Edwards's self-described career of self-less advocacy. Though he struggled to secure his lost economic privileges, while championing the larger cause of economic justice for Northern Nigerians, he seemed free of personal conflict. He transited between the personal and the public with ease, cleverly interweaving his personal plight with that of fellow Northern Nigerian colonial subjects also struggling to survive the economic upheaval. He saw himself as the voice of groups of Africans too intimidated or too subservient to speak out against harsh British economic recovery policies. "It was difficult," he argued, "to find those who go by their own judgment and [are] ready to give their honest convictions"—not even in the "churches and commercial houses."[7] Cole-Edwards asserted that Northern Nigerians suf-fered in silence because they cowered at the thought of voicing their concerns to the British.

In furtherance of his theme of selfless agitation, Cole-Edwards pointed to his earlier petitions demanding that the Northern Nigerian government invest in social infrastructure such as bridges, roads, and a "free water sup-ply." He believed that his troubles stemmed from these public-spirited actions of his as well as from his refusal to let a supposedly insolvent colonial state out of its social obligations. He was suffering personally because he insisted on a responsible, fatherly colonialism for Northern Nigeria. "In these efforts, displeasure was met in official circles and as previously said, I was misrepre-sented, misread, misjudged, misunderstood. As a result I have suffered treat-ments of the worst kinds, although in my humble opinion, I merited some recognition for the unselfish services I rendered, services which brought me no pecuniary gain."[8] Cole-Edwards's self-portrayal and his critical temperament did not make him as anticolonial as British officials might have thought. Indeed, he portrayed himself as a colonial insider invested in the colonial system. He wanted reform, not a revolution that would overthrow the system; he wanted to preserve the system by making it more responsive to local needs. He argued that his ultimate aim was to "assist the [colonial] administration to establish in our province peace and happiness."[9] He even went to great length to ingratiate himself with his perceived colonial persecutors, reminding them of one testament to his commitment to the colonial system: he had in the past counseled the government on how to improve the colonial system in Northern Nigeria and they had appreciated such suggestions: "There are records to prove that I have made proposals to Government that has been accepted, chiefly those submitted to Sir Hugh Clifford during his administration. This was done with the motive to assist the Officer Administering the Government."[10] Cole-Edwards had also invested in the colonial system as a contractor. His personal economic travail stemmed partly from this involvement in the colonial system and from the prevailing threat to it.

At the same time, Cole-Edwards emphasized his concern about deteriorating economic conditions for average Northern Nigerians, an aspect of his political engagement that perhaps made him something of a colonial outsider, despised by officials for drawing attention to colonial failings. But he was an accidental and circumstantial critic of colonialism, as his anticolonial advocacy was forged largely in the crucible of the worsening economic conditions in Northern Nigeria during the Depression. Cole-Edwards and his Northern Nigerian supporters must therefore be understood not only as disgruntled, excluded, and out-of-favor colonial outsiders but also (because of their investments and role in the colonial system) as invested internal critics of the system. As colonial auxiliaries, they understood the system's workings, and they critiqued the system from within at its most vulnerable time—during an economic crisis. Considering these realities, Cole-Edwards was both a critic of and a believer in the workings of the colonial system, a duality apparently lost on colonial officials eager to label him as an anticolonial rabble-rouser.

Cole-Edwards's dramatization of his grievance, and his argument that the Depression called for governmental economic paternalism, stemmed from both a personal encounter with the hardships of the Depression and what seemed like a genuine outrage at worsening economic conditions in Northern Nigeria. At both levels, his outrage, shared by Northern Nigerians of his ilk, acquired populist legitimacy because it grew out of prevailing conditions. Pay cuts, collapsing export prices, and retrenchments provided a tripod of evidence for anticolonial agitation. They offered a legitimate and popular basis for anticolonial complaints. Cole-Edwards thus had a platform for his grievances, whether or not his pontifications bespoke those of an opportunist. He—like his friends, most likely African merchants—would have personally felt the effects of some of the fallouts of the Depression. The decision of British produce-buying firms to use the foodstuff trade as an economic recovery strategy would have hurt them all. Cole-Edwards's antigovernment activism therefore increased as economic conditions deteriorated.

Although dismissive of Cole-Edwards's activities and ideas, the colonial authorities took him seriously as an agitator and as someone who (rightly or wrongly) embodied the collective local disapproval of the state's economic recovery policies. But what Cole-Edwards saw as economic injustice, the British considered mere fiscal conservatism and an aggressive revenue drive. Official suspicions of Africans like Cole-Edwards exacerbated this dissonance of perspective. The British authorities had reason to worry about Cole-Edwards; well educated, he had a reasonable knowledge of world and local economics and, perhaps more disturbingly, in September 1930 he began to publish Northern Nigeria's first newspaper, the *Nigerian Protectorate Ram.*

The newspaper was short-lived; it appeared weekly until November 1930, when officials ran its publisher out of Lokoja. Cole-Edwards fled to Onitsha, in Eastern Nigeria, where he published a few editions of the paper in 1931 as the *Nigerian Weekly Despatch.* Nothing in the records indicates that the newspaper had a readership beyond the small circle of Western-educated African colonial auxiliaries of Northern Nigeria. It also remains unclear whether there were other signatories to the petitions besides Cole-Edwards and his fellow pseudonymous writers. The newspaper gained its readership mostly among the African workers in the Northern Nigerian colonial bureaucracy, as well as the African, Arab, and Levantine merchants in the key Northern Nigerian urban centers of Kano, Lokoja, Kaduna, and Jos. The government itself discovered that this group of Northern Nigerians constituted both the readership of the newspaper and its funding base.[11] A secret British investigation concluded that the paper had a sizeable following among the Northern elite and that Cole-Edwards and his cohorts' petitions and newspaper activism would result in their ultimate ambition, to "create an anti-European political party."[12] Apart from one official's comment that the newspaper was "well-printed," available evidence does not support the existence of either a well-established mechanism or technical infrastructure for publishing, distribution, and circulation. This comes as no surprise, since the paper operated essentially as a clandestine endeavor, carrying risks to its publishers, distributors, financial and journalistic contributors, and readers.

Nothing indicates that the circulation of the *Nigerian Protectorate Ram* was large enough to pose a serious threat to the colonial authorities. However, Cole-Edwards and his cohorts managed to collect and discern confidential information from the colonial bureaucracy (where some worked or had worked) and had a provocative, emotionally appealing way of criticizing the government. In the perpetually paranoid minds of British officials, these attributes trumped their trifling anticolonialism, the small readership of the newspaper, the spasmodic nature of the petitions, and the crudeness of their methods.

To be sure, the colonial government in Nigeria had previously had a frosty relationship with educated Africans who ventured into newspaper publishing.[13] The newspapers of the South, especially Lagos, had, from their beginnings in the late nineteenth century, soundly criticized the government. Cole-Edwards's newspaper venture appeared more threatening because it seemingly marked the beginning of a "Southern" trend in Northern Nigeria. Though not nationalist in the classic sense, Cole-Edwards captured the burgeoning crystallization of a clear anticolonial sentiment. His campaign signaled the beginning of an articulated, radical critique of colonial practices and rhetoric in a region of Nigeria seen by the British as relatively conservative and quiescent. More important, Cole-Edwards's campaign came during an economic depression in which the control of information and knowledge seemed crucial to averting social unrest. An African-controlled print culture in Northern Nigeria portended the emergence of an arena of public discourse that could potentially define and explain the Great Depression and the government's handling of it.

The newspaper's first edition, published on September 22, 1930, criticized what it saw as an excessive tax burden on the depressed economies of Northern Nigeria and lamented the prevailing and worsening problem of unemployment. Understandably, this criticism outraged the Northern Nigerian colonial authorities. The resident of Kabba Province, under whose jurisdiction Lokoja (the newspaper's base) fell, wrote to the lieutenant governor informing him, among other things, that Cole-Edwards had not completed the necessary legal steps to obtain government approval for the *Ram*. Cole-Edwards, he noted, had violated the Newspaper Ordinance of 1917.[14] The resident's strategy—which the colonial authorities in Northern Nigeria came to support—entailed discrediting Cole-Edwards and the message of his newspaper, before stopping him altogether by invoking his breach of the ordinance. Cole-Edwards, the resident pointed out, "has been notorious . . . as an agitator," was "impecunious and has been trying to earn a living by persuading the more simple minded among the people that he is able to get any grievance they have redressed and he takes care to persuade them that they have a grievance."[15] He found an item on income tax collection in the first edition a "dangerous article in view of the possibility of repercussions."[16]

The resident accused the newspaper of "misstatement" and exaggeration, citing the paper's "attack on the United Africa Company" as a "deliberate attempt to foment discontent among the ring of Kola merchants," who were "at present well content" but could be "easily persuaded that they [had] grounds for grievance."[17] The newspaper had criticized the monopolistic buying practices of the United Africa Company. In an effort to remain viable by expanding its business to include food crop arbitrage (traditionally dominated by African and Middle Eastern merchants), the UAC contributed to rising food shortages and famines in the early 1930s. African criticisms of these UAC strategies had also led to a temporary withdrawal of official British backing and support for its operations.[18]

Although contemptuous of the paper's claims, the resident recognized their potential to cause trouble and to stoke anti-British feelings. His approach sought to undermine the intellectual and factual accuracy of the newspaper's stories and articles while not underestimating their capacity to influence or solidify anti-British public opinion.

In early 1931 officials invoked the Newspaper Ordinance against the *Ram*, resulting in a fine of £10. But when they realized that Cole-Edwards and his supporters could pay the fine and still continue publishing, they imposed a one-year prison sentence on him.[19] To escape imprisonment, Cole-Edwards fled to Onitsha, in Southern Nigeria, where he changed the name of the newspaper to the *Nigerian Weekly Despatch* and continued to publish for his Northern Nigerian readership.

"SUBVERSIVE" CRITICISMS

We may never know exactly why the authorities in Northern Nigerian suppressed the opinions and positions expressed in the *Nigerian Protectorate Ram*. One explanation may lie in the newness of what one might call intellectual anticolonialism in Northern Nigeria. This may explain both the knee-jerk reactions and the more articulate and rigorous responses of the British colonial authorities to the agitations and criticisms of Cole-Edwards and his group.

Indigenous newspaper publishing, which was new in the North, worried officials unaccustomed to dealing with or responding to criticisms in the press. Cole-Edwards's newspaper project caught them unawares, thus eliciting censorship before it provoked an articulate polemical response. Further, Cole-Edwards's anticolonial railings and criticism of the government's economic recovery policies, were also conveyed through other media, such as letters and petitions, reinforcing his newspaper's critical articles. The many forms of criticism meant that officials could not ignore its substance; it remained a constant irritant, coming at them from many different routes and in different forms.

The failure of British officials to minimize the spread of the burgeoning culture of public discursive anticolonialism was even more worrisome for the government. This anticolonialism went beyond a smug criticism of colonial policy. It offered what amounted to an inversion of familiar colonial rhetoric on development, welfare, accountability, and paternalism. Officials labored to identify the nodes of logistical support for the newspaper- and petition-writing infrastructure in Northern Nigeria. They came away knowing of a larger-than-expected community of discontented Western-educated Northern Nigerians engaged in publishing antigovernment opinions and commentaries.[20] The use of pen names in the articles and opinions published in the *Ram* had already made the task of identifying individual writers difficult for officials. Nothing short of the removal of the physical infrastructure of publishing seemed adequate as a solution.

Although the style and method of Cole-Edwards's anticolonialism bothered British officials and provoked some of their responses, colonial officials persecuted the *Ram* and its publisher mainly because of the poignancy of its articles, the currency and immediacy of the issues on which its articles focused, and the questions they raised. One of the uncomfortable issues raised by Cole-Edwards and his cohorts involved the exceptional tax burden of Northern Nigeria vis-à-vis the South. In the paper's first edition (September 22, 1930), an anonymous article called the attention of the administrators of Northern Nigeria to the exceptional hardship that the flat tax rate caused residents. The article argued that the people of "the Southern Provinces notably Enugu, Onitsha, etc.," had not incurred the flat rate "levied on us residing in the Northern Provinces."[21] The writer, while on a "study tour" of the South, had observed that "all women were exempted from taxation" in the Southern Provinces," a practice that "seem[s] unfair to those of us residing in the Northern Provinces," and hoped that the government would see the wisdom of granting similar privileges to all.[22] The writer raised the specter of mass migration from the North to the South, as Northern females who moved to the South had already enjoyed exemption and males had received a reduction in rates. The writer hoped that the government would intervene in the matter and "give less cause for grumbling."

The article, which was also sent to the chief secretary to the government of Northern Nigeria as a petition, received a response that editors published in the same edition of the *Ram*. The governor vehemently disagreed with the article's claims about excessive taxation.[23] But that did little to silence the critics. The governor's response elicited a rejoinder that was "not in agreement with . . . His Excellency's reply" regarding the issue of excessive taxation in Northern Nigeria. The rejoinder listed the different taxes and rents levied on the people of Northern Nigeria, especially in the urban centers. Northern Nigerian tax requirements included "Ground Rents," "Conservancy Fees," "income taxes," and "hawkers license" fees, among others.[24] The writer claimed that rather than from a desire to make frivolous demands, his motivation came from "the great poverty of the people" and that, in the prevailing economic situation, very few sources remained for men "to find and obtain [a] living." Whether or not officials admitted it, the power of the written word and its dissemination among locals had become quite decisive in determining the terms of colonial discursive confrontations. British officials found themselves inadvertently drawn into a public debate on Britain's role in the prevailing economic crisis. Once begun, such debates only expanded.

The petition went on to launch one of the most disturbing critiques of the government's economic recovery policy; it attacked the practice of taxation without social investment in the lives and communities of the taxpayers.

This criticism unsettled a colonial government unwilling to spend money on infrastructure and welfare projects, invoking the Depression as a justification for a cessation of social expenditure. The polemical coupling of taxes and development proved a particularly potent indictment of state-imposed austerity measures. The writer of the petition seemed determined to prick the social conscience of the colonial authorities by raising an uncomfortable question that struck at the heart of the age-old colonial debate on the true mission of colonialism: was colonialism for development and social progress or primarily for exploitation?[25] The author highlighted the amoral character of British Depression-era colonialism in Northern Nigeria. Another distinct character of this newspaper- and petition-centered public discourse was that it advanced not merely a criticism of colonial policy but also the discourse of economic entitlement and rights. What the writers of the *Ram* demanded as economic cushion for Northern Nigerian colonial subjects amounted to a colonial version of the welfare state, a demand at odds with the prevailing British consensus on fiscal conservatism.

The powerful and radical criticism of the state's economic recovery policy of nondevelopment was not powerful and radical because it was novel—it was not. Rather, its power came from its timing. The state wanted Northern Nigerians to believe that the dire financial situation made any form of investment in public infrastructures impossible and that even their taxes could not support such projects. The writer, using this newfound power, chose this time of crisis and the apparent absence of colonial economic paternalism to poke holes in the official "truths" disseminated about the Depression and its dramatized implications for the ability of the state to finance a program of economic relief.

As if to consolidate the momentum gained from the petition, the *Ram* carried another article, "Street Lights Should Be Provided in the Township and Native Town," which made specific infrastructural demands on the Northern Nigerian colonial authorities. This bold attempt demanded the social benefits of taxation and eloquently rejected the government's claim that infrastructural development was impossible in the Depression. The article argued that "in consideration of the taxes collected namely; Rates, Rents, Income Tax, Market Dues and Hawkers License, Street Lights should be provided as is the case of important towns in the South."[26] This and similar demands represented a new trend of challenging the depressed colonial state at its most vulnerable moment and questioning official truths about colonial events. No longer satisfied with merely criticizing official policy, members of the Northern Nigerian elite demonstrated their nonacceptance of the government's claim of insolvency by making material demands on the state. Discussion, analysis, and demands began to intertwine in this growing discursive space.

The article ended on a defiant and insistent note that foreclosed the possibility of reasoning with the government: "Tax payers throughout the entire civilized world [are] entitled to the benefits derivable from taxation."[27] The reference to the "civilized world" represented a stinging appropriation of the rhetoric of colonial modernity. The British often self-consciously advanced this expression of mutually beneficial obligations between the colonial state and subjects as a kind of social contract with responsibilities and benefits, but not the former without the latter. Local discussions of the economic crisis challenged the dual-mandate ideologies of the benefits of colonialism, while opening a window to the possibilities of governmental social intervention—possibilities that the government would rather keep shut. Local discussions of the state's economic recovery policy both challenged and insisted on the fulfillment of the dual mandate.

The criticisms of members of the Northern Nigerian elite indexed increasingly visible colonial failures. Furthermore, the *Ram*'s commitment to demanding the infrastructural benefits of taxation, in disregard of the state's commitment to fiscal conservatism, did not subsume its demand for tax relief. The two demands were compatible in the paper's polemical scheme. Even after Cole-Edwards left Lokoja and began publishing his newspaper as the *Nigerian Weekly Despatch*, in November 1930, the theme of tax relief for the people of Northern Nigeria continued to figure in the newspaper's agenda. In a particular article that caught the eye of colonial intelligence officers who made a clipping of it, a writer who went by the pen name of Langalanga wrote, "We are compelled in these days of the Depression to ask government to withdraw the collection of rates in the Township as it seems [a] hard measure and a change needed to meet the situation."[28]

In an article titled "A Call to Duty and Service," an anonymous writer laid out the questions that he thought needed answering in discussing recovery (or lack of it) from the Depression.[29] "We have now completed the half of the year and in taking stock have we reflected and ponder over surrounding circumstances and look backward and forward and have we asked ourselves the question: Have things change for the better or are they becoming worse? How are things progressing with the large number of unemployed? Is it on the increase? What steps are our leaders . . . taking towards these things?"[30] These rhetorical questions are a prelude to the criticisms and alternative explanations of economic health that the writer posits. He criticizes the amalgamation of the United Africa Company and John Holt, the two biggest British produce buyers in Northern Nigeria. They had merged early in 1930 as part of effort to minimize competition and to lower buying prices—all in response to the erosion of the companies' profits brought about by the Depression.[31] The writer sums up his criticism in a question: "Have we derived any benefits from the amalgamation of the two greatest business houses? . . . The man in the streets says the amalgamation has brought about deprivation of situation which once afforded comfort to our people and those depending on them."[32]

Having introduced the idiom of the man in the street, the writer uses it as a heuristic refrain on the quotidian, microlevel ramifications of British responses to the Depression. This concept defines his analytical trajectory and the ideological choice undergirding his commentary. He subtly repudiates the government's macroeconomic and abstract interpretation of the Depression as a crisis in budgeting and the balance of payments:

> The man in the streets says unemployment is on the increase. . . . He sees no prospect of things becoming better now and in the future. Again he sees trade becoming bad from day to day with our people. He sees that producers are not receiving their right dues from the fruit of their labour and hard toil. He sees that producers are compelled to deliver their kernels by weights in preference to bushels, fully knowing it is impossible for them to be able to work out by weights and measure the amount that should be paid to them.[33]

This sweeping commentary touches on most of the Depression-era grievances cited by the biggest segments of the Northern Nigerian population—peasants and workers. Peasants had fallen victim to the much-criticized buying practices of produce-buying agents, who, in their bid to sustain their operation and break even in the Depression, resorted to trade practices that mortgaged the economic survival of the farmer. Workers had lost their jobs as a result of the government's suspension of public works and retrenchments from government service and the tin mines.

The *Nigerian Protectorate Ram* and its publisher represented a major intellectual counterforce to the state in the volatile era of the Depression. To counter the state's public rhetoric of state budgetary woes and local sacrifice, the paper's writers produced their own alternate and transcendental narrative of the crisis, one that promoted tax relief and infrastructural development. For them, the economic crisis was not a reason to ignore Africans' needs; rather, it called for an unprecedented financial commitment to Africans' socioeconomic and infrastructural needs. When it suited their agenda, the writers ignored or sidestepped the state's economic recovery rhetoric to make disturbing demands that unsettled the emergency economic policy consensus in Northern Nigeria. Sometimes they came up with their own prognosis for the Depression and its unpalatable socioeconomic consequences for Northern Nigerians. They also produced their own indicators of economic health and recovery, discounting the esoteric macroeconomic paradigms of state bureaucrats. With such a ferment of local elite public opinion on the government's actions and inactions in response to the Depression, the Northern Nigerian colonial authorities—having had little success within the mechanisms and expressive constraints of officious response and persecution—waded into the debate publicly.

THE BRITISH RESPONSE

Cole-Edwards and other members of the Northern Nigerian urban elite who shared his ideals inadvertently opened a new front in the battle to control the public space for discussing the Depression, its effects on Northern Nigerians, and the government's handling of it. British officials, while harassing critics like Cole-Edwards, realized the potency of their messages and criticisms, which had a disturbingly populist appeal among Western-educated locals, who disseminated them to unlettered Northern Nigerians. In his memo to the resident of Kabba Province on the articles and petitions in the *Ram* and on Cole-Edwards, the secretary of the Northern Provinces suggested the publication of a regional newspaper with which to counter the so-called subversive articles of the emergent local press with what he called "judicious propaganda." "If it is the fact that there is a real demand for a local newspaper by certain sections of the N.P.s [Northern Provinces] population such would seem to add to the desirability of steps . . . to issue an authentic news sheet in which judicious propaganda can be employed against the ignorant or malicious misstatements of busybodies of the Cole-Edwards type."[34] In the period following Cole-Edwards's flight from Northern Nigeria, the state implemented the newspaper proposal, underscoring the anxieties that the petitions and articles in the *Ram* caused colonial officials. On November 14, 1931, the first edition of *Northern Provinces News/Jarida Nijeria ta Arewa*, a biweekly multilingual newspaper, appeared in Kaduna, the administrative headquarters of Northern Nigeria, and was distributed for free throughout the Northern Provinces.[35]

Northern Provinces News set out from its inception to disseminate a particular understanding of the Depression. The paper's writers and editors employed multiple strategies to that end. The April 9, 1932, edition contained an editorial, which, not surprisingly, focused on the Depression. It aimed to explain the Depression and the government's economic recovery measures to the Northern Nigerian people. The "judicious propaganda" in the article was as elaborate as its tone was pedagogic. It dripped with condescension in its appeal to local understanding; its purpose was instrumental and didactic. Against what the British regarded as the "misinformation" of Cole-Edwards and other local critics, the paper sought to contextualize the economic Depression, pointing out the global nature of both its origins and effects. They sought to emphasize the more profound implication of this line of argument: if the Depression had global origins, then Cole-Edwards and other critics had misplaced their efforts in indicting the government's economic recovery policies.

The global nature of the crisis also called for a global response and a global search for a remedy. Simply put, the problem was beyond the colonial authorities in Northern Nigeria. A Lagos-based newspaper columnist with the pen name Dan Zaki (Hausa for son of a lion) had famously criticized this colonial explanation as a "poor comfort" for Nigeria's suffering peasants.[36] Officials, however, continued to find the globalization of the crisis appealing as a strategy for deflecting and countering local criticisms and for writing British emergency economic policies out of local discussions of the crisis. The globalization of the crisis also served to remind Northern Nigerians that they belonged to a larger, multiracial, transatlantic community of suffering peoples, subject to a common imperial fate. Nigerians, the article argued, should thus find comfort in imperial economic solidarity.

In one editorial, the newspaper tried to justify the policy of pay cuts and special revenue levies on Northern Nigerian colonial auxiliaries: "Both the government and the native administrations have to find ways of reducing their expenditure and, after making all possible economies in other directions, it was decided . . . to introduce a 'levy' on the salaries of government servants . . . , which will, it is hoped, effect a saving of £100,000 a year. Many native administrations . . . are also reducing the salaries of their employees."[37]

To preempt and deflect criticism of these measures, the newspaper portrayed them as gestures of sacrifice proposed by local rulers as part of their contribution to imperial recovery. It claimed that "many Emirs have themselves suggested such a step" and that, "much as [the British] regret it, we recognise the necessity for it."[38] Another aspect of the government's "judicious propaganda" encouraged farmers to cultivate food crops alongside export crops to stave off hunger and destitution. "The man who relies for his livelihood on economic crops alone may, if the price falls or the demand slackens, find himself faced with disaster, but if, while growing these economic crops, he at the same time sows enough guinea-corn and food crops for himself and his family he will . . . never be reduced to destitution."[39] Here the editorial opinion of *Northern Provinces News* accorded with aspects of existing agricultural and economic policies of the government and contradicted others. It reinforced the existing policy of encouraging local farmers to bear the cost of their own recovery and subsistence by maintaining and even increasing existing levels of food crop production while expanding export crop cultivation. British agricultural policy in Northern Nigeria directed these policies mainly toward the cotton and groundnut farmers of the emirate sector of the protectorate. The editorial seemed in the same breath to contradict what the British in Northern Nigeria had (since the inception of colonial rule, at the turn of the twentieth century) prioritized as a major goal in the nonemirate, non-Muslim sector of protectorate: the conversion of non-export-oriented farmers from cultivators of food crops to cultivators of export crops.

This dramatic reversal of the decades-old colonial economic doctrine and practice offered a larger instructive purpose. It sought to convince the local readers of *Northern Provinces News* that the integration of export-oriented agriculture—which had exposed the peasants and the country to the effects of the Depression in the first place—with food crop production could in fact become a source of strength and economic resilience. In this thinking, agriculture, especially when it involved both food and export crops, simultaneously linked Northern Nigerian peasants to global economic crisis and made them resilient against it. It is not clear, though, how much purchase such a nuanced explanation had with Northern Nigeria's suffering peoples.

Subsequent articles in the newssheet advanced self-help, communalism, and mutual aid, projecting them as distinctly African attributes that must be cultivated and used in the face of economic difficulty. Such articles asked Northern Nigerians to "regain prosperity without self-seeking," while also "helping the less fortunate of their fellow countrymen."[40] This reification and valorization of communalism and collectivism—two socioeconomic realities that were previously constructed by some colonial believers in profit-oriented individual agricultural enterprise as obstacles to Nigerians' assimilation into a rational, capitalist colonial order—is instructive. In their quest to relieve the state of the burdens of individual economic recovery, the authorities in Northern Nigeria advanced the African communal and collectivist social ethos as a pragmatically tolerable alternative to the colonial capitalist fixation on the creation of profit-motivated agricultural individualism.

This temporary refinement in British colonial economic philosophy indicates the extent to which the economic Depression had begun to refashion colonial rhetoric and practice in accordance with the imperatives of austerity and economic recovery. Colonial pronouncements became more modest. In the non-Muslim sector of Northern Nigeria, where the British had set out to construct a sociopolitical and economic edifice of Hausa-British modernity,[41] these pronouncements completely reversed the policy. They tolerated and even recommended alternative economic rationalities in place of a market-oriented rationality that had been the model of colonial engagement with African agricultural systems. Originally committed to the goal of civilizing "backward" Africans via Western modernity, officials began to promote nativism as a form of economic and social protection.

The spectacular valorization of tradition, culture, and other such collective constructs resulted from the state's commitment to thrift. Communal economic and social support supplanted governmental responsibility in the British economic recovery imagination. The polemical and practical utility of tradition in the economic recovery regime of the British reinforces what Steven Pierce describes as an ironic British discomfort with tradition, in which official critiques of "backward" African traditions were offset by a reluctant acknowledgment of their practical uses in colonial governance. Northern Nigerian colonial authorities, Pierce argues, often enlisted tradition in its own transformation.[42] This ad hoc project of advocating a reinforcement of tradition through what seemed like a rhetorical British disengagement from the agricultural cash economy may appear contradictory. But the British were being true to their own tradition. In British settler colonies, where the regular face of economic extraction resembled the economic configuration in Depression-era Northern Nigeria, the practice had always been to release the government from the financial burdens of peasant welfare by constructing the physical and cultural domain of the "natives" as a self-contained, self-supporting, "traditional" communal sphere. The Northern Nigerian colonial state had no choice but to maintain this rhetoric of egalitarian functionalism and communal support spirit if its goal was to make locals bear the burden of economic recovery.

BRITISH PROPAGANDA STRATEGIES

In countering local insinuations and polemics on the government's handling of the Depression, British writers employed what the French Parliamentarian Paule Brousse has called "propaganda of the deed."[43] This entails the strategic media projection of so-called good deeds—building schools, clinics, bridges, roads—to win the hearts of minds of those inclined to view a power formation unfavorably. Articles in *Northern Provinces News* recounted and sought to revive memories of what the state saw as the transformative and modernizing influence of British rule. Without fresh evidence of British developmental activity in Northern Nigeria—since public works had all but been halted at the onset of the Depression—officials published numerous pictures of wells dug, bridges built, and roads constructed before the economic crisis. In this thinking, the economic crisis and the attendant break in the modernist project of British colonialism became a footnote in the larger narrative of a purported British transformation of Northern Nigeria.

British Depression-era propaganda in Northern Nigeria revolved around the themes of progress and welfare. To counter the criticism that the government had retreated from the traditional British colonial promise of socioeconomic progress for Africans, the state again turned to *Northern Provinces News*. The paper published lengthy articles chronicling the "social progress" and improvements brought to Northern Nigeria through British colonialism. As in the wartime propaganda of World War II,[44] the articles promoted the king of Britain as a symbol of progress, uplift, and modernization whose reign had transformed Northern Nigeria into a colony with modern amenities and life-styles. They presented a modernity interwoven with progress, in the form of objects with positive contents. An article in the newspaper in November 1935 spoke of the numerous improvements recorded in the last twenty-five years, a time frame that coincided with the reign of King George V (1910–36). As a result of the crown's commitment to Northern Nigeria's progress,

> motor roads with good permanent bridges radiate in all directions and it is possible to motor practically anywhere in the Northern Provinces. Motor cars of all kinds from Baby Austins to two-and-half-ton Albions and other large lorries are seen everywhere on the road. Most of the chiefs have good motor cars and nearly every native administration has at least one motor lorry; Kano native administration has a fleet of twenty-six lorries. To give an example of the road facilities nowadays, a man can leave Bida at seven in the morning by car and be on the Marina at seven [the] same night. Also for some years now the people have seen aeroplanes in the sky.[45]

In addition to these improvements, the British presence resulted in other advances:

> Fine buildings of stone and cement are springing up everywhere. Look at the buildings in Kano, Sokoto, and Bida—to name only a few—and compare them with the mud buildings of 1910. Pure drinking water supplies are now being provided in all the large towns and there is already electric light at Kano, Maiduguri and Kaduna.[46]

The association of British colonialism with material advancement became the central focus of a well-orchestrated propaganda campaign meant to as-suage local frustrations and an escalating anti-British resentment. From direct "developmental" actions of the British to more indirect consequences of the British presence, officials shifted their gaze to anything that could illustrate the noble intentions and commitments of British colonialism. Officials dug into the state's documentary archives to recover any evidence of the transfor-mative and modernizing influence of British colonialism. The overarching goal of this effort was to replace current economic gloom and stagnancy with past glories—in the minds of Northern Nigerians.

THE CURRENCY OF THE LOCAL VOICE

Another strategy employed by the colonial authorities in Northern Nigeria involved employing local voices—especially those of educated and respected personalities—to translate, disseminate, and reinforce the government's "judicious propaganda." Articles written by members of the local elite that were sympathetic to colonial policies received strategic prominence and were advanced as a counterpoint to the views of Cole-Edwards and his peers. Articles written by locals in *Northern Provinces News* for the most part leaned charitably toward British colonialism. Coincidence played no part in the overtly political articles written by locals in the newspaper, which praised the British and their policies. These articles suited the government's justification of its economic recovery policies and highlighted the achievements of British colonialism. The public commentaries of local interlocutors came in handy for a government harried by local criticisms of its management (or lack thereof) of the Depression.

Responding indirectly to the widespread local criticism of government taxation in a time of economic crisis, an article by Mallam Abubakar Tafawa Balewa, the future prime minister of Nigeria, published in the October 15, 1934, edition of the newspaper, attempted to explain the reasons for and benefits of tax collection. In "Rashin sani ya fi dare duhu" (Ignorance is darker than night), Tafawa Balewa stated that he wrote the article because "it is important for everyone in this country to know the reasons why taxes are paid." He found his resolve to enlighten his compatriots on the importance of taxes strengthened "after a heated argument with some of my friends who are not educated":

> One day, one of my friends visited me during the collection of taxes. We sat down to chat and he said to me: "Honestly we are really being oppressed by this tax collection." On hearing this I asked him why he pays taxes every year. He was silent for a while and finally he said he only pays because he has no choice; he also said that it had been many years since he started paying and he was yet to see any benefit of the money.[47]

Tafawa Balewa expressed surprise that his fellow countrymen saw taxes as a means of oppression and could not see "the ways that this money [tax proceeds] is being spent," especially since "they are not hidden." Tafawa Balewa's aim in the conversation was to "explain to him [his friend] why he is being asked to pay taxes."

> The first thing I reminded him of is the peace in the country—there is presently no war in the country, there are no robberies, thefts have declined, forceful dispossession has ceased; policemen have been detailed to protect our property and to apprehend thieves. Guards

have been posted to keep watch over us; no matter how dark it is there are soldiers guarding/protecting our country. Hospitals have been built to help heal our diseases; bridges have been built over our rivers. Another important thing to bear in mind is the major roads present everywhere to ease mobility. There are also the Judges, the palace workers, and their assistants, who are now very many.[48]

Mallam Tafawa Balewa's thesis rehashed the standard British justification for taxes. Coming from a respected member of the local elite, however, it carried more credibility and may have helped reduce local hostility toward colonial taxation at a time of unprecedented colonial economic crisis. Tafawa Balewa argued that ignorance and illiteracy made taxes seem oppressive and colonial authority exploitative. Taxes, in his opinion, carried no inherent harshness or unfairness. Having listed the expenditures of government and the personnel that the government had to support, Tafawa Balewa confronted his friend: "I asked him where he thought the money for all these things came from." His friend answered, "Oho!" (I don't know). That response gave Tafawa Balewa the opportunity to inform his friend that "all these personnel are paid from no other source than taxes that we pay every year." His friend was "so surprised." Tafawa Balewa concluded by proposing that the best way for "this kind of people [un-educated locals] to know how their tax money [was] being spent" was to ensure that "everyone in this country enrolls in a school and learns how to think."

In another article, published in January 1937, Tafawa Balewa praised the Europeans for "transforming our country." Among other virtues, Tafawa Balewa reminded readers that upon conquering "our land they did not try to destroy our religion," nor did they denigrate local customs and traditions. He considered the Europeans noble and gracious conquerors: "Instead of forcefully demanding our obedience, the Europeans cajoled us. These Europeans know what they are doing."[49] Here we see the convergence of Tafawa Balewa's and the colonial authorities' appropriation of tradition as a substitute for the provision of tangible (and monetarily costly) welfare to suffering colonial subjects. The preservation of "our religion" thus becomes a highlight of British achievement, subsuming the avowed British project of economic improvement. The conduct of the British after the conquest was even nobler.

> After the conquest of the entire land, they began to establish agricultural plantations. At first the levy placed on people was small. In no time we started seeing our country enter *haske* [enlightenment/modernity]. Our trade and economy grew; roads opened and people from other lands started coming to our country. Roads that facilitated safe travel opened everywhere and we got a better and easier means of transporting goods.

Channels of knowledge opened to us and our religion was strengthened as a result. Before the European conquest, only a few could make the pilgrimage to Mecca. Now, due to the opening of roads many are making the pilgrimage annually. This is indeed a great blessing for us.[50]

Tafawa Balewa argued that in addition to these tangible benefits of British rule, the colonial authorities had "established big schools in our country with the purpose of teaching us the wisdom [wayo] of the world." They had similarly "strengthened the hand of our justice system by entrusting judges with the dispensation of justice."[51]

These local testimonies to Britain's redemptive and "developmental" mission in Northern Nigeria, however contrived and mediated by colonial concerns, represented invaluable propaganda gains and served to reinforce the government's responses to the groundswell of elite Northern Nigerian opinion on the economic crisis. Did this deployment of surrogate propaganda and other strategies employed by the government in its intervention in the Depression debate undermine the print culture and discursive anticolonialism of the Northern Nigerian elite? The answer remains unclear, especially since the trail of anticolonial criticisms blazed by Cole-Edwards and his cohorts would shortly be followed by a vocal, radical segment of the Northern Nigerian, Hausa/emirate, Muslim intelligentsia, led most prominently by Sa'adu Zungur and his Bauchi Discussion Circle.[52]

The 1930s saw a tremendous outpouring of articulate local criticism of the colonial state's handling of the economic Depression and of its economic management principles. These criticisms and demands—polemically and intellectually grounded and at times factually and statistically unassailable—introduced a sphere of public discourse in which members of the Northern Nigerian elite expressed their perceptions of British colonialism, their aspirations, and their economic visions.

Cole-Edwards and other members of the Northern Nigerian Western-educated class of colonial auxiliaries and merchants wrote petitions and newspaper articles to demand that the avowedly bankrupt colonial state come to the aid of economically depressed Northern Nigerians. Although they themselves had become casualties of the colonial state's cost-cutting policy of retrenchment and budget cuts, Cole-Edwards and his supporters managed to construct a narrative of demands and criticism that seemed to transcend their personal economic adversities by linking their travails to those of Northern Nigerian peasants, laborers, and chiefs. This small, emergent elite appropriated colonial paternalism to articulate an anticolonial message grounded in economic hardship. This ad hoc, crisis-driven anticolonialism remarkably demanded more, not less, colonial paternalism. The critics strategically embraced the rhetoric of colonial benevolence and lamented the dwindling of what had sustained them before the Depression: colonial exploitation of surpluses and profits. Cole-Edwards and his group asked the state to bear the burden of economic recovery by reducing the taxes of Northern Nigerians, to make more social investments in the lives of Northern Nigerians, and to create jobs instead of eliminating them.

The largely reactive response of the colonial state treated the critics of the state's economic recovery policy as troublemaking enemies of British colonialism. Cole-Edwards and his cohort of anticolonial critics became the subjects of colonial persecution, harassment, and surveillance. In addition, the colonial authorities sought to undermine the populist messages of the critics by establishing their own Depression-era propaganda medium in the form of a regional multilingual newspaper, *Northern Provinces News/Jarida Nijeria ta Arewa*.

As trenchant as their criticism was, Cole-Edwards's group never criticized the colonial expropriation of profits and surpluses—or colonial exploitation as we know it. As colonial employees, contractors, clients, and members of colonial patronage networks, they were invested in the colonial system of profit extraction temporarily truncated by the Depression. Instead, provoked by the widespread cash squeeze, they directed their assault against the unavailability of surplus and profits and the government's insistence on extracting revenue from collapsing rural production sectors. Like most Northern Nigerians, the members of the elite discussed here protested little, if at all, before the Depression, when profits and surpluses were enough to go around, even if disproportionately. Then, as rural export-oriented agriculture expanded, many locals—perhaps grudgingly—tolerated sharing their profits and surpluses with colonial authorities, British and African produce buyers, and African colonial clerks like Cole-Edwards. Northern Nigerians only criticized the economic system when it became dysfunctional. In short, Cole-Edwards and his peers were not protesting against colonial exploitation; they were ironically lamenting the absence of conditions favorable to colonial exploitation.

Confrontations and disagreements between the colonial state and Northern Nigerians on the economic hardship were not always as civil as those between the Northern Nigerian critics and British officials. The confrontations between state efforts to implement the government's economic recovery policies in Idoma Division—a colonial backwater that had not been integrated into the taxpaying and export crop–producing economy of colonial Northern Nigeria—and the determination of the Idoma people to resist this new regime of exaction was fraught with violence, raids, and revolts.

5 ⌒ The Periphery Strikes Back

Idoma Division, Colonial Reengineering, and the Great Depression

THE ECONOMIC crisis was experienced in the Northern Nigerian economic mainstream as a collapse of the export economy. The anticolonial commentaries and critiques of the period bear this point out (see chapter 4). This economic collapse resulted in mine closures, a drastic reduction in household incomes in export crop–producing regions, retrenchments, criminal and legitimate self-help initiatives, and anticolonial activism. Outside the Northern Nigerian economic mainstream — in areas such as Idoma Division,[1] export-oriented agriculture was the exception rather than the rule, and colonial taxation had been only tenuously and halfheartedly implemented. Indirect rule, the pillar of colonial economic schemes, was chaotic in the absence of homegrown centralized political institutions. These economic and sociopolitical realities made the Depression experience in Idoma Division uniquely volatile, violent, and devastating, as the relative unfamiliarity of colonial exaction and intrusion produced a series of instructive, if depressing, encounters between the Idoma and fiscally desperate colonial officials.

Idoma Division's marginality in Northern Nigeria conditioned and constrained its experience of the Depression. Marked by the peculiar production, consumption, and exchange preferences of the Idoma people, this marginality did not entirely originate with British colonial policies and attitudes. It followed from ecological circumstances, social organization, and the economic and political configurations of the Idoma area. However, the desire of the Northern Nigerian colonial officialdom in the early colonial years to politically and economically remake the division in the image of the emirate sector of the protectorate paradoxically accentuated the uniqueness of the Idoma area and resulted in a failed experiment in economic and political reengineering. This failure further damaged

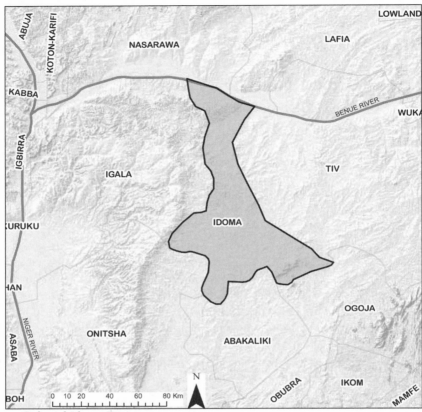

Colonial Idoma Division

whatever credibility the British had with the Idoma people, jeopardizing colonial control and undermining the power of the state in this remote colonial outpost.

The failure of this early project of reform led to a British disillusionment and to a political and economic disengagement from Idoma Division in the early 1920s. This retreat, however, came with a renewed commitment to a cultural and educational project designed to liberate the Idoma people from what officials deemed a congenital backwardness and cultural degeneracy. The project focused on the propagation of formal colonial missionary education and Christianity in Idoma Division.[2] The attempt by the British to move away from this costly project and to reimagine Idoma Division as a revenue-yielding participant in the economic recovery scheme of the 1930s set the stage for a variety of encounters between the Idoma and the British and also produced an array of unexpected responses from the Idoma.

The Depression ravaged the Idoma economy, mostly because of the economic primacy of food crops, which uniquely lost value in domestic markets, and because of the local currency, brass rods (which lost more than 80 percent of their value). Impoverishment worsened because the division, a marginal economic domain, relied on the vibrancy and prosperity of other economic spheres for its own survival. The tin mines suffered terribly during the Depression and the Southern Nigerian port cities experienced a similar decline in prosperity due to retrenchment and unemployment. Several Idoma communities exported yams to these centers of mining and trade before the Depression.

These unique economic vulnerabilities of the Idoma complicated their experience of the Depression. The extent of impoverishment produced crises and dynamics that tasked the imagination and management abilities of colonial officials and confounded their economic recovery measures. First, officials' cost-saving measures, such as the suspension of monetary subventions to missionary colonial institutions drew criticism from missionary educators. They considered this withdrawal a betrayal of the Union Jack, the king, and the avowed policy of cultural uplift in a quintessentially "backward" part of the British Empire. Second, the effort to substitute Hausa clerks and Igbo teachers with an emerging educated Idoma elite boomeranged. While the move saved the government money—the Idoma clerks received much less pay than the Hausa and Igbo imports—the relative economic stability of the new Idoma clerical cadre in an economically unstable polity pointed to possibilities previously unimagined by the Idoma and provoked unprecedented interest in Western education and colonial missionary schools. This interest translated to demands by communities for schools and educational goods. The colonial authorities had neither the resources nor the will to meet this unforeseen and unprecedented surge in demand for missionary schools.

The peculiar hardship experienced by the Idoma during the Depression bred in them a disturbing economic xenophobia, leading them to blame non-Idoma settlers in the division for the unprecedented fall in the price of their agricultural goods. Some of them attacked the settlers, demanded their expulsion, and attempted to revoke their access to farmland. The hardship also forced young Idoma men to migrate in unusually large numbers to the cocoa belt of Western Nigeria. This migration not only gave them respite from tax responsibilities in their home districts but also enabled them to earn cash and weather the Depression. This migratory process ultimately led to the emergence of agricultural wage labor in Idoma Division.

In trying to reconfigure Idoma Division to serve British economic recovery goals during the Depression, the British ignored history. They overlooked the failure of a similar attempt in the 1920s to bring the division into the economic and political mainstream of Northern Nigeria. That failure had compounded the homogenizing ambitions of colonialists, forcing them into compromises with different cultures and political economies within Northern Nigeria. In one compromise struck with the Idoma, officials, while lamenting their eccentricity and deviation from a preferred economic and political paradigm, let the Idoma inhabit an economic and political universe of semisubsistence and political fragmentation. Before the Depression the Idoma were largely left alone and out of the economic and political policies of the Northern Nigerian colonial government. For instance, colonial authorities did not assess taxes in Idoma Division until 1921, and for most districts tax collection did not become a yearly affair until 1925.[3] The attempt by colonial officials in the 1930s to force the Idoma into the new regime of economic recovery by seeking to integrate them into taxpaying institutions and autocratic political arrangements that propped up taxation caused backlash and fomented crisis. This crisis-induced effort to reinvent the economic relevance of peripheral economic zones would set in motion a bewildering series of social upheavals at the colonial grass roots. Idoma Division is emblematic of these marginal but instructive Depression experiences.

To understand the struggles of the Idoma against British economic recovery and austerity measures, one has to understand how colonial discourses and actions had made Idoma Division a backwater in Northern Nigeria; how colonial authorities had constructed and reinforced its status as a periphery over the early and middle period of colonial rule; and how that configuration became an obstacle to British economic recovery objectives during the economic downturn.

THE MAKING OF A PERIPHERY

One fundamental assumption that guided the British conquest of Northern Nigeria (1900–1907) was the unspoken belief that the Sokoto Caliphate had jurisdictional influence over all the territories that came to be known collectively as colonial Northern Nigeria. The assumption had an inherent flaw. Several provinces and divisions, including Idoma Division, had not come under any significant political control or cultural influence of the caliphate before the British conquest. Within the Sokoto Caliphate, the events following the capture of Sokoto in 1903 did bear out the British strategy, as Sokoto's collapse signaled the end of formal military resistance in the caliphate areas. But the caliphate excluded as many people as it included. Bordered by peoples who had neither accepted the suzerainty of Sokoto nor been conquered by its military adventurers, the caliphate was big but it was not wholly representative of Northern Nigeria. Resistance in the caliphate to the European conquest waned with the capture of Sokoto. In the nonemirate areas, however, the fall of Sokoto marked the beginning of the struggle to maintain sovereignty in the face of British expansion.

Idomaland, Northern Nigeria's southernmost division, covered an area of over three thousand square miles with a 1921 population of over one hundred thousand.[4] Here the conquest proceeded by fits and starts until the 1920s, although most of Idoma had already come under the direct and indirect sway of the British by 1910. Administrative fragmentation in Idomaland and in most of the areas outside the caliphate demanded several separate "patrols" and a piecemeal approach to "pacification." This strategy took time and effort. The conquest of Idomaland concluded only in 1922, when the final resistance to the British was crushed in the Igedde area of what would later become Idoma Division.[5] Although the conquest of Idomaland and other nonemirate areas disproved the theory of precolonial caliphal hegemony in all of Northern Nigeria—the collapse of the caliphate proving inconsequential to the British "pacification" efforts in the nonemirate areas—the official administrative attitude toward the Idoma still reflected the notion of precolonial caliphal jurisdiction.

British officials sought to infuse the nonemirate areas with the economic and political institutions of the caliphate by appointing chiefs where none existed. They urged the Idoma to abandon food-based agriculture for the export-oriented agriculture of the emirate areas. Neither differences in ecology, organization of labor, agricultural methods, nor the historical dynamics of Idomaland mitigated this colonial resolve.[6] This thinking formed the basis of early colonial policy in Idoma Division, as it did in other noncaliphate areas.

This is the ideological genealogy of the initial reforms embarked on by colonial administrators in Idoma Division—reforms that antagonized the Idoma and earned them the reputation of being difficult, troublesome, backward, and irremediable. But before the colonial authorities resigned to this defeatist denigration of the Idoma, they attempted to integrate the Idoma into the socioeconomic and political mainstream of Northern Nigeria—defined in normative caliphate terms.

The British sought to create a measurable, manageable, and profit-oriented economy in Idoma Division. They sought to engineer the evolution of an economy governed and driven by Western principles of economic rationality, a goal integral to British imperial formations elsewhere.[7] The end result was envisioned as an economic and political system resembling that of the emirate zone of Northern Nigeria. Officials sought to create, disseminate, and entrench the idea of a working organic economy among the Idoma, but such systemic stricture in economic life had little appeal among Idoma peasants, who had the distinct liberty of engaging in need-based exchange and of applying agricultural logics scripted by ecology, culture, and locally situated social realities. The economic minimalism of the Idoma conflicted with both caliphal economic practices and British economic goals.

Believing that Idoma agricultural and exchange practices remained localized, closed, and self-contained, officials "imported" hundreds of Hausa traders into Idoma Division to stimulate trade by buying Idoma products and selling imported European and local (emirate) goods to the Idoma.[8] But, having imported these "foreign" traders, the government lacked the personnel to monitor their activities. As a result, their documented practices of price fixing and currency hoarding went unchecked. Many officials considered the exchange practiced by many of the Hausa traders crudely unequal and exploitative. The traders, by the accounts of colonial anthropologists and administrators, took away much of the colonial currency that managed to get into Idoma Division, leaving it without the capacity to become monetized in colonial currency terms.[9]

As direct colonial income taxation took off in Idoma in the early 1920s, wage labor on the construction of the Eastern Railway (which passed through Idoma Division) and on the tin mines on the Jos Plateau arose to supply some of the cash needed for tax.[10] Many of the Hausa traders cultivated exchange relations that had the effect of taking away much of the cash remittance sent to the division from the Idoma laborers on the railway and in the mines. Colonial officials also encouraged the traders to introduce Idoma cultivators to groundnuts and other exportable crops that formed the basis of market transactions in emirate areas. The Hausa traders, far from becoming heroes of colonial economic revolution and agricultural proselytization, became despised economic interlopers associated with the British presence.

The projection of Idoma economic anxieties unto the colonially sanctioned Hausa traders produced the first major backlash of the economic reform of the colonial state in the division. In 1924 the people of Igedde District, disenchanted with the perpetual removal of currency from the district by Hausa traders and the attendant crisis of tax payment, murdered one of the traders to, as they claimed, register their displeasure. Colonial troops, as protectors of the traders, moved into the village of Ainu, the site of the murder, to disarm the villagers, who violently resisted. Officials quickly quelled the ensuing uprising that had engaged all of Igedde District. But in 1927 locals murdered several more Hausa traders in a renewed effort to scare them out of the division. This time the British concentrated their efforts on arresting Ogbuloko, the leader of the rebellion. The rebellion lasted till 1929, when Ogbuloko was captured by British forces.[11]

Rather than alert officials to the burgeoning problems of currency scarcity and the creation of unfamiliar economic cycles of dependence among the Idoma—both facilitated by Hausa traders and the larger transnational trade networks in which they participated—the reaction of the Idoma and the subsequent failure of early reform fed into their supposed preference for economic isolation. Colonial officials facilitated the entry of the mantra of Idoma economic notoriety into the descriptive and ethnographic register of the Northern Nigerian colonial bureaucracy. Take, for instance, the statement of W. R. Crocker, an assistant district officer in Idoma Division in the early 1930s: "Trading in the local markets—and there is little such market trading in comparison with what is done throughout the Moslem parts of the country—is, saving a few cheap trinkets and cloths hawked by Hausa peddlers, a matter of one household exchanging its surplusses [*sic*] (e.g tomatoes) for those of another (e.g paw paws), and with the exception of pennies and tenths legal currency is little (if ever) used. The normal exchange media are brass."[12] This statement sums up the official perception of Idoma economic practices. Authorities saw the Idoma as teetering precariously on the edge of subsistence, a position from which they needed to be rescued. Successive colonial officials tended to repeat these common statements without question. Rehabilitated as ethnological facts in official reports, they produced the hyperreformist impulse ultimately brought to bear on Idoma Division.

In response to the perceived economic recalcitrance of the Idoma, British officials appointed Hausa chiefs to act as colonial political enforcers. The imposition of this superstructure of Hausa-caliphate chieftaincy—the Fulani system, as Alvin Magid calls it—promised a usable constellation of political centralization, strong chieftaincies, economic regulation, export-oriented agriculture, and other socioeconomic qualities deemed necessary for the difficult task of making the Idoma, like caliphal peoples, contribute revenue to the British recovery effort.[13] The attempt to build an emirate-type indirect rule system in Idoma Division had an economic underpinning: "develop[ing] Native Authorities . . . to be responsible for tax collection."[14] Another response was that officials relapsed into an extreme version of the apathy and denigration that had prompted the failed project of transformation in the first place. This rhetoric authorized a twofold British political and economic disengagement in the early 1920s.[15]

First, officials abandoned efforts to forge an export crop economy as a substitute for the food crop agriculture and instead began to promote export crop production more as a rational, capitalist option that would evolve with time. Second, they entrusted an important plank of the colonial economy—taxation—to the inchoate and shaky authority of local chieftaincies, as British officials fell into the familiar rhetoric of Idoma Division as a tax-loathing, administratively difficult division.[16] This pre-Depression colonial economic apathy toward Idoma Division is crucial for understanding the difficulties that ensued with taxation and other revenue schemes during the economic crisis.

THE DEPRESSION IN IDOMA DIVISION

As in other divisions and districts in Northern Nigeria, the economy of Idoma Division lost value due to the collapse of economic prices during the Depression. However, the division's economy lost more value than those of most other divisions due to its status as a food crop–producing zone. It therefore struggled more in trying to overcome economic adversity and to cope with the state's new revenue offensive. Contemporary colonial sources confirm Idoma Division's economic peculiarity as one of only a few divisions in colonial Northern Nigeria that did not produce export crops. The people of Idoma Division cultivated mostly food crops such as yams, cassava, grains, and vegetables, unlike peoples in divisions further north. Sesame, a marginal export crop, was cultivated, but much of it was consumed locally.

The Idoma had no craft industry capable of earning much cash. In addition to producing mostly food crops, a semisubsistence ethic had a hold on the people. Market calculations did not drive Idoma agriculture. Agriculture had limited potential to earn cash, and locals still used brass rods as a standard of value, as well as the barter system.[17] From the oft-repeated colonial lamentations about the refusal of the Idoma to let the market dictate production choices to the contemporary simplistic reification of the food crop/cash crop dichotomy and its connotations, Idoma economic practices attracted colonial derision. These characterizations missed the fact that Idoma ecological conditions and cultural realities favored the cultivation of food crops and that this alternate economic rationality and ecological logic helped preserve agricultural and economic equilibrium in the division.

Colonial sources—including annual reports, the diaries of colonial officials, and correspondence—lamented the tenacity of the food crop agricultural economy of the Idoma, while historians of the Idoma colonial experience (like V. G. O'kwu and A. P. Anyebe) have celebrated it as a mark of Idoma resistance to colonial economic pressures. Neither understanding entirely captures the dynamics at work. An alternate or parallel economic rationality was at work. The discourse of Idoma economic backwardness was dramatized to the point of eliding the ecological and historical dynamics that produced what was being described as backwardness. Such a discourse also occludes the regime of economic and political valuation that undergirded the rhetoric of backwardness itself.

Beyond the previously noted colonial missteps that bred resentment toward colonial attempts at economic reforms, the failure of officials to provide an economic incentive for export crop cultivation (relying instead on the compulsive pressure of taxation) doomed official efforts to promote export crops and a concomitant cash economy. The economic disengagement of the 1920s exacerbated this economic alienation and convinced Idoma cultivators of the continued rationality of the food crop economy. Thus, by 1930, when the Depression hit, agriculture remained very much based on the cultivation of food crops, with a few enclaves that cultivated the exportable but largely locally consumed sesame crop.

When prices of the major export crops fell, those of food crops fell three times as much.[18] For a division like Idoma, for which food crops were both the mainstay of its economy and a means of sustenance, this radical drop in prices meant the loss of both food security and the route to cash. In turn, these losses led to massive depreciation in the value of discredited but widely circulating local currencies like brass rods. The problem for peripheral economic units like Idoma Division lay in the tenuous connections of an isolated agricultural economy to larger regional, national, and international economic systems that provided insufficient protection against economic crisis while carrying their own risks. As an economy that depended "almost entirely on the production of foodstuffs for sale in other parts of Nigeria,"[19] the worsening of the Idoma economic situation happened incrementally, corresponding to falling demand and decreasing prices in the foodstuff market. But the division's dependence on the prosperity of other economic domains (the tin mines mainly) meant that it received the accumulated burdens of a collapsing national colonial economy.

By 1934 the price of sesame, the only export crop cultivated in the entire lower Benue Valley, had fallen to 36 percent of its 1929 value. At the same time colonial currency, which could sometimes be obtained for tax purposes by selling some sesame from the local food barn, "became very scarce."[20] The sesame price collapse also applied to neighboring Tivland, the other actor in the subregional economy of the Benue Valley. There the prices had, "owing to the world slump, dropped catastrophically."[21] H. P. Elliot, a staff member of the colonial bureaucracy in Benue Province between 1933 and 1935, was struck by "the hardship suffered by sweating women carrying heavy loads of beniseed for as much as 15 miles to get a few pence (I think the price had dropped to 3p. a cwt), and wanting to buy soap, salt, koresine [kerosene] or a bit of cloth in the canteen. It was my first experience of what I began to regard as exploitation by overseas companies, who had no alternatives but to drop the prices they paid, but did not drop proportionately their generous profit margins."[22]

In Idoma Division, where sesame was not cultivated primarily for export, the collapse of the market for yams contributed the most to economic losses. In financially healthier times, significant brass-rod payments allowed yam cultivators in the division to exchange some of them for British currency, to pay taxes, fines and fees and to purchase manufactured goods. But the currency problem became particularly acute in Idoma Division, where the "lack of an economic crop" and the prevalence of brass rods as the means of exchange had exposed the people to a uniquely severe economic adversity. As cash became a fetish of sorts during the Depression, lack of or diminished access to it (whether conditioned by noninvolvement in a cash-earning vocation or by a non-export-oriented agricultural system) threatened the economic existence of

Idoma colonial subjects. Before the Depression the Idoma economy, though anchored on brass rods, managed to get by because the relative fiscal comfort of the colonial state led it to overlook the division in its revenue calculations and because a market existed in the industrial centers for yams and other food crops originating in Idoma Division.

Brass rods were volatile instruments of economic transactions. The rate of fluctuation in their value increased with official disregard for their economic utility, and they seldom became scarce. On the contrary, a constant surplus in supply kept their exchange value low against the British currency. Brass rods became almost worthless against the pound during the Depression. Before the crisis, Idoma peasants exchanged their brass rods for cash in the neighboring Southern Provinces.[23] As the Depression intensified and the state mopped up silver currency, however, even the Southern Provinces began to suffer a scarcity of cash, resulting in a massive devaluation of brass rods. By 1931 the rods had lost 80 percent of their value.[24] For economies like Idoma Division, in which wealth was measured in brass rods, this meant the erosion of a significant amount of both inheritable and circulating wealth.

This currency scarcity in Idoma Division would produce a receptive and sophisticated market in counterfeit coinage. (See chapter 6 for the implication of this acute scarcity of cash during the aggressive revenue drive of the Depression.) The insistence of the colonial authorities on transacting revenue business exclusively in British currency caused problems. In addition to taxation, revenue payments included court fines, vaccination fees, and other novel regimes of fines and fees too fuzzy for exploration here.[25] The departure from the pre-Depression tolerance for brass rods, florins, and other local currencies inaugurated the consciousness and reality of cash scarcity in Idoma Division. It created panic, speculation, hoarding, counterfeiting, confiscation, and more scarcity — in short a vicious circle of currency troubles. Officials acknowledged the widespread use of brass rods but as early as the 1930s began to counter that acknowledgment with a rejection of their use in transactions with the state.[26] This new intolerance for local monetary alternatives to British currency was particularly hurtful to the Idoma.

The loss of revenue that previously accrued to Idoma Division came through other unsavory routes. The wave of retrenchments and mine closures on the Jos tin mines[27] had two devastating effects on access to cash in Idoma Division. The closures, explained by the tin-mining companies and the government as measures necessitated by the entry of Nigeria into production quota arrangements of the international tin agreement, resulted in the drastic fall in the price of tin on the international market.[28] The retrenchment of the small number of Idoma men who had migrated to the mines and begun remitting cash to their kin at home diminished access to cash in their home communities and undermined the ability to pay taxes. Although their number was small, the return of retrenched miners and their reintegration into the cultivation of yams, the division's major crop, must have caused some further depression in its prices in local markets. The loss of cash as a result of the mine closures and retrenchments on the construction of the Makurdi bridge affected communities on the railway—communities like Otukpo, Otobi, Igumale, and Utonkon.

Since most Idoma districts far from the railways did not enjoy the cash benefits of the labor migration to the mines, this wave of retrenchments had a limited impact on the larger Idoma economy. Instead, the mine closures drastically reduced the number of residents on the mine compounds and in their vicinity, which in turn reduced demand for yams and worsened Idoma peasants' insolvency. The trade in yams to the tin mines had served as the major cash earner for most peasants in the division. Buying agents would traverse the entire division, exchanging brass rods for yams and employing porters to transport their cargo to railway stations, from where they continued on to the tin mines and to Port Harcourt, in the east.

The Idoma found this trade economically palatable because it merely tapped the surplus of a staple crop. By the time of the Depression its nexus had expanded throughout the division, and the loss of this market proved economically crippling. A colonial official in Idoma Division characterized the problem succinctly: "The Depression has meant the loss of their old market for yams at Oturkpo railway station, en route to the tin mines, and it is hard for them to sell other things to the extent of getting in the two or three shillings assessed on each adult male [as tax]."[29]

Like other divisions in Northern Nigeria, Idoma Division faced an economic recovery regime that rested on the extraction of revenue without its avowed benefit—socioeconomic development.[30] But here again the division found itself haunted by a state that considered it—in all respects except in the economic recovery plans—a periphery. It thus experienced a peculiar lack of development during the Depression. Part of the problem originated with an assumption that the economic fate of a periphery did not constitute a recognizable indicator of colonial failure. Nowhere did officials pursue the policy of nondevelopment with more vigor than in Idoma Division. For years, the colonial authorities, working from the theme of the division's geographical isolation, proclaimed the absence of access roads as the biggest obstacle to development and "material progress." During the Depression this lack of infrastructure came in handy as both an alibi for noninvestment in social services and as a self-fulfilling prophecy. Officials transitioned from talking about a "road system" as an element of material progress or a facilitator of it, to talking about roads as a precondition for other social investments. "Material development, which would speed up administrative, cultural and economic progress" was being "held up by complete lack of a road system." And since roads were structures "which the Native Treasury could afford to maintain but for the construction of which neither are Native Treasury Funds nor Government funds available,"[31] the suspension of social investments was deemed justified and inevitable. The resident of Benue Province concurred with the assessment that "material development in Idoma Division is indefinitely held up pending road construction."[32]

A web of cyclical connections sustained this logic of nondevelopment in Idoma Division, and its explanatory value suddenly came alive (not to say handy) during the Depression. Economic and "material development" depended on a road system, which in turn depended on the availability of funds, which in turn depended on government solvency, which in turn depended on government revenue. Everything was connected and without one the others ceased to exist. This thinking demonstrated the depth of official justification for suspending public-works projects in an area that, going by official rhetoric, needed infrastructures more than any other in Northern Nigeria. Superior colonial officials responsible for providing and supervising policy directions detected the seemingly infinite negativism implied by this logic of nondevelopment. The resident of Benue Province moved to remove the gloom from the canvas of developmental impossibility painted by officials serving in Idoma Division. The division's colonial administrators did not require, he noted, a suspension of infrastructural and social spending for its own sake or, for that matter, for the sake of the British economic recovery efforts. The absence of a road network, the amelioration of which the Depression had foreclosed, hindered material development, he conceded. But "financial policy in Idoma Division should continue to be the accumulation of extra Reserve" for "subsequent" post-Depression "expenditure on development."[33] Certainly the Idoma wanted roads and the sources indicate that, like other people in Northern Nigeria, they requested them. The benefits of roads constructed to link villages and towns in the division had after all become quite clear; they facilitated local trade and human mobility. As Elliot stated, "the Idomas . . . wanted development. Unfortunately, a tight-fisted Treasury meant that we could do little. . . . It was a penny-pinching affair."[34]

Authorities followed the advice of the resident to the letter: the accumulation of "extra reserves" for future "development'" became a substitute for a development agenda for the present, which was now foreclosed for the duration of the Depression. Officials achieved accumulation of these extra reserves through budget cuts. In 1932 they canceled a £200 budgetary allocation toward the building of a central school in Otukpo to fulfill the "necessity for economy."[35] They also postponed the construction of a dispensary and a "road northwards from Oju," saving the government £195.[36] They then advanced the savings from these budget cuts as reserves accumulated through prudent management. These were, however, far from innocuous reserves. The colonial authorities transferred most of these funds to Britain and "invested" them with the crown agents and in fixed-deposit accounts.[37] For instance, in 1932, the second most difficult year of the Depression (after 1933), they placed £9,000—out of a total revenue of £11,509 collected from Idoma Division—in British financial institutions as "investments," "fixed deposits," and "savings bank" deposits.[38] These deposits represent an injection of about 80 percent of Idoma Division's revenue into the British financial system under the guise of accumulating reserves for future developmental projects. Because this revenue was collected not from the profits of trade and agriculture—which had all but fizzled out—but from the rainy-day reserves and livestock wealth of the Idoma, its removal from the division and the resulting nonfulfillment of administrative and infrastructural needs in the division were devastating.

THE DEPRESSION AND EDUCATION IN IDOMA DIVISION

British officialdom was convinced that the Idoma needed social elevation and schooling to make them receptive to political centralization, chiefly authority, export-oriented agriculture, and taxation. This vision constituted a civilizing mission within the civilizing mission.[39] It produced a modest project of social elevation requiring Hausa auxiliaries, teachers from Eastern Nigeria, and British Christian missionary educators.

The colonial disengagement from Idoma Division in the early 1920s swept away what V. G. O'kwu has called a "nondescript class of 'aliens'"[40]—Hausa chiefs and traders brought in to make the Idoma more suitable for indirect rule and the needs and obligations of the colonial economy. The disengagement, however, left some of the Hausa auxiliaries and Igbo teachers who staffed the clerical and educational arms of the colonial bureaucracy intact. By the time of the Depression, these groups of colonial agents already constituted an expensive layer in the colonial bureaucracy. The government had also motivated them to go to an officially designated colonial backwater with modestly attractive monetary incentives. Since Idoma Division never attracted a significant number of British administrative officials, because of its reputation and the obscurity of official service there,[41] this class of indigenous colonial expatriates ran much of the colonial machine in the division with British supervision.

As the Depression hit hard, officials rethought the presence of these subimperial African expatriates; the transformative visions that had necessitated the presence of the Hausa clerks and Igbo teachers in Idoma Division gave way to an economically pragmatic assessment of the cost of such an arrangement. The Hausa-dominated colonial bureaucracy and the Igbo-dominated teaching cadre no longer fit with colonial priorities of saving money. This reality necessitated a "policy of substituting Idomas for Hausas in court clerk-ships and other colonial auxiliary services."[42] Igbo teachers and, later, colonial missionary educators would gradually find themselves sacrificed in this exercise of crisis-inspired indigenization. The move to dismantle the sub-colonial infrastructure of African expatriates was far-reaching, thrust upon the government by economic crisis rather than by the achievement of the avowed goal of preparing the Idoma to take over the subordinate roles of the indirect rule system.

Officials implemented this policy most vigorously in the area of missionary education. The missionaries of the Primitive Methodist Mission, headquar-tered in London, dominated the missionary field in Idoma Division. Along with the Roman Catholics, they helped the colonial authorities discharge the proclaimed educational obligations of British colonialism.[43] While the colonial authorities refrained from supporting missionary educational efforts in the emirate North for fear of offending Muslim sensibilities,[44] no such anxieties constrained them in Idoma Division and other non-Muslim parts of Northern Nigeria. This operational latitude resulted in an open alliance between missionary educators and colonial officialdom; the latter gave an annual monetary allocation to the missions to promote educational work. The mis-sionary educators in Idoma Division thus functioned partly as an arm of the colonial establishment, relying partly on donations and subventions from sup-porters in Britain but enjoying considerable financial and logistical assistance from the colonial authorities.[45]

The Depression eroded the government's capacity to meet its obligations to missionary educators, which tested the relationship between the two arms of colonialism. This strain, expressed through missionary frustration and complaints, resulted as much from the state's financial woes as it did from the Idoma's attempts to grapple with the economic difficulties. As early as the beginning of 1930 missionary educators began reassessing their financial position and lamenting their dwindling fortunes.

The first indication of financial problems with the colonial education proj-ect in Idoma Division emerged in 1930, when missionaries learned that they would not receive the money already approved by the colonial bureaucracy for various educational projects in the previous year's budget.[46] This discovery caused both disappointment and outrage among the missionary education staff. They felt that the colonial bureaucracy had unfairly targeted their activities for budget cuts. They further decried the practice of retroactive cuts in edu-cational subventions. In correspondence between Rev. Dodds, the minister in charge of the Methodist mission in Idoma Division, and Mr. Ayre, his superior at the mission's headquarters, the latter noted that they must make the colonial education department in Northern Nigeria "realize that we expect them to carry out their [budgetary] decisions and not withhold payments already approved." He described the sudden financial decisions of the colonial political bureaucracy as "playing 'ducks and drakes' with us" and thus confusing and confounding missionary educational plans.[47]

Six months earlier Rev. Hutchinson, a prominent missionary educator in Idoma Division, had warned of a growing situation that threatened to defeat the educational enterprise of the Methodist mission: "We are faced with a grave problem [and] financial stringency is upon us all."[48] Hutchinson foretold a troubling contradiction: "putting down [more] agents" in Idoma Division was no longer feasible because of the financial problems, but "the people are eager to have schools opened" in their districts.[49]

As the Depression deepened, so did anxieties about the loss of missionary educational territory. Missionary educators began to realize that many of the seemingly infinite educational opportunities would remain unmet because of financial handicap: "there is scope and opportunity but we lack the labourers and the means to go up there and possess the land."[50] Hutchinson, for instance, saw "great visions and ambitions for our work in . . . Idoma land" and wished "that the means were available to develop at the rate the demand is coming to us from the people."[51] Educators lamented the inability to "follow the beckoning of opportunities" because "we are suffering from a severe attack of financial cramps."[52] In correspondence between missionary educators in Idoma Division and their home sponsors and among missionaries in different parts of the division, the language of financial management replaced that of missionary education. Missionaries engaged more in economic talk than in educational or religious discussion. The Depression cast a shadow over the activities and conduct of educators. The economic situation even colored personal communication, with missionaries hoping that their colleagues had "so many things to cheer [them] in spite of the difficulties that the financial Depression has caused."[53] At the heart of all these anxieties was an unprecedented Idoma demand for colonial missionary schools—for Western education.

The political arm of the colonial bureaucracy urged patience and prudence. So did the Methodist mission's headquarters, which was strapped for cash, as donations to it had decreased. Responding to financial and logistical complaints and requests from the "field," mission officials in London, Uzuakoli, and Port Harcourt (the three hierarchical superiors to the mission in Idoma Division) recommended thrift, cutbacks in projects, and, starting in 1933, retrenchment of staff. In response to the complaint by Dodds about the adverse repercussions of budget cuts for the educational work in the division, Ayre, his superior in London, noted that the mission understood that "the reductions now made necessary would not only be difficult . . . to carry out, but will involve grievous loss to the work as a whole."[54] He argued, however, that the situation, "which is a challenge to us all," demanded a reassessment of the composition of missionary educational work. He wanted missionaries to "review the whole of their position" and come to what he considered a realistic conclusion—that the finances of the Methodist mission in Britain and the colonial government could no longer sustain many of them, since the two entities had suffered a decrease in revenue.[55] Missionaries, he advised, should consider handing over their educational work to "their colleagues who are nationals in the country in which they are working and to the local church." Ayre suggested the devolution of roles to less expensive, educated local converts where possible in order to reduce the cost of maintaining the educational presence of a large expatriate missionary. Not only would the locals help save the mission money; they would be "compelled" to do more for themselves and their missions "than in the past" and would "depend less on outside help."[56]

It remains unclear whether this invocation of self-help, indigenization, and devolution of roles caused the wave of retrenchment that befell the missionary educational enterprise in Idoma Division in the 1930s. Officials had already implemented Ayre's recommendation in the division: young Idoma men who had passed through the educational institutions of the missionaries had taken charge of schools while their British superiors went to Britain on compulsory leaves and were laid off or retired. [57] This Depression-inspired partial Africanization of the missionary educational institutions in Idoma Division deviated from the standard narrative of the Africanization of colonial missionary institutions, which originated in the restiveness of Africans in the missions in the 1900s.[58] In Idoma Division, unlike in South Africa and Southern Nigeria, the anxieties of financial strain—not the need to accede to the demands and protests of African mission–educated Christians—drove this process.

The downturn persisted through the 1930s. As schools closed, educational supplies became scarce, and retrenchment occurred, missionaries became more apprehensive about the sustainability of their educational work and about the security of their careers. Missionaries on the ground in Idoma Division began to respond to superiors' pleas for realistic repositioning in the face of economic adversity. Some educators expressed their frustration at the dwindling logistic and financial incentives and at the lack of appreciation on the part of bureaucratic superiors of the enormity of the educational challenge in Idoma Division. These missionaries inundated their sponsors and the colonial authorities with complaints.

Retrenchment proved a particularly bitter pill to swallow for idealistic missionary educators because it coincided with a paradoxical boom in demand for colonial education. The unwillingness to accept retrenchment as an option for dealing with the financial crisis colored the outbursts of the on-ground missionaries. Most of them believed that further budget cuts would stave off retrenchment but wondered if that was an option, since "people are experiencing difficult times" and "requests are coming to us to start work in different towns."[59]

Faced with financial difficulties and admonitions for thrift, some missionaries subtly protested. In 1934 Dodds replied to advice from Rev. Norcross, a pioneer of missionary educational work in Idoma Division, by noting the expansion in missionary educational responsibilities without corresponding increases in funding. The division's missionary work, having already lost £80, took a £125 budget cut, while its revenue from the sale of books, offerings, and other religious and educational materials, he projected, would decrease from the previous year's total of £111 because "our people are suffering terribly hard times."[60] Dodds wanted the synod to devise new ways of improving its revenue.

Overwhelmed by unusual numbers of financial complaints, Norcross felt that the Northern Nigerian authorities had abdicated their role as supporters of the educational project in Idoma Division: "we naturally think it is unfair that the government should squeeze a Missionary Society as it has been doing in some of these matters, where the financial responsibility should be theirs."[61] The subtle strain emerging in the partnership between colonial officials and missionary educators did not merely stem from the perceived failure of either of them to adjust to the crisis or to fulfill their obligation. The problem stemmed partly from local realities and thus loomed larger with on-ground missionaries, who were closer and more sensitive to it than administrators and missionary bureaucrats. And they conveyed the problem eloquently.

An anonymous missionary educator in Idoma Division wrote to the local Methodist headquarters, in Port Harcourt, to declare that officials had breached a reasonable threshold of prudence: "We have now come, I think, to the point where our economies can go no further, and with industrial Depression in this country so keen I fear we shall have decreased rather than increased revenue."[62] The unidentified missionary educator and others sought to communicate to their superiors the utter futility of the advice for increasing locally sourced revenue. He foreclosed the idea of raising funds from impoverished local students and converts and underscored the difficulty of making the schools self-sustaining.

The complaints from on-ground missionary educators reflected a different set of realities than those conveyed by their superiors' budget-balancing efforts and innovations. Missionaries confronted "village schools . . . weak in numbers" in areas with a "growing desire for schools" but where a lack of teachers and "the inability to pay fees and buy books" and the withdrawal of government subsidies toward those ends continued to undermine the mission's educational work.[63] Hutchinson succinctly articulated the dilemma of on-ground missionaries on the one hand and the dissonance between the admonitions of London-based superiors and the practical challenges of carrying out educational work in an economically depressed colonial outpost on the other. Hutchinson saw a fundamental contradiction in cutting back educational involvement in Idoma at a time when demand for colonial missionary education had hit a peak: "We have something like 7,000 in membership. . . . We have only two Central Schools, and we need at least six—the people are clamouring for the type of education our mission gives, and we have to tell huge districts that we are not able to help them."[64] The contradiction that he pointed out ran deeper. It raised the question of the fate of the avowed project of socially raising a declared periphery to the level of the Northern Nigerian mainstream. Colonial officials had previously advanced the educational enterprise as both a replacement and a precondition for economic and political reform in Idoma Division. The budget cuts and the resultant inability of educators to open more schools and run existing ones effectively broached the question of whether economic crisis had led to a suspension of this supposedly necessary project of social uplift.

For Hutchinson, the missionary educators needed to "prevent [further] retrenchment" rather than encourage it: he wished that "our people at home [British donors] could realize that retrenchment out here means hauling down our flag in districts for which we are . . . responsible."[65] By tying the decline of the missionary educational project to a decline or an abandonment of the British civilizing mission, Hutchinson invoked imperial sentiments and underscored the mutually reinforcing roles of political and economic colonialism and missionary colonial education.

Neither Hutchinson nor other missionary educators could see the bigger picture; a collage of many dynamics triggered by the Depression complicated the work and visions of both colonial officials and missionary educators. The situation went beyond the failure of British donors to sustain the missionary educational enterprise or the failure of the Northern Nigerian colonial authorities to fulfill their financial obligations to the project. At play was a classic case of unintended consequences—the results of hurried and halfhearted policies and the rhetoric of cultural uplift. The colonial authorities and missionary educators had unwittingly set off an overwhelming demand for missionary education among the Idoma.

Not only did the colonial authorities replace Hausa clerks and administrative assistants in Idoma Division with newly educated Idoma as a way of saving money, they also sought to replace the eastern Nigerian teachers employed as part of the educational offensive, although as missionary educators were retrenched or returned to Britain on compulsory leaves, some of the easterners found themselves reengaged. As a result, Idoma youths who passed through the missionary schools found employment in clerical positions at lower salaries than the ones paid to the British and Igbo teachers. Their economic position was comparatively good nonetheless; they had a fixed, steady income. The emergence of a new cadre of salaried Idoma workers who were propelled into these new positions by their education aroused interest all over the division in missionary education. As one missionary put it, "boys and youths in other towns have noted this and wish to qualify for similar jobs."[66] In 1931 the division's native authority recruited thirty-three educationally enthusiastic "boys" from all over the area for the central school at Otukpo. Villages and towns from where these candidates were selected eagerly contributed the £2 required to maintain them in the school each year. Missionaries hailed this gesture as a strategic alliance that could satisfy the desire for education in the division and saw in it an opportunity for both conversion and education.[67] For them, the willingness of communities to pay £2 made their case that there was an unprecedented hunger for Western education in Idoma Division and that the British colonial bureaucracy was responsible for satisfying it.

Two years later, as villages and towns inundated missionaries with requests for schools, the excitement turned into anxiety. The fact that these towns and villages eagerly paid the £10 mandatory contribution toward the cost of starting schools in their locales at once excited and troubled missionary educators.[68] With a depleted workforce and a reduced budget, the Methodist mission in Idoma Division struggled with the difficulty of dealing with a sudden, dramatic reversal of what they had earlier understood as an abiding indifference to colonial education among the Idoma. Some educators now questioned the complacency that this belief in Idoma educational apathy had bred in missionaries. A reversal of roles had occurred: the Idoma had become the seekers of colonial missionary education and the missionaries and colonials had become the apathetic ones denying it to them.

The growing interest in and unprecedented demand for missionary education bothered missionaries and colonial officials alike. One question kept suggesting itself (which officials somehow missed): why would people in an impoverished economic periphery during a period of economic adversity suddenly develop an interest in colonial education and be willing to sacrifice scarce resources to secure it? Philip Zachernuk has articulated an instructive answer to this question in his analysis of the education boom in Depression-era Lagos. According to Zachernuk, the paradoxical development of unprecedented interest in colonial education during the Depression bespoke the "attempts to find more diverse and stable economic foundations."[69] He describes how "demands for [Western] education multiplied" as merchants and educated Africans, stung to varying degrees by the Depression, sought to provide their wards with a firmer and more secure economic foundation by sending them into educational pursuits.

In Idoma Division a similar dynamic obtained. Not having a merchant class or an established elite meant that the equation of Western education with economic stability and financial security was even more firmly entrenched in Idoma Division than in Lagos. For the Idoma, the precarious economic existence of the Depression meant that only those with a stable income—salaried workers like teachers, clerks, and other government employees—could cope with the economic crisis. Since graduation from the missionary schools guaranteed a government job (as the substituting of Idoma clerks and teachers for Hausa and Igbo ones had become a cost-saving measure), Idoma people came to develop a new conception of and attitude toward the colonial missionary schools. The schools became economic refuges and ceased to be perceived as colonial impositions on society. The economic hope invested in the missionary schools during the Depression became so great that one missionary remarked that in the "newest places" where schools opened, the Idoma "look[ed] upon school as a sort of employment and expect[ed] to be paid for attending."[70]

The biggest challenge confronting the Methodist missionaries as economic hardship took its toll came not from meeting the rising demand for education but from trying to keep existing schools open. The financial problem that confronted them compelled them to look more than before to local converts and enrolled pupils for financial support. But new Christian converts had yet to internalize the spiritual logic of giving monetary offerings, and the Depression was scarcely the most opportune time to induct them into this Christian practice. Pupils dropped out of school when asked to buy their own books and pay fees that conflicted with their or their parents' dwindling incomes.[71] The missionary educators thus became their own principal supporters, relying on their own "collections" for sustaining their educational work. But even that soon proved insufficient and, as Hutchinson noted, became "conspicuous in its absence."

Desperate and overwhelmed by need, the missionary educators turned to the Igbo teachers retained or reengaged to work in place of British teachers retrenched or sent back to Britain on compulsory leave. In June 1933 they appealed to Igbo teachers to make a pledge of ten shillings per month from their salaries toward the sustenance of the various educational stations. The teachers rejected the move and "for nearly a week went on strike." The management of the strike fell to Hutchinson, the missionary in charge of Idoma Division, who described the experience of dealing with the striking teachers as "unpleasant." Two of the striking teachers "got violent and abusive" during negotiations and "had to be discharged"; another resigned.[72]

Experiences like these served to further reacquaint the missionaries with the depth of local hardship and made them even less receptive to the counsel of superiors, who relentlessly urged thrift, revenue drive, and retrenchment.

They were conflicted in several respects. The source of their dilemma was complex: they had become small players in the dynamics unfolding before them. Their work was caught between the colonial policies of drastic budget cuts, the crisis-inspired substitution of non-Idoma African colonial auxiliaries, and the dwindling of donations from economically troubled donors in Britain. All this produced a situation that tasked the missionaries' idealism, rendered their work ineffective, and removed them from the haughty pedestal of educator-civilizers that they had self-consciously occupied in Idoma Division before the Depression.

IDOMA REACTIONS TO THE CRISIS

The Idoma were not passive observers of the realities of the economic Depression and of the state's actions and inactions. They responded to economically adverse conditions through their overwhelming demand for colonial missionary education, which they saw as a gateway to economic stability. They responded to the downturn in other ways as well. The unraveling of the state's economic recovery policy in Idoma Division assumed elaborate forms and sparked other dramatic confrontations (see chapter 6). Here the concern centers on local initiative and agency as propellers of local economic recovery actions.

Idoma peasants took new initiatives toward recovering some of their lost means of income. The people of Igedde began, from 1932, to take loads of tobacco and mats to the market at Makurdi, the provincial capital. The economic benefits of this trade as well as its potential as a cash-earning activity for peasants excited colonial officials in the division, who still bore illusions of the failed economic transformation project there. To colonial officials this positive development represented a triumph of the market over subsistence. It did not matter if it had its origins in economic adversity rather than in an all-conquering market rationality. Officials hoped that this new trade would become, with the construction of an access road, a source of cash flow into the division. Nothing in the records indicates that the idealistic hopes of officials materialized, but the commencement of this trade signaled a growing desire on the part of the Idoma to look beyond their locale for economic opportunity, recovery, and sustenance.

Idoma peasants also reacted to the Depression difficulties by actually enacting the economic xenophobia previously ascribed to them. This time, though, they were not rejecting the economic pedagogy of British-backed Hausa traders. They were instead blaming settlers in the division for their economic woes. Most notably they cited the drastic, unprecedented fall in the price of yams, Idoma Division's staple and its major cash earner. Stung by the Depression, non-Idoma Africans in the division—who before the Depression had worked on the railway and in other colonial institutions and had experienced retrenchment at the onset of the state's budgetary problems—engaged in the cultivation of yams and grains in order to get by. Idoma peasants blamed the settlers' agricultural activities for the glut in the produce markets, to which they ascribed the collapse of prices. Consequently, antisettler hostility, directed mainly at the Igbo and Tiv, who had been forced into farming by the Depression, became rife. Fueled by a new refrain that considered the settlers strangers and agricultural interlopers in Idoma Division, this hostility grew in step with rumors that settlers had begun selling their produce below prevailing market prices. Capt. R. J. Lynch, an assistant district officer in the division captured the problem: "Owing to the trade Depression many of the industrials in the Oturkpo stranger settlement had been forced to resort to farming in order to tide over the difficult period. The local who largely relies on the market in the settlement as an outlet for his produce attributed the collapse in prices and stagnation in trade, which Oturkpo is experiencing in common with the rest of the world, to these farming activities. There is no land shortage in the District and the Oturkpo people have acquiesced in farming by strangers for some years past."[73] The relatively harmonious coexistence among different ethnicities and indigenes of different Idoma districts shattered when mutual distrust and an invocation of the stranger factor emerged to shape the attempt to make sense of an economic crisis whose origin remained a mystery. The real causes of the economic difficulties originated in distant lands, in world capitals, and in the international market, but the remotest fringes of the British Empire had to grapple with their real-life implications. Most of the inter- and intra-ethnic conflicts in 1930s Idoma Division fell within the matrix of peasant colonial subjects attempting to seek local explanations for an empirewide problem.

In September 1932 locals destroyed farms belonging to "strangers" in Otukpo, the divisional headquarters. This attracted the intervention of colonial authorities who fined the "guilty villages" to cover the damage. Captain Lynch, the assistant divisional officer, did not share the Idoma peasants' sentiments about settlers' role in the prevailing economic problem, as he, after all, understood its international origins. Nonetheless, he knew that with such deep-seated sentiments officials could not explain the Depression in purely economic terms and in its global context to impoverished Idoma peasants. Internationalizing the crisis could also indict the entire colonial economic system and further discredit the declared merits of the export economy. Such a corrective explanation would likely redirect the economic hostility of the Idoma from "settlers" toward institutions that embodied the international and colonial economies.

Lynch thus found himself with little room to maneuver when it came to situating the Depression and its origins for the cognitive benefits of frustrated Idoma peasants. He settled on a measure that validated the Idoma peasants' interpretation of events, but not because he believed in it. The imperative of law and order informed his decision. Lynch instructed the native authority "to place a restriction . . . on the extent of farming [by settlers]." He also instructed the native authority not to consider applications from new arrivals for land in the settlers' quarters.[74]

Lynch's instruction most likely did not result in a divisionwide dousing of economic and social tensions originating in Depression hardships. There is no evidence to indicate that the category of stranger and its refraction through the idiom of economic crisis receded with the intervention of colonial authorities. In other parts of the division tempers flared against so-called strangers who were accused of depressing prices through their agricultural ventures. In 1932 other antistranger uprisings occurred. In Igumale District pressure from indigenous farmers forced the district head to post notices in public places "intimating that no stranger farming would be allowed in Igumale District next year."[75] Similarly, so many confrontations erupted between "strangers" and "indigenes" in Akpa District that the district court had "much difficulty" in adjudicating them. Overwhelmed by both the volume and intensity of these conflicts, it sought the intervention of higher colonial juridical instruments.[76]

In another reaction to the crisis in the Idoma hinterland, young men migrated to centers of export crop production. Migration was a widespread response to the hardships of the Depression (see chapter 3). The search for previously ignored economic opportunities, especially labor demands in distant lands, took Idoma youths mainly to the cocoa-producing groves of western Nigeria, where they hoped to earn the increasingly elusive British money.

Pioneered by young men from Agatu District in the early 1920s, the migration of young Idoma men to the cocoa farms of western Nigeria increased remarkably during the Depression.[77] The boom in cocoa production, which defied the Depression,[78] was both a cause and an effect of the influx of cheap labor from the Benue Valley. Labor recruiters and agents, seeking cheap labor and hoping to make money as middlemen in labor negotiations, swarmed Idoma Division, signing young men to short- and long-term contracts.[79] Recruitment became a big part of the emigration process. A fairly big business, it involved infrastructures of mobility as well as cooperation between recruiters and cocoa farmers. Wealthy cocoa farmers often purchased trucks, and those who could afford to maintained a stable of them for moving laborers from Idoma Division to the cocoa belt and between farms. In 1932 colonial authorities intercepted two such trucks and were shocked at the organizational sophistication of what they called the "child smuggling syndicate."[80] The 1930s witnessed a perfection of the networks that sustained the migratory flow from Idoma to the cocoa belt.

Young Idoma men sought to escape the burden of taxation and the new punitive measures that tax default attracted. In the cocoa belt, the government assessed employers' taxes along with those of employees, which officials deducted at the source from cocoa revenue.[81] Historians of both the entrepreneurial and migrant-worker aspects of the cocoa industry have confirmed that the influx of the 1930s also partly stemmed from hunger. Young men arrived at the cocoa belt malnourished, telling of food stocks depleted due to tax demands and raids of reserves by tax agents.[82] Although migrants sometimes took their wives and children along with them, most of the married men left their wives and children behind, in Idoma Division. The women had to both provide for children and elderly relatives and engage British tax raiders in violent encounters (see chapter 6). Like the women of Kabba District, the wives and female relatives of the Idoma cocoa belt migrants navigated the revenue-gathering intrusions of colonial agents while many males migrated in search of cash. For both the women and the colonial agents, these novel encounters were fraught with tension. The absence of many young men forced colonial officials to deal with women, a change that generated conflict and violence while upsetting their Victorian assumptions about gender and African women's roles.

Apart from producing several generations of migratory communities of Idoma people in geographically distant southwestern Nigeria—the study of which is outside the scope of this work—the migration proved instrumental to the development of agricultural wage labor in most of Idoma Division. As most of the migrants worked on seasonal, short contracts, they soon completed their duties and returned to their districts in Idoma Division. These young men were used to working for money and wanted to continue on that path instead of cultivating personal agricultural plots, whose yield had become economically less rewarding due to the collapse of prices. Chiefs and other financially solvent notables began to hire these young men to cultivate their plots. Soon, returnees from the cocoa belt would go around neighboring towns and villages securing agricultural work contracts, which they would execute alone or with other returnees.[83] Part-time and largely target oriented, this work did little to disrupt the patterns of agricultural production and thus soon became popular.

Convinced that the path to prosperity during the Depression ran through cocoa fields, ambitious returnee migrants sought to recreate the cocoa plantations of the west in their districts. Experimental cocoa farms started by migrants in Utonkon, Agila, Igumale, Agatu, and other Idoma districts failed to live up to the expectations of the planters. Evidence of these failed cocoa projects still exists all over Idoma Division today, a further testament to the ecological unsuitability of Idoma Division to the export crop economic doctrine of British officials. The cocoa fields thus not only offered a source of cash at an economically difficult juncture in Idoma Division, they insinuated a range of economic possibilities into the economic imagination of young Idoma men. Impoverished Idoma peasants invested their hopes and anxieties in the youthful bodies of the new migrant class. Paradoxically, these experiments in agricultural transplantation reenacted the idealism and fantasies that undergirded similar colonial schemes in the early years of British rule in Idoma Division. The failure of some of these possibilities to materialize does not detract from the fact that the economic crisis produced a situation in which Idoma people, acting outside the economic purview of the state, imagined alternate economic fates outside the economic configurations of their locales. More important, they acted outside the reformist visions of interventionist colonial officials.

↩

At the heart of the tense relationship between the Idoma and British economic recovery schemes lay a fundamental difference between British and Idoma priorities. For as long as the Depression lasted, the British wanted to preserve a measure of budgetary equilibrium at the expense of infrastructural development, missionary education, and other advertised social benefits of colonial rule. While withdrawing these benefits, British officials sought to integrate the Idoma into the export crop and taxpaying culture of mainstream Northern Nigeria—to incorporate the Idoma economy into imperial and world markets. The Idoma, on the other hand, wanted more, not less, missionary education as a way of improving and stabilizing their incomes in the Depression. Contrary to colonial aims, the Idoma did not want to increase their participation in the colonial economy through tax payment or the substitution of export-oriented agriculture for semisubsistence. Nor did they want to make sacrifices to colonial economic recovery. They wanted to gain access to the social benefits of colonialism in order to improve their prospects of economic survival and future prosperity. This problem of divergent priorities and aspirations contributed in no small way to demystifying British colonial economic potency and paternalism. It set the stage for the violent encounters and scorched-earth confrontations analyzed in the next chapter, confrontations in which the Idoma showed little regard for British economic instructions and compulsions.

6 ⇌ Economic Recovery and Grassroots Revenue Offensives

THE PERIPHERAL stigma attached to Idoma Division returned during the Depression to constitute a site of crisis mediated by the British attempt to recapture and reexplore the division as a valuable, revenue-generating colonial unit. Not only a hurried afterthought, this effort became a policy alternative authorized by the economic recovery strategy of revenue generation and the bolstering of solvency. This revenue-centered exploration of the Idoma countryside went beyond rhetoric. It was also practical. The rhetoric of Idoma backwardness gave rise to the supposed imperative of integrating the division into the Northern Nigerian economic mainstream. This imperative in turn authorized the violent invasion of the Idoma countryside in the name of revenue generation.

In Idoma Division colonial officials attempted to allay their financial anxieties through tax raids, setting off tense encounters between the Idoma and the British. Revenue generation through taxation emerged in economically depressed Idoma Division as a central colonial project that almost displaced the traditional social and economic preoccupations of British colonialism. The combustive mix of local demands and the official inability and refusal to meet them troubled and sometimes truncated these traditional colonial commitments during the Depression (see chapter 5). Officials pursued taxation and other forms of revenue generation as if they constituted a substitute regime of colonial govermentality.[1] It seemed that, in the face of an official retreat from investments in education and other social projects, taxation and its intrusive bureaucracies came to serve as a cheap, fiscally rewarding mechanism of political control, an alternative to financially costly, familiar preoccupations of British colonialism.

Seeking revenue on behalf of a financially depressed colonial state, the violent tax raiders provoked a dramatic backlash as the Idoma resisted with both

146

crudely novel and sophisticated strategies of escape and mockery. Colonial officials rationalized the violence that characterized the tax campaign as a form of economic discipline, necessary in an economically backward colonial backwater. However, like most economic recovery measures of the Depression, the raids elicited local reactions that served to further frustrate colonial goals and to burden colonial officials with an incipient social disorder.

More important, the raids underscored the dramatic erosion of whatever control the colonial bureaucracy had built in Idoma Division. The expeditions made up for, and emanated from, a frustrating realization of the paucity of colonial control and the tenuousness of the local embrace of colonial economic and political rhetoric. The reactions of the Idoma to the raids demonstrated in very stark terms their perceptions of British colonial economic distress. The reactions buttressed the view that British rule was a crumbling imperial system that could no longer exploit or control its subjects without crude violence at the grass roots. The economic crisis and the reaction of both the British and the Idoma to it exacerbated the crisis of control that plagued British rule from its inception in 1900.

COLONIAL FINANCIAL ANXIETIES IN IDOMA DIVISION

In a 1932 report Capt. R. J. Lynch, the assistant district officer in Idoma Division, informed his boss, the resident of Benue Province, that trade in the division had reached a standstill and that he "anticipated" that "considerable difficulty [would] be experienced in collecting the necessary currency to meet tax demand."[2] This statement illustrates the degree of frustration with the limited success of efforts to revive trade and bolster revenue in Idoma Division.

The captain and the resident appeared more concerned with the implications of the trade depression for tax revenue and with the "embezzlement" of tax money by chiefs—the local intermediaries in tax collection—than with the impact of the crisis on the Idoma economy. Though acknowledged, colonial discourses represented the impoverishing of the Idoma as an inevitable consequence of their supposedly noncapitalist economic practices. The difficulties in tax collection that Lynch anticipated for the 1932–33 tax season stemmed from an apprehension informed by the difficulties of the previous season, which was marked by incidents such as that involving two "hamlet Heads who embezzled . . . sums of money . . . [and who were] sentenced to imprisonment for three months by the Native Court."[3] The district officer also informed the resident of the £7 10s. of tax money from Utonkon District he had to write off "on account of embezzlement."

Embezzlement became a recurring theme in officials' anxious discussions on taxation. It appears that the topic of embezzlement became both a statement of fact and an administrative rationalization of empirical, perhaps insurmountable, obstacles in tax collection in the face of cash scarcity.[4] The colonial obsession with revenue, according to Steven Pierce, helped produce corruption in colonial Northern Nigeria.[5] Officials sought convenient explanations for their inability to squeeze tax out of economically depressed villages. This led to some buck-passing in which African tax agents—the hamlet heads and chiefs—bore the blame for taxes that they could not practically collect.

When tax revenues did not meet estimates, embezzlement increased, but a curious ambivalence was evident in the tone of the allegations, suggesting an exaggeration of the extent of the problem. For instance, the district officer reported to the resident in late 1932 that of the £40 of tax money not accounted for, £15 "was apparently stolen" while the balance was "thought to have been borrowed by village Heads."[6] It is plausible that chiefs used "borrowing" as way to stabilize their incomes in the face of falling prices of agricultural goods in lo-cal markets and dwindling personal incomes. Officials may have conveniently confused this practice with embezzlement, especially when the chiefs could not pay back the amount borrowed. The exaggeration appeared strategic.

Interestingly, when districts did meet tax estimates, the discourse of em-bezzlement was sublimated. Captain Lynch's annual report for 1932 trium-phantly hailed improvements in tax collection and revenue generation. "Tax," he stated, "has come surprisingly well. Our unduly gloomy prognostications made at the beginning of the year have been confounded."[7] The resident re-sponded on an equally positive note: "In the years I have been in the province I have noticed this tendency in Idoma Division in other matters than tax. I appreciate the hard work done and the discomforts endured, but I should like to see more optimism. Pessimism must react on the object—the Idomas; so would optimism. Very definite progress is being made. Rome was not built in a day."[8] Apparently emboldened by his boss's sympathy and appreciative remarks, Lynch now saw little use in invoking embezzlement as a self-exonerating strategy. The resident had not reprimanded him on the shortfall in taxes, and so the self-exoneration that seemed to undergird the allegations of embezzle-ment gradually vanished from his reports.

THE ECONOMIC BLIZZARD AND THE REVENUE IMPERATIVE

By early 1932 the effects of the Great Depression had registered profoundly on the Idoma economy. In the annual report for 1932, Lynch observed, "Idoma Division like the rest of the world has not escaped the effects of the economic blizzard. The price of yams, the staple crop for consumption and export, has reached a record low level. In recent years a substantial export trade in yams had been developed but owing to Depression and unemployment in the industrial areas of the Jos Plateau and Port Harcourt the trade is now stag-nant."[9] The yam trade to the tin mines on the Jos Plateau as well as labor migration to the mines constituted sources of cash for the Idoma, as Freund confirms. He notes that yams on the mines "were brought in mainly from Benue Province."[10] The mine closures of 1930–31 and the subsequent loss of jobs represented an economic setback for an already cash-strapped colonial enclave. By 1932, therefore, anyone could observe the situation that Lynch reported. Lynch went further to provide details of the effects of the Depression on the Idoma economy: "In 1929 1086 tons of yams were railed from Utonkon station; in 1930 the figure was 1027 tons and in 1931 1009 tons. The figure for 1932 has not been supplied by the railway. It is feared that there has been a considerable shrinkage in trade."[11]

Two export crops, beniseed and groundnuts, could have helped provide the Idoma with much-needed cash. They, however, only cultivated them on a small scale, for "unfortunately the Idoma has not yet responded to the propaganda indulged in to induce him to develop the cultivation of these crops." But even if the Idoma had embraced the cultivation of these export crops, they would have had trouble selling them, "since there are no facilities for the disposal of the crops as the canteens [produce-buying centers], which formally existed at Utonkon and Oturkpo were closed down in 1931."[12]

This situation seriously affected the fiscal health of the division and became further aggravated by some attributes of the Idoma economy. Chief among them was the predominant use of brass rods as currency, in defiance of the monetization drive of the British. Colonial authorities pursued monetization though taxation and what colonial documents recorded as export crop propaganda. The Idoma opposition to both strategies frustrated attempts to promote colonial money and entrenched brass rods firmly as the most popular currency in Idoma Division. The Depression caused a sharp depreciation in the value of brass rods, making revenue generation unusually difficult (see chapter 5). In June 1932 one colonial official reported to the resident of Benue Province that the fall in value of brass rods, circulating widely in the division, had become a "great embarrassment." "The value of rod," he complained, "is at present 1½ d and is likely to fall to less than 1d when collection starts in earnest." He lamented that Idoma could no longer convert brass rods to the colonial currency for tax purposes as they had always done because they could not obtain good exchange rates from the Southern Provinces, which had suffered a shortage of currency due to tax collection.[13]

For all the concern that officials expressed about the persistence of non-British currencies—and though they certainly preferred a monetized economy and sought to create one in Idoma Division to promote revenue generation—the circulation of brass rods was not in itself the problem. Before the Depression the British appeared content with partial monetization, or what Felicia Ekejiuba calls the multiple-currency system.[14] As she argues, the colonial government, understanding the reluctance with which some Nigerians accepted and used the British currency, struck a compromise after 1912 that allowed the use of brass rods and manillas (brass or copper armlets) in transactions between Nigerians. The colonial authorities' only assault on local currency before the Depression was the effort to fix the rate of exchange at levels strategically calculated to limit the attraction of the local monetary units and to diminish their status as legal tender.[15] During the Depression, however, the issue of monetization took on a new urgency. In 1932, Captain Lynch reported to the resident that the use of brass rods as a form of currency had become "the main obstacle to economic progress" and that "the only way in which this form of currency can be ousted is the substitution of nickel and alloy and this can only be achieved by means of trade with the outside world."[16] Lynch admitted that in terms of external trade "ground has been lost in the last twelve months." Overwhelmed and confused by the lack of fiscal and economic order and predictability in the division, and, unwilling to tolerate local reluctance to seek out colonial currency for tax payment, officials initiated a brutal tax campaign as a way to extract the much-desired revenue and to compel the Idoma to embark on cash-earning endeavors.

A major source of concern stemmed from the fact that a "large proportion of the tax was being paid in nickel," a practice that caused "an embarrassment to the government and Native Treasuries." Lamenting the £4,500 worth of nickel that officials disposed of during 1932, Lynch noted that though a larger proportion of tax came in alloy, the payments included "numerous florins," which he said indicated that the people had begun to use their rainy-day reserve in order to meet their tax needs.[17] However, such instructive, if subtle, admission of local financial strain hardly resulted in a downward reassessment of tax rates. On the contrary, officials netted an almost 10 percent increase in tax rates in the division between 1931 and 1933. Nor did the knowledge of soaring tax rates amid depressive economic conditions mitigate the severity of the violent tax campaigns that Lynch's successors resorted to in order to collect taxes that local rulers could not and refused to collect.

Several factors constrained the tax campaign. First, currency counterfeiting increased as the exchange of brass rods for colonial coinage became difficult due to the massive confiscation and transfer of silver coinage from the Nigerian economy at the onset of the Depression. The depletion of British currency in neighboring Eastern Nigeria through tax collection also contributed to the illicit activity. An unprecedented cash scarcity hit Idoma Division and the other food crop–producing divisions in Northern Nigeria. It developed into a potential cause of friction between the colonial authorities and Idoma peasants, whose tax-paying ability rested on the availability of British currency. The new British effort to discredit the brass rod as a legal tender compounded the volatile situation.

The emergence of the counterfeiting industry (see chapter 3) quickly filled the currency void created by British currency withdrawals. Though widespread, the counterfeiting problem did not uniformly affect Northern Nigeria. In the emirate divisions, where opportunities to earn cash existed in export crop production and wage labor, however diminished, counterfeiting arose merely in response to the fluctuations in the volume of circulating currency and in response to seasonal problems of acute cash scarcity. This especially occurred during the tax/harvest season. In those areas, it was much easier to simply criminalize the problem. In Idoma Division counterfeiting emerged as an alternative fiscal domain that rendered useless the discourse of criminality so integral to the colonial characterization of local adjustments to the economic crisis. Counterfeit coinage became a perennial and unavoidable presence in the Idoma hinterland from 1930. The acute cash scarcity in the division and the widespread circulation of counterfeit coinage led to extensive policy discussion on the problem in the early 1930s. Officials often referenced Idoma Division to illustrate the complications and difficulties of controlling the counterfeiting cottage industry.[18] Colonial discussions on the problem of counterfeit coinage in the domain of taxation centered on Idoma Division, which the government auditor argued provided a template for understanding how counterfeiting compromised the state's revenue aims. The Idoma case study revealed the pragmatic dilemmas inherent in dealing with the counterfeiting problem.[19]

With time, the British became victims of their own efforts. Their revenue-generation aims now stood imperiled by previous efforts to reintegrate Idoma Division into the state's revenue scheme after a lull; to increase the solvency of the home economy by exporting silver coins from Nigeria; and to restrict the use of local currencies, especially in Eastern Nigeria, where most of the counterfeit coins in Idoma Division originated.[20] This problem would haunt the tax campaigns of the 1930s.

The mandate given to local chiefs to act, once again, after the political disengagement of the mid-1920s, as agents of state economic recovery—as tax gatherers—also constrained and complicated the tax campaign for the British. Officials did recognize the tenuousness of chiefs' powers in Idoma Division. They further understood that chiefs would be ineffective participants in the tax campaigns. Nonetheless, the pragmatics of saving money through the reduction of British colonial staff forced British officials to rely, albeit partially, on the brittle powers of local leaders in an increasingly volatile division. This leadership crisis, the continuous growth of the counterfeit industry, and the increasing use of violence as a tax collection tool would impede the British effort to extract scarce cash from Idoma Division through a tax and revenue campaign.

No better evidence exists for the violence-driven tax campaigns of the early 1930s than the journals of colonial officials who played key roles in the tax raids. One of these journals came from W. R. Crocker, who served in Idoma Division in 1933. The graphic descriptions in these journals allow us to reconstruct the nature and complications of the campaigns. Having convinced himself that the Idoma people and their leaders needed weaning from "the pampering with which they have been treated in the past by the [British] Administrative personnel here"[21]—a reference to the administrative compromise of the mid-1920s, Crocker set out to do two things. First he sought to jolt the weak Idoma leaders into a new sense of fiscal responsibility. Second, he readied himself to override their power and take the tax-gathering initiative into his own hands. A violent tax campaign ensued. Crocker, and other officials after him, rationalized these decisions by depicting local leaders as too weak, illegitimate, and incompetent to enforce taxation by themselves. Similarly, they considered peasants too shifty and too removed from the bureaucratic and economic institutions of the colonial government to be trusted with voluntary compliance with tax requests.

Between June and December 1933, Crocker, together with an entourage of servants, armed guards, scribes, and enforcers, traversed the length and breadth of Idoma Division. They enforced a relatively novel tax regime whose brutality was accentuated by the lull in taxation that preceded it. Convinced that local leaders needed prodding and that peasants needed compulsion, Crocker pioneered a method of tax gathering that would become the modus operandi of British tax gatherers for the next few years: tax raids. Colonial officials carried out the raids with a violent ferocity that caused further economic dislocation and injured the economic fabric of Idoma villages.

The confrontations that the tax campaigns produced offer an instructive snapshot of the tensions generated by the British attempt to recast Idoma Division as a significant tax-yielding division. As Crocker went from village to village and hamlet to hamlet, locals expressed to him and his entourage the extent of their impoverishment. Such dramatization of local poverty served, it seems, only to harden Crocker's resolve to enforce the tax-gathering imperative. One of the first districts to receive Crocker and his entourage was Oglewu. Disappointed that the district head had collected only £15, Crocker urged him to increase his rate of collection. The frustrated district head, having reached the limits of his persuasive ability, told Crocker on behalf of his subjects, "there is scarcely any currency in the district this year."[22] Unconvinced, Crocker urged a more vigorous collection effort. Two weeks later Crocker and his men invaded Offoi, where the district head, the village head, and all the hamlet heads were "summoned and spoken to about tax." Here, as in Oglewu, they had collected less than 5 percent of the tax. The villagers pleaded the no-currency defense, which Crocker conceded was "admittedly true in part" but which did little to earn them reprieve. Crocker directed them to find work and earn money.

As village after village pleaded no currency and repeated the emotional appeal for empathy, founded on poverty and depressed prices, Crocker grew more aggravated and less empathetic with the plight of Idoma peasants. Appeals and prodding receded gradually in the methodological hierarchy of Crocker and his entourage. Patience faded and a retreat to the stereotype of the Idoma's propensity for malingering and trickery in tax matters ensued.[23] For Crocker the Depression merely exacerbated what was historically true of the Idoma: "there is always difficulty in collecting tax among the Idoma even in the boom years."[24] But this frustration produced neither retreat nor surrender in taxation matters. It proved to Crocker once and for all that the Idoma still resorted to their trickery and maintained their irrational opposition to institutions of British economic and administrative rationality. It also made the direct involvement of British officials in tax collection inevitable. For, as Crocker rationalized of his method of tax gathering, "normally, [tax] has to be collected by [British] political officers themselves and with the aid of Government Police."[25] That, of course, violated the spirit of indirect rule.

Crocker decided that only force would break what he saw as the cycle of Idoma recalcitrance in taxation matters. In November he launched the inaugural tax raid in the district of Otukpa. The raid itself resulted rather fortuitously from an unexpected frustration on Crocker's part. He had arranged to meet with elders and adult males of the village for the purpose of tax collection. Frustrated that only the district head turned up and that "not a penny of tax had been paid," Crocker's "20 labourers," his messenger, and other members of the colonial police fanned out across the district and its villages seizing goats, fowl, yams, and any other valuable property they could find. Owners, who had apparently hidden in the bush to escape from Crocker and his tax-gathering entourage, could either redeem their property by paying, or they would find it auctioned off to cover their taxes. Crocker's own account details the raid: "For the 5 hours we collected as many goats (over 50) fowls (over 50) and yams as we could: we could collect no more as the rest had been taken off and hidden just as the houses of the owners were deserted; they had absconded. The owners of the property restrained were informed that on paying their tax to their Village Head at Otukpa this afternoon, they could recover their stock."[26] At Otukpa Bariki only two men came to redeem their property—an indication of the security and economic threat that the tax raids represented in an already impoverished division. This development forced Crocker to rethink his anthropological explanation of the Idoma people's noncooperation in tax matters. Gradually, as he confronted irrefutable evidence of poverty and economic desperation, the fabled Idoma predilection for escaping official exaction and for malingering gave way in his mind to rare moments of self-reflection. Crocker acknowledged not just the fact of poverty but also the potentially counterproductive effect of the raids: the devaluing or taking away of rainy-day wealth stored in goats, fowl, and other products, which doubled as emergency cash earners and sources of sustenance. "This afternoon came and only 2 men appeared with their 2/6. Hence the livestock remains on my hands. What can I do with it? What can I do with all the rest that is to be collected in this neighborhood alone? The market will be glutted. The Otukpa people haven't enough currency to pay their tax let alone to buy extra goats."[27] It emerged that the people of Otukpa had put up fierce resistance in the face of Crocker's tax aggression. In addition to hiding food and livestock, they had sunk stakes and erected booby traps "near their goat pens," which injured three of Crocker's men as they tried to reach for the livestock. Crocker deliberated on what to do with the culprits. Was their action legitimate self-defense or a criminal assault on servants of the colonial state? "What again is to be done with people who staked the ground near their goat pens?" The tax raids aroused palpable hostility in the Idoma countryside. Shortly after the raid at Otukpa Bariki, locals beat up two members of Crocker's dreaded native authority police and an official messenger; all three were on their way to draw some water for Crocker.

Cocker remained unfazed throughout the dire situation. He managed to auction off the confiscated properties by pricing them below prevailing market prices. This enabled him to raise money to show for his checkered tax drive, which in turn nudged him on in the quest for more tax money. On November 23, Crocker and his entourage invaded Effiom and "seized all the goats [we] could find—34." The party would have confiscated more goats and fowl but the people of Effiom had gotten wind of the impending raid and had "run away and taken the goats with them and hidden them in the *Kurmi* [forest]." Crocker and his men searched but could not find any more livestock in the undergrowth.[28] By now news of the raids had circulated through the Idoma countryside, and villages and hamlets organized their escape and strategies of livestock concealment. When Crocker and his men reached Eifole, for instance, they found "not a human being except the decrepit aged left in the hamlet and not an animal."[29] Similarly, "the raid on Ogenago was futile [as] every goat had been taken and hidden" and "not a thing was left in the hamlet except a few fowls and some yams." At Aioga, simply "no goats" remained; the stock had either been hidden or removed in an earlier raid. The diminishing success rate of Crocker's raid forced him yet again to reevaluate his method to make the raid more effective as a tax-gathering instrument.

As they progressed, the raids became victims of their own success. First, locals, always on the alert, stood ready to hide property and themselves and to stay one step ahead of Crocker and his entourage. Second, repeating the raids in one area diminished the area's stock of livestock and foodstuffs or, at the very least, facilitated the transfer (through auction) of confiscated valuables to relatively wealthy local potentates, thus exacerbating a volatile economic differentiation in the Idoma countryside. Crocker soon realized that, for a raid to succeed, "it must be secret—that is, not divulged beforehand" and that "it can't be repeated in the same neighborhood."[30] This realization did little, however, to mitigate the confidence of Crocker in the raids themselves as instruments of tax collection. He returned frequently to previously raided districts, villages, and hamlets. On December 1, 1933, he returned to Oglewu, the district where he had carried out the inaugural tax raid. The second raid there yielded a "haul of 30 goats," many of which officials auctioned off in Oglewu and neighboring districts. On December 14 he also returned to Otukpa, where, "learning of the doings of the two previous days [the people] had hidden [their goats]," leaving only fowls, which Crocker had pronounced not worthy of confiscation as "they die a few hours later."[31] On the way to Otukpa, Crocker stopped over at Agbaha and "distrained [confiscated] all property I could lay my hands on, the owners of which had not paid their taxes."

There is no clear evidence on the tensions and troubles that the auctioning process caused between buyers and the former owners. However, it is clear that losing goats (described by Crocker as the Idoma's "most valuable [movable] property"), fowl, and foodstuffs—the rainy-day wealth of the Idoma peasantry—agitated those who lacked the money to redeem them. The testimony of Crocker himself is instructive in this regard. Describing the chaos of the auction process, Crocker, provides a telling illustration of the trauma brought to owners of confiscated property: "Dogarai [native authority policemen] mixing up the different parcels and adding a confusion of their own to the general; competing buyers shouting out their bids against one another; goats bleating and fowls screeching; and some of the ex-owners crying (one, when his goats were offered for sale, came into the ring and said that he was going to do 'this'—'this' being conveyed by running his hand across his throat)."[32] Whether the individual in question actually committed suicide or whether suicide had become a widespread response to such loss of household wealth remains uncertain. But the frustration of the raids and the raucous auctions constituted a constant irritant to Crocker, who wondered, as it became increasingly difficult to find villagers and their property, whether he should consider burning down the huts of deserting tax defaulters as a punitive measure.[33] As H. P. Elliot, who was posted to Idoma Division in 1935, confirmed, British officials indeed used arson to punish tax evaders: "often they outwitted us and we would arrive at an empty village. Some of my colleagues in cases of extreme defiance went so far as to set fire to the grass huts."[34]

In 1935, Elliot confronted a similar massive tax default and pleadings of no currency and poverty from locals. He attempted to use the threat of arrest and prosecution to extract outstanding tax from Idoma peasants, warning village after village that he would return to arrest tax defaulters if, after a given deadline, they did not pay in full. Neither that nor the threat of Crocker-style confiscations brought any significant changes in the tax situation. Youths complained that they had no money to pay their own taxes and talked about asking the elders to pay for them, while elders cited the lack of currency with which to pay taxes.[35] In November, Elliot began to arrest tax defaulters and household heads in Angul, Otukpo Nobi, and other districts. But, as in the days of Crocker, most villagers began to escape to the bush on the approach of Elliot and his party of tax gatherers. Not even the arrest of village heads as surety for the defaulters proved effective in fostering tax accountability. Nonetheless, Elliot continued to arrest defaulters that he could catch. For most of November, arrests and detention of tax defaulters preoccupied Elliot and his crew. But as the novelty of the arrests and detention wore off, locals began to resign themselves to their fate. This created a dilemma for Elliot, who began to take the locals' claim of poverty, dwindling incomes, and lack of currency more seriously. "It is probable," he said, "that they [locals] simply have not the money." He also explained that "in 1935, the Idomas were getting lower prices for their crops because of the world slump and did not like paying tax. Their own currency was brass rods, which in those days were still in circulation. These Government would not accept. So there was resistance. Touring officers had . . . to be accompanied by Government police armed with rifles."[36]

In spite of such proclamations of prevalent hardship and cash scarcity, Elliot remained firm in his belief that the "village elders" resorted to "trying . . . various tricks—to avoid paying taxes."[37] Occasional acknowledgments of the severity of the economic conditions in Idoma Division tempered the indictment of the Idoma character, which in turn justified the violent approaches to tax collection. Elliot came to the conclusion that the villagers "had clearly not the slightest intention of doing anything and took it quite for granted that they would be imprisoned."[38] Whether true, or whether the resignation of locals to arrest and detention indicated financial helplessness on their part, we do not know for certain. We do know, however, that Elliot deployed a novel method of pressure when he arrested male defaulters and encouraged their wives to sell off goats and other valuables to pay their husbands' taxes in order to secure their freedom.

This method of blackmail met with limited success, although many of the women who were "good market traders . . . produced the cash and ransomed their men."[39] Soon, very few Idoma avoided arrest by hiding in the forests. Elliot concluded on November 24, "it is now becoming very difficult to catch anyone." As a result of this apparent frustration, he resorted to Crocker's method of raids and confiscation. Elliot surmised that since the Idoma had become too elusive, confiscation of "their goats is the only alternative."[40] From then on, Elliot traversed the countryside, arresting those too old to escape or those caught unawares. His "string of prisoners and large herd of goats" followed him from village to village, swelling as the raids progressed and as "representative collection[s] of goats [were] made." Most of these confiscated goats went unredeemed by their owners. The ensuing auctions proved just as rowdy and as traumatic for owners as they had been in the time of Crocker. Like Crocker before him, Elliot believed that the Idoma's resistance to the tax campaigns, though enhanced by the hardship of the Depression, resulted from the British leaving the Idoma alone for too long and not schooling them in the utilitarian values of taxation as an institution of modern governance. Unlike Crocker, Elliot set out to disseminate what he called "tax propaganda," helping locals to estimate their own taxes based on household production and delivering lectures to tax defaulters in prisons on what "tax was meant for" and "what it was expended on in colonial Idomaland."[41]

Elliot's tax propaganda was unlikely to make extracting taxes from the Idoma easier. Until November 1936, Elliot continued the tedious routine of raids and arrests. And he continued to confront the same levels of desperation and number of complaints and pleas for reprieve that had marked his earlier encounters. The convoluted path of revenue requisition in a division arguably hit worst by the Depression in Northern Nigeria did not lead to the fiscal outcomes desired by officials. As noted earlier, several reasons accounted for this quagmire, including an illusion of local chieftaincy internalized by colonial officials and the unrealistic expectations placed on rulers who must, as a matter of tradition and necessity, remain weak to remain rulers in the division (see chapter 5).

RAIDS, RULERS, AND REVENUE

Official ambivalence regarding the role of local leaders in this revenue scheme emerged as one of the major problems of the tax campaigns of the 1930s. Officials concluded very early that local rulers inefficiently gathered revenue and therefore resolved to carry out raids themselves, commanding the revenue offensive directly. As Elliot put it, "the Native Authority, consisting of warrant chiefs in charge of districts representing the different clans of the Idoma people, was weak and inefficient at the unpopular task of tax collection."[42] But the lack of adequate British tax-gathering personnel—the colonial establishment in Idoma Division remained "always short of staff" during the

Depression[43]—ensured a place for the rulers in minor roles as persuaders and collectors. Officials had to rely on the local rulers to the extent that theoretically they had to work among their own people as tax agents, although their perceived lethargy and weakness ruled them out as the main driving force of the revenue offensive.

Several factors hamstrung the local rulers and complicated their position within this novel regime of taxation. Colonial officials—despite admitting that local peasants suffered the effects of the Depression and that currency had indeed become scarce—clung to the prose of tax evasion, the standard leitmotif of their characterization of the Idoma attitude toward the British revenue offensive. As a result, when local rulers returned to their British supervisors with sad tales of local poverty and inability to pay taxes, officials interpreted their failure as weakness at best and abetting of tax evasion at worst. The authorities convinced themselves that local rulers, wittingly or unwittingly, merely validated the lies of their tax-evading subjects. This mindset fit well with the extant official views on the supposed generic incompetence of the typical Idoma ruler: "it goes without saying that he [the Idoma ruler] has no presence or personality of any sort. Nor has he a little 'public sense': his chieftainship is something to be enjoyed without contributing anything himself toward the cost of the enjoyment."[44] This lamentation on the perils of Idoma kingship was widely held in colonial circles.

Both Crocker and Elliot accused the rulers of sitting by idly while their subjects defied their instruction to pay their taxes. In Otukpa Bariki, Crocker was incensed with the district head, "who hasn't lifted a finger until I came here to get tax, not even in his own hamlet." Crocker lamented the degeneracy of the variant of indirect rule practiced in Idoma Division. The district head, Crocker argued, would not qualify as headman on a road project in a "Hausa Emirate," let alone head of a district. Elaborate explanations abounded as to the unsuitability of local Idoma rulers for the revenue ambitions of British officials. As hamlet head after hamlet head reported to Crocker that "their people refuse[d] to listen to them to pay up [their taxes]," Crocker found two reasons for the attitude of the rulers. First, the chiefs exhibited the "deceitfulness of the Idoma." Second, they had been pampered in the past and allowed to merely enjoy the prestige of their offices.[45] The chiefs feigned "ignorance as to their being permitted to distrain property of tax defaulters." Crocker similarly lashed out at the district head of Otukpa for failing to carry out tax-related instructions: "I left him with a carefully mapped-out programme as to which places to go to, when, and how. He hasn't done a tap—hasn't moved from his house. At first he said he had arrested and collected tax from seven villages (not those he had planned), but he later denied this."[46] Elliot took his outrage a little further than Crocker: he prosecuted local rulers who failed to fulfill their tax obligations. In August 1935 he prosecuted the hamlet head of Agineka in the native court for "hopeless incompetence and slackness."[47] In November he ordered the arrest of several hamlet heads for failing to collect the taxes due from their hamlets. When the hamlet heads "escaped to the bush," he arrested the village head "as surety for their appearance."[48] In addition to the perceived incompetence of the chiefs, Elliot also dealt with a recurring dilemma of the tax campaigns: what to do about discrepancies in collected taxes.

Like colonial officials before him, Elliot believed that local rulers continued to embezzle taxes that they managed to collect. From January 1936 he began to complain consistently about such embezzlement. Officials sometimes founded these allegations on presumption and sometimes on established evidence. On January 17 he ordered the prosecution in the native court of two hamlet heads, Ochai and Oibeche, for allowing tax money to go "unaccounted for and apparently lost." Questioned on the loss, the two hamlet heads claimed to have taken out counterfeit coins from the collected tax, but "the presumption was strong that they had embezzled certain sums."[49] Embezzlement also plagued the tax returns of Obiokpa, the head of Ikikra; Oto, the head of Ikpoke; and Akoji and Akumu. As late as November 1936 the problem of embezzlement trailed the accounting process of amassing revenue from the Idoma countryside. Prosecution and arrests of hamlet heads remained common.

The discourse of embezzlement and chiefly greed congealed into the trope of the weak and incompetent Idoma ruler. Authorities saw Idoma headmen and chiefs as profiteers interested only in personal profit, preferably from taxation, not in the fulfillment of colonial tax obligations. There was some truth to this. At Crocker's auctions chiefs schemed to buy goats and fowl cheaply to swell their own flocks. Crocker narrates how a district head tried to abdicate his role in one of the auctions because "I refused to allow [him] to buy a parcel of goats . . . (his interest all along has been the possibility of securing a series of splendid bargains: the collection of tax money hasn't entered his head)."[50] The tax raids seem to have indeed presented chiefs and hamlet heads with the opportunity of "picking up some cheap bargains on goats and fowls."

Missing from the harsh, albeit fairly accurate, indictment of local rulers by British colonial officials was a sense of perspective. Unwilling to ask why local rulers could not collect taxes effectively, why they made poor persuaders on tax matters, and why the chiefs sought to profit from an unprecedented economic despoliation of their domains, colonial officials sought a sociological explanation that focused on collective character and blamed previous official policies of "pampering," compromise, and indifference. Officials curiously ignored the fact that the chiefs and headmen did not receive a salary for their efforts, partly because the British did not regard them as chiefly allies in colonial administration, as they did chiefs in the emirate sector. As rulers not recognized as fit for leadership but necessary only to maintain a facade of consistency in the practice of indirect rule across Northern Nigeria, the chiefs did not benefit from the remunerative privileges of chiefs in the Muslim emirates—the real chiefs in the British imaginary. When, in August 1935, Idoma chiefs asked for salaries like their counterparts elsewhere, Elliot, the assistant district officer, told them that "there was none for them at present."[51] It was not until October 1936 that officials decided to pay the chiefs a salary, basing this review of policy on the principle of "no work no pay," as Elliot put it. The chiefs would be paid only if they fulfilled their responsibilities to the colonial regime—namely, "tax collection" and the production of defendants, judgment debtors, and tax fugitives.[52]

Indeed, a causal link, however tenuous, did exist between the economic predicament of chiefs and their reluctance to gather taxes on behalf of the colonial state. Jane Guyer provides an instructive parallel here. She argues that in Depression-era south-central Cameroon, the attempt by the colonial state to reduce the range of revenue available to chiefs and thus to downsize their economic status provoked widespread resistance, which aligned chiefs with their subject against colonial officials and undermined the partnership between chiefs and colonial authorities. The assault on chiefly privilege and perquisites turned chiefs against the state's effort to make revenue generation the cornerstone of its economic recovery policy. It also made them begin to "speak about the interests of their people . . . oppose tax increases, ask for a reduction in court and market fees, and wonder how their people were to sell their cash crops when there were no buyers."[53]

One can reasonably tie the perceived greed and profiteering of the Idoma chiefs to their lack of a stable income as compensation for their locally dreaded roles in the revenue offensive. Strengthening this contention is evidence of a rise in the number of incidents of unauthorized and unofficial extortion by African agents of British colonialism in Idoma Division, a phenomenon known as *sojan gona* (lit., farm raider). Both Elliot and Crocker reported several cases of sojan gona. Their reports suggest two possibilities: first, that agents of the state opportunistically exploited the revenue campaigns to extort money and materials from locals in the name of the state; second, that these local agents used their positions on the margins of colonial officialdom to make up for lack of steady official remuneration.

The proliferation of the sojan gona problem during the Depression may have escaped the detection of petty British officials, who wondered why their Hausa-speaking Idoma and non-Idoma auxiliaries and interlocutors commanded more respect, awe, and fear in local eyes than did British officials, who possessed real, tangible power. Crocker marveled at the "significant amount of deference" that Itodu, his messenger, got from the Idoma. While greetings for

Itodu included genuflection and an *agaba* or *zaki* (Idoma and Hausa for lion, respectively), the highest terms of respect in colonial Idoma Division, Crocker and other Europeans got "a surly stare, [and only] sometimes an *agaba*."[54] Crocker and other British officials did not realize that, as interlocutors between non-Idoma-speaking British officials (who spoke Hausa poorly, if at all) and the Idoma colonial subjects (who spoke little or no Hausa), Hausa-speaking local auxiliaries imposed a great deal of personal whim and interest on colonial conversations about power relations. Their significant roles meant that they determined whose goats and fowl officials confiscated and whose they spared. They could also misrepresent official directives for personal benefits or launch unofficial raids to enrich themselves. Local testimony has it that this was the real source of the colonial auxiliary's seemingly inexplicable power and of the fear and deference he inspired in the Idoma.[55] This subtle power operated with particularly devastating effects in the non-Hausa-speaking districts of Northern Nigeria—mainly Kabba, Igala, Idoma, and the districts of Ilorin Province. The fact that British officials posted to these districts often spoke neither Hausa nor the local language well—Hausa being the official language of colonial power relations in Northern Nigeria—gave interpreters and Hausa-speaking auxiliaries enormous control over colonial instructions. This control enabled them even in more prosperous times to carry out extortionist activities in the name of British colonial officialdom. An anecdote from Constance Larymore, who toured Kabba Division in 1909 with her husband, a newly arrived colonial district officer, illustrates this contention.

On the Larymores' arrival at the village of Lukpa, a crowd of locals, who appeared to be excited at seeing the British officials (but whose excitement also betrayed a sense of agitation), mobbed the Larymores. Constance recalls,

> I was, by that time well accustomed to creating a sensation wherever I appeared, no white woman having been seen previously; but these people struck me as having more than salutations in their minds and on their clamouring tongues. I had been six weeks in the country, my knowledge of Hausa was confined to salutations and a few simple words, so I summoned our interpreter to help me to entertain my visitors. They chattered, shouted and gesticulated at "Paul," who eventually explained to me, smilingly, that they had never seen a white woman before and were anxious to offer me a personal welcome. I nodded and smiled in high gratification, thanked them cordially, and, when I had exhausted my small stock of polite salutations, told the interpreter to give them leave to go home. This they did, somewhat reluctantly, I thought; but after describing the interview with some amusement to the Sahib, I dismissed the matter from my mind. Six weeks later we

passed through Lukpa again, on our way back from Lokoja, and found it deserted—not a man, woman, or child, not a goat, not a fowl—all gone, obviously fled into the bush! I felt distinctly hurt at this churlish behavior on the part of my late admirers, and learnt, long afterwards, that on our first visit, our precious interpreter and others of our party had seized and killed every goat and fowl in the village! The wretched owners had rushed up to the rest-house to complain and implore protection, and all they got was: 'thank you! Thank you! Yes, that's all right! You can go home now!' I am not ashamed to confess that I cried when I made that discovery! The lesson, however, went home to us both, and drove us to work ceaselessly at the Hausa language, knowing there could be no security for ourselves, or justice for the people, until we could be independent of dishonest interpretation.[56]

Like the people of Lukpa in Larymore's story, the unofficial exactions of the sojan gona phenomenon worsened and complicated the economic predicament of the Idoma during the revenue campaigns of the Depression.

The choice of Hausa as an administrative and operational language by British colonial officialdom in Northern Nigeria invested Hausa-speaking interlocutors with unintended manipulative political capital and alienated Idoma Division and other non-Hausa-speaking divisions. It also further confirmed their status as peripheries of the Hausa-speaking emirate mainstream of British Northern Nigeria. The problem of colonial interpretation has assumed a prominent place in discussions of the colonial encounter in Africa and elsewhere.[57] However, this reconsideration of the layering of colonial encounters and its quotidian outcomes for ordinary colonial subjects has yet to embrace the ways in which state proclamations and priorities, especially during difficult and tumultuous junctures, unwittingly gave African colonial agents authorization to extort and oppress subjects at the colonial grass roots.

The official obsession with fiscal results (and its equation with administrative effectiveness) extended beyond the institution of local chieftaincy. The British reconfigured institutions of colonial governance, such as the judiciary in Idoma Division, to serve the need for revenue.

COLONIAL JUSTICE AND REVENUE

In the effort to fully integrate Idoma Division into the economic recovery schemes of the state, officials sought to mobilize the full range of revenue potentials in Idoma Division. In this regard the judiciary acquired additional importance as a site for generating revenue. Numerous complaints about the performance of the native courts differed in substance from those before the Depression. British officials in Idoma Division expressed concern that Africans' patronage of the courts had declined and that courts had either begun hearing cases unofficially or were refusing to enforce their rulings—especially when such rulings involved the payment of fines.[58]

Beneath these expressions lay a concern with dwindling revenue from the courts. As the Depression lingered, the British increasingly gauged the performance of native courts by the amount of revenue they generated rather than by the justice they dispensed. The 1932–33 financial report for Idoma Division complained that court fines produced £127, against an estimated £200, and that court fees yielded only £187—far less than the projected £300. Colonial officials attributed such failures to a failure of the judiciary and attempted to mitigate the problem. The report blamed the fall in fees and general court revenue to the unwillingness of courts to enforce their judgments (often fines), a fall in summons fees due to the refusal of the Idoma to use the courts, and a devaluing of the fines and fees collected due to the depreciation of brass rods.[59] Available records do not indicate a decline in the frequency and intensity of civil and criminal conflicts during the Depression. In fact the contrary appears to have occurred. Idoma peasants, it seems, did, however, remove themselves from the colonial organs of judicial redress and sought conflict resolution in alternative local institutions and mechanisms that did not involve or result in the payment of fees or fines. The court fees and the increasing ease with which the courts imposed fines led to widespread unpopularity for the colonial courts and for other revenue generating colonial institutions. The annual report shows that colonial officials came gradually to prefer fines to imprisonment during the economic crisis.[60] As the assistant district officer put it, "Sentences of imprisonment mean that the services of a youth are lost to his parents or householder during his period of detention. In the case of a fine the father usually has to pay in the end and the culprit gets off free."[61] The prioritization of judicial fines and fees recalibrated the colonial courts for revenue generation, but this proved counterproductive, as patronage dropped and the Idoma strategically shunned the institution, to the disappointment of British officials.

⤳

In the history of the Idoma experience with British revenue offensives during the depression, two themes are intertwined: the rediscovery, through tax raids, of Idoma Division's revenue-generating potentials as a result of increasing fiscal desperation on the part of the colonial state, and the novel responses of Idoma peasants to the revenue-inspired invasions of their private domains. In the colonial economic recovery imagination, especially in the colonial obsession with revenue generation, Idoma Division's reputation as an economically inconsequential colonial unit gave way to a determination to forcefully make the division contribute to colonial solvency through taxes and fines. This determination authorized violent tax raids on Idoma villages. Officials justified the raids through a sociological logic that cast the Idoma as backward loathers of taxation. The notion that Idoma chiefs were too weak and incompetent to help the state squeeze taxes from impoverished Idoma peasants completed the dual justification for the tax raids. In persecuting and displacing the chiefs, intrusive colonial officials were doing violence to the mainstay of an inchoate indirect rule system in Idoma Division: the nascent chieftaincy institutions.

As taxation took its place at the center of the government's economic recovery policy, the British increasingly measured colonial success and the effectiveness of petty British officials by their ability to generate revenue. The Idoma found themselves suddenly thrust into the nexus of colonial fiscal obligations, from which they had managed to partially escape before the Depression. Previously "abandoned" as unprepared for indirect rule and its economic corollaries, the Idoma had become participants in an unfamiliar, relatively novel regime of revenue requisition, conceived as a service in aid of the state's economic recovery effort.

The unfolding of the revenue drive in Idoma Division was complicated by several factors, not the least of which included the sheer brutality of the tax raids. The government attempted to explain this unforgiving method of revenue generation adopted by petty colonial officials in the division with the rhetoric of Idoma aversion to taxation and to anything colonial and governmental. Weak local chiefs and their new role constituted an important aspect of the revenue offensive. Previously denigrated, poorly supervised, and unpaid, colonial officials now expected them to perform as revenue agents. This raised important questions of chiefly ethics and local legitimacy. It exhibited a facade of indirect rule, while colonial officials used the weak rulers merely as scapegoats and their predictable failures in revenue generation as an excuse to carry out well-organized and often prearranged raids and property confiscation. As chiefs took advantage of their new roles and powers to profit from tax raids and to boost their income through tax collection, colonial officials accused them in the same breath of laziness and greed.

Faced with a threat to the foundation of their economic existence, Idoma peasants adopted imaginative, crude methods of escape, subversion, and resistance. They hid themselves and their animals in the bush and set traps for the tax raiders. These responses made the raids socially volatile and economically unrewarding. Ultimately the raids revealed not so much the backwardness, economic desperation, and antitax sentiments of the Idoma as the desperation of a harried colonial project temporarily unable to exploit surpluses and profits from peasants.

This incarnation of colonial power dispensed with the rituals and pretenses of indirect rule and became direct, intrusive, and desperate. This desperate colonialism contradicted the familiar rhetoric of colonial legitimacy, which rested on nonintrusion. The story of this chapter also illustrates a colonial failure to achieve declared economic recovery ends in the revenue domain because of local innovations and acts of self-preservation. The desperation and frustration of British officials prefaced their pathetic resort to the confiscation of goats and other domestic animals in a forlorn effort to boost state solvency. A colonial project reduced to the chasing of goats and chickens in rural colonial districts does not demonstrate the effectiveness of colonial power. It underlines the temporary failure of colonial exploitation and the desperate, counterproductive colonial actions that this failure inspired. In essence it highlights a weak colonial system in urgent need of reform.

Epilogue

THIS BOOK is not about colonial success in exploiting Africans to cushion metropolitan economic anxieties and problems; that story has already been told. Rather, it is about the colonial failure to exploit Africans—in spite of a desire to do so—in the service of metropolitan economic recovery, and the multifarious fallouts of that failure. What I have tried to do here is write a history of colonial failure and its social, economic, and political effects on the colonized. This is however not a counterfactual exercise in establishing the might-have-beens of colonial economic and social management, since the failure explored here is a real one: the failure to extract nonexistent surpluses and profits from Northern Nigeria in a period of economic barrenness. This book is a history of what colonialists could not do during the Depression and the myriad consequences and repercussions of that brief moment of colonial economic impotence. The narrative raises methodological and theoretical questions about how to document imperial failure in an intellectual environment saturated with discourses of imperial omnipotence. These questions call for more empirical, microlevel studies of colonial failures and retreat.

My analysis is obviously set against the backdrop of an impressive and illuminating outpouring of histories of colonial exploitational successes and consistency in Africa and elsewhere and perhaps should be read as a counterpoint to those histories. But the book's essential argument is not necessarily at variance with the thrust of radical colonial historiography, which contends essentially that colonial powers enjoyed unchallenged and rarely disturbed access to profits and surpluses in Africa. My overarching point is that the consequences of colonial exploitation—during boom years—and of the momentary failure or inability to exploit during the Depression are uncannily similar. This momentary inability of colonialists to exploit, like their ability to extract profits and surpluses in years of economic expansion, resulted in suffering and hardship for African colonial subjects. The economic recovery policies that the financial crisis inspired led to more, not less, suffering for Northern Nigerians. The drastic reduction in state revenue from export surpluses and profits authorized a new regime of indiscriminate grassroots profiteering and exaction in which European, Arab, Levantine, and African merchants took financial advantage of peasant tax obligations to mop up rural food supplies, leading to famine and destitution (chapter 2). This is an outcome that has been traditionally associated in colonial studies with colonial exploitation, not with its cessation. The consequences and legacies of colonial exploitation should therefore not be emphasized in disregard for or in denial of equally devastating fallouts from the failure to exploit. This outcome is an unlikely possible point of convergence for radical colonial historical interpretations and the new, revisionist histories of imperial apologia.[1]

Denial is not the exclusive province of revisionist scholars seeking to rehabilitate imperial traditions and intentions. It finds expression in the works of radical historians of colonialism in Africa. The argument that the Great Depression represents a period in which "nothing [except exploitation] happened" in colonial Africa stems from a similarly escapist reluctance to give analytical prominence to facts that complicate an established paradigm.[2] Contrary to this denial, the contention of this book is that the inability of the Northern Nigerian colonial state to exploit nonexistent profits did not generate a lull in familiar colonial activities but that it resulted in several significant events and encounters. These confrontations occurred as a result of the frustration and anxieties of colonial bureaucrats at the Northern Nigerian grass roots who could no longer engineer the flow of elusive profits. The Depression decade is therefore not an unremarkable period of African colonial history; it is one of the most important decades in the colonial life of Africa and should be treated as such in scholarly discussions on, and the teaching of, African colonial history. Colonial economic frustration intermeshed with and exacerbated the familiar brutalities and exactions of colonial power relations. Without an understanding of the changes that the Depression inaugurated in grassroots colonial relations and in African engagement with colonial power, it is difficult to cultivate an accurate understanding of the rapid advance to political independence after the Depression.

The story of the momentary failure and absence of colonial exploitation in the 1930s is a tale of colonial frustration. It is, of course, difficult to gauge frustration, or any other emotion for that matter, that may reside, even if temporarily, at the heart of any power structure. But the consequences of British colonial despair in Northern Nigeria were visible, far-reaching, and fairly measurable. The first casualty of this colonial desperation was the complacency with which British colonial officials regarded the profit-generating economic regime of colonial Northern Nigeria. The Depression shook officials out of that complacency, spawning policies and ad hoc interventions designed to overcome the fiscal and social problems of the Depression. An even more important aspect of the story, one that each chapter of the book documents, is the convoluted effects of British economic recovery efforts on Northern Nigerian colonial subjects, as well as the efforts of Northern Nigerians — legal and illegal — to defeat, confound, or escape the government's economic recovery schemes. Colonial authorities in Northern Nigeria, like colonial authorities elsewhere in Africa, sought to incorporate peasants more deeply into the imperial system through efforts to boost export crop cultivation, encourage the patronage of colonial economic institutions and markets, and compel the fulfillment of economic obligations to the state. These efforts were inspired not by African concerns, anxieties, and priorities, but by the financial anxieties of an economically insecure state worried about its solvency. Northern Nigerians had their own anxieties, goals, and strategies of self-preservation. Their reaction to the state's economic recovery efforts were shaped in part by these economic fears and aspirations.

In defiance of state aims, Northern Nigerian peasants, craftsmen, and laborers strategically removed themselves from economic networks and markets sanctioned and supervised by colonial authorities and inserted themselves into more locally grounded, safer economic vocations and transactions. Similarly, they adopted novel strategies to escape the nodes of state revenue generation, which became exceptionally impatient with African resistance during the Depression, especially in places like Idoma Division, where colonial taxation had been a sporadic presence at best before the Depression.

It is in this tense contrast between colonial economic recovery strategies and objectives and the economic aspirations and fears of Northern Nigerians that we can situate a discussion of how the Depression and the encounters it generated inspired a new form of colonial power. The colonialism of the Depression period expressed its power more directly than a theoretical understanding of the British policy of indirect rule would suggest. Frustrated by Northern Nigerians' inability and refusal to *help* the colonial state recover by fulfilling fiscal obligations and making required sacrifices, colonial officials increasingly violated the principle of indirect rule by sidestepping local chiefs and taking matters of fiscal exaction and social order into their own hands. This was a colonialism baring its fangs and applying violence and compulsion in correspondence to local resistance of dreaded British economic recovery schemes. This was British colonial power at its crudest, most direct, and most autocratic. It is this Depression-induced form of colonial power that was nurtured over the next three decades and that continued to authorize the occasional violation of indirect rule under the guise of achieving overarching state goals into the post–World War II period. This is perhaps one of the origins of the autocratic and centrist power formations of postcolonial Africa. Recent discourses on the evolution of power in postcolonial Africa have identified such colonial continuities but have yet to identify the specific colonial moments and junctures from which this form of power emerged.

In the end, though, this new show of colonial power only deepened Northern Nigerians' repertoire of creative resistance to and selective participation in colonial economic institutions. It also increased the spate of local demands for the advertised benefits of colonial rule: infrastructure, schools, prosperity, and so on. This strategy of self-help, self-insulation, and demands for social goods frustrated colonial economic recovery aims and made colonial officials even more desperate, intrusive, and disrespectful of local chiefs — the bedrock of indirect rule. This is thus a story of how rural exaction through a new variety of colonial power not only failed to yield the desired economic recovery ends but also suggested many anticolonial strategies to Africans, strategies that were perfected through the 1930s and sometimes carried forward through the 1940s. Ultimately, then, the Depression represented a weakening of colonial power and control, in spite of appearances to the contrary, as more, not fewer, African challenges accompanied the desperate impositions and coercions of colonial officials.

The 1930s saw significant socioeconomic and political changes and shifts. The interwar period witnessed both practical and rhetorical changes in the encounter between Northern Nigerians and British colonizers, although in much of the historiography of colonial Africa the period is presented as a lull, a period of stoppage and "lost opportunities."[3] But some of these changes come into sharp relief only when juxtaposed against the events and encounters of the subsequent periods. By examining some of the events of the immediate post-Depression period, one uncovers direct and indirect legacies of the crisis.

Recovery from the Depression was well under way by 1936. However, the empirical, experiential, and rhetorical legacies of that difficult period had remarkable staying power, surviving through World War II. One example of this is the problem of currency scarcity and the concomitant growth of a previously insignificant cottage industry in counterfeit coinage. Until 1941 this unintended consequence of a seemingly benign economic recovery policy of withdrawing silver coins from circulation in Nigeria and shipping them to Britain continued to trouble colonial bureaucrats in Nigeria.[4] There is no indication that monetary stability returned to Nigeria in the 1940s and beyond or that the problem of counterfeiting was ever stamped out.

Another example of the lingering legacies of the Depression and of the government's economic recovery policy was the fact that the rhetoric and idioms invoked by Northern Nigerian elites to criticize the colonial state's economic recovery policies—financial conservatism, suspension of social spending, and an aggressive revenue drive—outlived the political relevance of these elites. These idioms of anticolonial criticism reincarnated in the subsequent anticolonial activism of Northern Nigerian elites.

The anticolonial discourses of Samuel Cole-Edwards and his fellow petition writers provided both an organizational and an intellectual example. While Cole-Edwards and other Depression-era anticolonial activists hardly found a voice in the post–World War II nationalist struggle, the rhetorical strategies, criticisms, ideological blackmail, and material demands they insinuated into the colonial public arena were amplified by Mallam Sa'adu Zungur, Aminu Kano, Gambo Sawaba, and other Northern Nigerian postwar nationalist radicals. British officials proudly displayed Alhaji Tafawa Balewa's pro-government views as a counterpoint to the views of Cole-Edwards and his group of economically impoverished colonial auxiliaries (see chapter 4). Tafawa Balewa's was not the only Northern Nigerian, emirate view on the government's handling of the Depression and on the nature and unfolding of British colonialism in Northern Nigeria.

Three years after the emergence of the *Nigerian Protectorate Ram* and in the thick of the Depression, an intellectual anticolonial circuit was emerging among a group of Muslim, Hausa Northern Nigerians who had been educated in Northern Nigeria's colonial educational institutions and had therefore been expected by the British and the emirate establishments to endorse and function within the colonial status quo. The nucleus of this group formed around Zungur, and came to include Aminu Kano, Alhaji Ibrahim Baba-Hallah, Abubakar Sadiq Zukogi, Mustapha III Ibn Sanda, Raji Abdallah, Gambo Sawaba, and others.

Zungur, the son of a Bauchi emirate official and Islamic scholar, started moving away from the emirate tradition of self-interestedly cooperating with and pragmatically accepting colonial policies on November 19, 1934, when he sent an individual petition to the Northern Nigerian colonial administration.[5] The petition was a general criticism of colonialism and an indictment of colonial exploitation rather than a commentary on a specific colonial policy, although it would not be far-fetched to suggest that the hardship of the Depression may have insinuated the theme of colonial exploitation into Zungur's inaugural anticolonial discursive activity. Zungur would go on to organize a collective petition to the Bauchi native authority and to organize the first public demonstration against the colonial authorities in Northern Nigeria.[6]

Without making a direct causal connection, one could argue that the discursive ferment engineered by Cole-Edwards and other Depression-era anticolonial activists stirred up the atmosphere for the emergence and growth in the emirate public sphere of anticolonial criticism and Muslim, Northern Nigerian nationalist thought. The trend resulted in the formation of the Northern Nigerian Youth Movement in 1939, which became the Northern Peoples' General Improvement Union two years later. This organization provided a forum in which Western-educated emirate Northerners articulated and sharpened their commentaries on colonial policies. It also led to the formation in 1943 of the Bauchi Discussion Circle (BDC), a public sphere of discussion where leading Northern anticolonial figure Mallam Sa'ad Zungur and his fellow Western-educated Northerners subjected colonial practices and policies to intense debate. The BDC's strident criticisms of both the colonial authorities and their emirate allies led to its suspension by the emir of Bauchi in December 1944.[7]

The demise of the BDC precipitated the emergence of its successor, the Bauchi General Improvement Union (BGIU), whose objectives mirrored those of the BDC and included the desire "to voice out the sentiment of the local intelligentsia by way of representation, through proper channels, to the authorities in all matters affecting the progress and welfare of the people . . . educationally, socially, and economically and otherwise."[8] This ambitious and somewhat vague declaration of commitment to colonial accountability and local welfare recalled the rhetoric of Cole-Edwards and other Depression-era anticolonial activists. The BDC and the BGIU were the precursors of a movement that later metamorphosed into an Islamo-populist, antiemirate, anticolonial political party, the Northern Elements Progressive Union.[9]

The 1930s witnessed the emergence of a small but radical group of Northern Nigerian anticolonial activists, whose anticolonial rhetoric was legitimized by the growing economic failures of British colonialism. It is fairly clear that subsequent radical anticolonialism in Northern Nigeria, which, according to one author, even enjoyed the secret patronage of emirs and Islamic leaders,[10] benefited, however indirectly, from the atmosphere of colonial retreat and vocal anticolonial criticism that Cole-Edwards and other supporters of the *Nigerian Protectorate Ram* had helped create.

One could argue that the anticolonial critical activism of the Depression was one of the inspirations for a new kind of colonialism after World War II. It was a period in which the concept and practice of development and "native" welfare came to inhere in the practice of British and French colonialisms in Africa.[11] The embrace of so-called developmental colonialism has been linked with a postwar urgency to save empire in the face of international criticisms, especially those from the two new superpowers, the United States and the Soviet Union.[12]

Although acknowledged by scholars of decolonization in Africa as one of the impulses for postwar decolonization, much less attention has been paid to the way in which the crises of the Great Depression—the labor crisis, dramatic confrontations in the revenue domain, the production and spread of poverty, the cessation of social spending, the rise of crime and destitution, and the emergence of articulate local anticolonial criticism and demands as a result of all these crises—impressed on colonial officials the necessity for a developmental agenda that could undo the damage done to British colonialism in the eyes of Africans during the economic crisis. At issue after the Depression was British colonial anxiety about restoring some credibility to the familiar rhetoric and claims of British colonialism, which had been greatly undermined by the economic downturn. Before the Depression, British rule had not been fully routinized in many parts of Africa and still struggled to gain the obedience of locals. The Depression exacerbated that crisis of legitimacy. It exploded the foundational rhetoric of British colonialism as a civilizing and progressive mission capable of improving the lives of Africans while exploiting their resources. The so-called dual mandate of British colonialism was in ruins in the Depression's aftermath and needed to be repropagated through a rhetorical, if not practical, commitment to developmental colonialism.

My analysis of Northern Nigeria's experience of the Depression shows that the damage to British colonialism in local eyes was quite extensive, so extensive that any effort to explain the practice of colonial development in Northern Nigeria in the postwar period would be incomplete without an acknowledgment of how this practice was in fact a necessity thrust forward by the bruised image of the British in the course of the Depression. The colonial crises of the 1930s (strikes and labor unrest in Central and southern Africa and the Caribbean from 1935 through 1939), which Frederick Cooper credits with forcing a rethinking of policy in the British imperial metropole had precedents in Northern Nigeria between 1931 and 1934. The Depression triggered volatile and violent colonial confrontations in the labor and trade domains and at the colonial grass roots throughout those three years (chapters 3–5). From the Northern Nigerian example, then, one could argue that "developmental colonialism," to borrow Frederick Cooper's term, was as much a product of the Depression as it was of recovery (1935–39) and of a burgeoning Cold War rivalry that made colonial accountability an international agenda.

In remote outposts of British colonialism in Northern Nigeria, such as Idoma Division, the post-Depression period witnessed an active effort by the British to win back some local confidence after years of tax raids and revenue-motivated colonial brutality had left the Idoma countryside devastated and the Idoma people bitter. The rapid expansion of educational institutions in the division, the acceleration of yam importation from the division to feed African-British troops during World War II, the recruitment of many Idoma into the British army as salaried potters, and the withdrawal of the resented Hausa bureaucrats could be interpreted as acts and processes of rapprochement.

In much of Northern Nigeria the British didn't have to do much to reestablish the economic viability and appeal of the export crop economy. The recovery of raw-material prices in the world market restored profitability to the production of groundnuts, Northern Nigeria's biggest export crop, and rapidly led to the groundnut prosperity epitomized most prominently by the famous groundnut pyramids of Kano.[13]

The Depression had a bearing on the momentous periods that followed. But it was also, in its own right, a significant period in the history of British Africa, marking the escalation of the tensions and crises of colonialism, illustrating the limits of the colonialism of exploitation and repression, and serving notice of the local discontent that awaited colonizers. The post-Depression period bore the imprints, if not the causal signatures, of the Depression. The latter, after all, was a period in which the very basis of the British colonial system, the concept of dual mandate, was called into question, while the liberal pretensions that underlay the policy of indirect rule lost their relevance. This is an illustration of just how thin was the line between direct and indirect rule, a line that the British continued to transgress until Nigeria's political independence, in 1960.

Notes

ABBREVIATIONS

Afr. S.	African Studies
Afr. T.	African Studies "T" Section (MSS African Texts)
AH	Arewa House Archives
LOKOPROF	Lokoja Provincial Office
MAKPROF	Makurdi Provincial Office
NAK	National Archives of Nigeria, Kaduna
NMMDA	Norcross Memorial Methodist Diocese Archives
Otudist.	Otukpo District Files
Otudiv.	Otukpo Division Files
PMMC	Primitive Methodist Mission Collection
RH	Rhodes House Archives
SNP	Secretariat of the Northern Provinces
SOAS	School of Oriental and African Studies, London

Unless otherwise noted, all translations are mine.

INTRODUCTION:
CRISIS, COLONIAL FAILURE, AND SUBALTERN SUFFERING

1. Rhodes House Archives (hereafter cited as RH), African Studies (hereafter cited as Afr. S.) 1073, W. R. Crocker, diary entry (hereafter cited as Crocker's journal), November 14, 1933.

2. Claude Ake, A Political Economy of Africa (Harlow, Essex: Longman, 1981); Samir Amin, Accumulation on a World Scale: A Critique of the Theory of Development, trans. Brian Pearce (New York: Monthly Press, 1974); Bill Freund, Capital and Labour in the Nigerian Tin Mines (London: Longman, 1981); Walter Rodney, How Europe Underdeveloped Africa (Washington, DC: Howard University Press, 1981).

3. Michael Hardt and Antonio Negri, Empire (Cambridge, MA: Harvard University Press, 2000), 322–28.

4. Patrick Manning, for instance, argues that in francophone sub-Saharan Africa, the economic crisis of the 1930s was the peak of French imperial power, as "the authority of colonial governments went almost unchallenged within their borders and without." He goes on to argue that, while enforcing economy measures on

African peasants, French colonial authorities prospered and successfully consolidated their power. Manning, *Francophone Sub-Saharan Africa, 1880–1995*, 2nd ed. (Cambridge: Cambridge University Press, 1998), 82. A recent work informed by this assumption of imperial economic omnipotence and exploitational expertise is Alvin O. Thompson, *Economic Parasitism: European Rule in West Africa, 1880–1960* (Barbados: University of the West Indies Press, 2006).

5. Jeffery Herbst, *States and Power in Africa: Comparative Lessons in Authority and Control* (Princeton: Princeton University Press, 2000), chap. 3.

6. Catherine Boone, *Merchant Capital and the Roots of State Power in Senegal, 1930–1985* (Cambridge: Cambridge University Press, 1992), 32–35.

7. Manning, *Francophone Sub-Saharan Africa*, 51.

8. Catherine Coquery-Vidrovitch, *Africa: Endurance and Change South of the Sahara*, trans. David Maisel (Berkeley: University of California Press, 1985).

9. Mike Davis, *Late Victorian Holocausts: El Niño Famines and the Making of the Third World* (London: Verso, 2002), chap. 5.

10. The most prominent example of a new kind of imperial history that advances a revisionist disavowal of colonial exploitation as a discursive framework for evaluating imperial systems is Niall Ferguson, *Empire: The Rise and Demise of the British World Order and the Lessons for Global Power* (New York: Basic Books, 2003). This new history of imperial nostalgia, as one of its critics, Frederick Cooper, has called it, has many detractors. Cooper, "Empire Multiplied: A Review Essay," *Comparative Study of History and Society* 46, no. 1 (2004): 247–72. One of the most direct, empirical critiques of Ferguson's revisionist claims about colonial exploitation and its consequences is Matthew Connelly, "The New Imperialists," in *Lessons of Empire: Imperial Histories and American Power*, ed. Craig Calhoun, Frederick Cooper, and Kevin W. Moore (New York: New Press, 2006), 19–33.

11. RH, MSS African Texts (hereafter cited as Afr. T) 16, S. M. Jacob, "Report on the Taxation and Economics of Nigeria, 1934," 14.

12. See Michael Watts, *Silent Violence: Food, Famine and Peasantry in Northern Nigeria* (Berkeley: University of California Press, 1983).

13. For portrayals of the 1930s as a period of unprecedented colonial exploitation in Africa, see Monique Lakroum, *Le travail inégal: Paysans et salariés sénégalais face à la crise des années trente* (Paris: L' Harmattan, 1982); Hélène d'Almeida-Topor, *Les jeunes en Afrique* (Paris: L'Harmattan, 1982).

14. See John E. Flint, *Sir George Goldie and the Making of Nigeria* (London: Oxford University Press, 1960); R. A. Adeleye, *Power and Diplomacy in Northern Nigeria, 1804–1906: The Sokoto Caliphate and Its Enemies* (New York: Humanities Press, 1971); Obaro Ikime, *The Fall of Nigeria: The British Conquest* (London: Heinemann, 1977).

15. Timothy Mitchell, *Rule of Experts: Egypt, Techno-politics, Modernity* (Berkeley: University of California Press, 2002), chap. 3. Mitchell's analysis of a similar British project in Egypt is instructive.

16. For a detailed discussion of the land tenure question, debate, and reforms in Northern Nigeria, see Steven Pierce, "Looking for the Legal: Land, Law, and

Colonialism in Kano Emirate, Nigeria" (PhD diss., University of Michigan, 2000). See also Anne Phillips, *The Enigma of Colonialism: British Policy in West Africa* (London: James Currey; Bloomington: Indiana University Press, 1989); Robert Shenton, *The Development of Capitalism in Northern Nigeria* (London: James Currey, 1986), chap. 3.

17. For an explication of the Native Revenue Ordinance, its initial implementation in the emirate areas of Northern Nigeria, and its subsequent modifications, see Florence Adebisi Okediji, "An Economic History of Hausa-Fulani Emirates of Northern Nigeria: 1900–1939" (PhD diss., Indiana University, 1970), 97–210.

18. For the British effort to promote cotton cultivation in Northern Nigeria and its fate, see Marion Johnson, "Cotton Imperialism in West Africa," *African Affairs* 73, no. 291 (1974): 178–87. For a discussion of the groundnut promotion campaign of the British colonial government and its mercantilist allies, see Gerald Helleiner, *Peasant Agriculture, Government, and Economic Growth in Nigeria* (Homewood, IL: Richard D. Irwin, 1966); Jan Hogendorn, *Nigerian Groundnut Exports: Origins and Early Development* (Zaria: Ahmadu Bello University Press, 1978). A. G. Hopkins, *An Economic History of West Africa* (New York: Columbia University Press, 1973), while decidedly triumphalist in its characterization of colonial export promotion in West Africa, is meticulous in its documentation of the course and crisis of agricultural export promotion.

19. The noncaliphate peoples of Northern Nigeria were the constant targets of British efforts to rule the protectorate on the ethnographic assumptions gleaned from studies of the Sokoto caliphate. The peoples of Ilorin, Benue, Kabba, and Plateau provinces, and other noncaliphate peoples subsumed within the administrative jurisdiction of Muslim emirates have managed to forge a loose geopolitical identity in contemporary Nigeria. Under the regime of Gen. Sani Abacha, Nigeria was divided into six geopolitical zones. The north-central zone, popularly known as the Middle Belt—a term popularized by a political movement of Northern Nigerian minorities in Nigeria's First Republic (1963–1966)—was one of them. The contemporary Middle Belt corresponds roughly to the Middle Belt of the early postcolonial period and more loosely to the non-Muslim section of colonial Northern Nigeria.

20. For an explication of the dependency paradigm, see Amin, *Accumulation*. See also Immanuel Wallerstein, *The Capitalist World-Economy: Essays* (Cambridge: Cambridge University Press, 1979); Wallerstein, "Africa in a Capitalist World," *Issue* 3, no. 3 (1973): 1–11; Andre Gunder Frank, *Capitalism and Underdevelopment in Latin America: Historical Studies of Chile and Brazil* (New York: Monthly Review Press, 1967).

21. See, for instance, Ian Brown, ed., *The Economies of Africa and Asia in the Inter-war Depression* (London: Routledge, 1989). Most of the articles in this volume endorse the idea that the fluctuations of the world economy crushed local peasant production, the latter having been integrated into, and made vulnerable to, the forces of global capitalism. See also Catherine Coquery-Vidrovitch, "'L'Afrique coloniale française et la crise de 1930: Crise structurelle et genèse du sous-développement,' l'Afrique et la crise de 1930," *Revue d'histoire d'outre-mer* 63, nos. 3–4, numéro spécial (1976): 386–424.

22. For a detailed critique of the underdevelopment, dependency, and world-system paradigms, see Frederick Cooper, "Africa and the World Economy," in *Confronting Historical Paradigms: Peasants, Labor, and the Capitalist World System in Africa and Latin America*, ed. Frederick Cooper, Allen F. Isaacman, Florencia E. Mallon, William Roseberry, and Steve J. Stern (Madison: University of Wisconsin Press, 1993), 93–109.

23. June Nash, "Ethnographic Aspects of the Capitalist World System," *Annual Review of Anthropology* 10 (1981): 406. See also Theda Skocpol, "Wallerstein's World Capitalist System: A Theoretical and Historical Critique," *American Journal of Sociology* 82, no. 6 (1977): 1075–90.

24. Clifford Geertz, *Agricultural Involution: The Process of Ecological Change in Indonesia* (Berkeley: University of California Press, 1963).

25. See Frederick Lugard, *The Dual Mandate in British Tropical Africa* (Edinburgh: W. Blackwood and Sons, 1922); Alice Conklin, *A Mission to Civilize: The Republican Idea of Empire in France and West Africa, 1895–1930* (Stanford: Stanford University Press, 1997).

26. Conklin, *Mission to Civilize*, introd., chap. 7.

27. Quoted in Frederick Cooper and Randall Packard, eds., *International Development and the Social Sciences: Essays on the History and Politics of Knowledge* (Berkeley: University of California Press, 1997), 6.

28. For an exploration of the concept of developmental colonialism, see ibid. See also Frederick Cooper, "Modernizing Bureaucrats, Backward Africans, and the Development Concept," in Cooper and Packard, *International Development and the Social Sciences*, 64–86. He argues that the aggressive colonial investments in colonial welfare and infrastructure in the post-Depression period and especially after 1945 was a new approach to colonial development and was thus more disruptive in its unfamiliarity and intrusiveness than it was a stabilizing, relegitimizing tool. The development preoccupations of the previous period were not as extensive and thus largely preserved the status quo.

29. Coquery-Vidrovitch, "Afrique coloniale"; David Anderson and David Throup, "The Agrarian Economy of Central Province, Kenya, 1918 to 1939," in Brown, *Economies of Africa*, 8–28; Wolfgang Dopcke, "'Magomo's Maize': State and Peasants during the Depression in Colonial Zimbabwe," in Brown, *Economies of Africa*, 29–53. This is one point on which both radical and neoclassical scholars of colonial economic policy in Africa tend to agree.

30. See Frederick Cooper, *Decolonization and African Society: The Labor Question in French and British Africa* (Cambridge: Cambridge University Press, 1996), 49–50, 57–58.

31. See Mahmood Mamdani, *Citizen and Subject: Contemporary Africa and the Legacy of Late Colonialism* (Princeton: Princeton University Press, 1996); Achille Mbembe, *On the Postcolony* (Berkeley: University of California Press, 2001).

32. The view of Idoma being a "punishment division" was widely expressed in the Northern Nigerian colonial bureaucracy, not least by those British officials who actually served there. See, for instance, the journal of H. P. Elliot, who asserted that no

one wanted to end up in Idoma Division because such a posting was done to either get rid of incompetents or to punish disloyal subordinates. Elliot and several other British officials who served in the division also commented extensively on the supposed backwardness of the Idoma, especially their lack of social, political, and economic institutions suitable for indirect rule and an export-oriented agricultural economy. RH, Afr. S. 1336, journal of H. P. Elliot, assistant district officer, September 5, 1935.

CHAPTER 1: FROM EMPIRE TO COLONY

1. Starting from 1867, Britain entered a period of economic cycles characterized by brief spells of prosperity punctuated by spells of recession. This state of affairs culminated in two depressions, one lasting through the 1870s and the other starting in 1921 and lasting to 1923. See Franklin Roosevelt Library, Alexander Sachs Papers, Economic Cycles. The mentality that emerged from this cycle of crisis was constant national economic panic, which in turn led to a national paranoia that inspired a host of institutions and economic sentiments. One such institution is the dole (unemployment benefit), which was designed to serve as a safeguard against the all-too-familiar tides of economic hardship.

2. See Franklin Roosevelt Library, Alexander Sachs Papers, Depression Studies, article in the British-based *Monthly Review* (author and title unknown), 1933. See also Sachs Papers, Depression Studies, 1933–66.

3. Arthur Schlesinger, in "The Great Depression and Foreign Affairs," film script, show 5 in the series *Between the Wars* (Los Angeles: Alan Landsburg Productions, 1978).

4. See, for instance, Sir George Parish, "Nationalism and the Cause of the World Depression: American and European Jealousy Threatens Trade and Credit Breakdown—An Interview with Sir George Parish," *Barron's*, June 1, 1931.

5. One of the most vocal of such groups was the United Empire Trade League, which published the *Imperial Review*, a London-based monthly journal widely read by the British trading, merchant, and investment elite. Another publication of similar inclination was *The Empire Illustrated: The National Review*. Other less vocal but equally active groups and publications were part of the ferment of opinion favoring imperial economic solidarity.

6. See, for instance, Financial Editor, "The Need of Stability in Empire Currencies," *Imperial Review* 1 (October 1934): 12.

7. Thomas August, *The Selling of the Empire: British and French Imperial Propaganda, 1890–1940* (Westport, CT: Greenwood, 1985), 20.

8. Nigeria, *Report on the Economic and Social Progress of the People of Nigeria, 1932* (Lagos: Government Printer, 1933), 39.

9. In analyzing the threat posed by Japanese products to those of Britain, contemporary British commentators appeared unanimous in locating the problem in the much lower prices of Japanese textiles. See "Japanese Competition in Empire Markets: Co-operation If the Dominion Essential of Flood of Cheap Goods Is to Be Checked," *Imperial Review* 1 (October 1934): 16. See also "Men and Matters," *Comet: A Weekly News Magazine of West Africa*, September 1, 1934).

10. *West African Mail and Trade Gazette*, January 25, 1930, 8.

11. *West Africa Mail and Trade Gazette*, January 18, 1930.

12. Our Trade Commissioner, "Ocean Transport and the West African Trade," *West Africa Mail and Trade Gazette*, January 25, 1930, 8.

13. "Elder Dempster and Co. and the United Africa Company," *Nigerian Protectorate Ram*, September 22, 1930, 6.

14. Ibid.

15. "Men and Matters," *Comet*, September 1, 1934, 1.

16. Arewa House Archives (hereafter cited as AH), SNP1 12, 307, "Draft Estimates for the Financial Year, 1931–32."

17. Bill Freund, *Capital and Labour in the Nigerian Tin Mines* (London: Longman, 1981), 121–30.

18. Ibid. See also Zakariah Goshit, "The Impact of the Great Depression on the Jos Plateau: A Case Study of the Tin Mine Fields in the 1930s," *Mandeng: Journal of Middle Belt History* 1, no. 1 (2001): 72–86.

19. Nigeria, *Economic and Social Progress*, 33.

20. Ibid., 32–33.

21. In fact groundnut exports rose between 1929 and 1932, stabilizing only in 1933. See ibid., 32.

22. This was especially so in the northernmost part of Northern Nigeria, where it was mostly produced. The crop featured and still features in several diets of the Hausa, Nupe, Kanuri, and other peoples of Northern Nigeria.

23. *Nigeria Gazette Extraordinary* 18, no. 42 (July 1931): 413.

24. Ibid., 415.

25. Ibid., 417.

26. For comprehensive, department-by-department data on retrenchments in the colonial public service, the biggest employer of labor in the country throughout the colonial period, see *Nigeria Gazette Extraordinary*, February 8, 1932, 88–104.

27. AH/NL/A5, sessional paper 46, 1935, "Report of the Committee Appointed by His Excellency the Governor to Enquire into the Question of Unemployment," 1.

28. *Nigeria Gazette Extraordinary*, February 8, 1932, 70.

29. Ibid., 76.

30. Ibid., 76.

31. Ibid., 85.

32. Ibid.

33. *Nigeria Gazette Extraordinary*, April 27, 1933, 255. The justification for the levy was the unexpected further fall in the prices of agricultural produce, which caused "a serious decline in the estimated revenue of the year."

34. Nigerian National Archives, Kaduna (hereafter cited as NAK), Kano Provincial Office, KPN 02481, "Circular: Purchase of Goods of Empire Origin by Native Administration," August 1932.

35. Kweku Ampiah, "British Commercial Policies against Japanese Expansionism in East and West Africa, 1932–1935," *International Journal of African Historical Studies* 23, no. 4 (1990): 619–41.

36. Ibid.

37. Marion Johnson, "Cotton Imperialism in West Africa," *African Affairs* 73, no. 291 (1974): 178–87.

38. Ampiah, "British Commercial Policies."

39. Ibid., 634.

40. *Nigeria Gazette Extraordinary*, (July 1931, 414.

41. In Northern Nigeria this effort to incorporate all classes of Africans into the government's taxation system started in early 1931. It was consolidated over the next several months. See NAK, Secretariat of the Northern Provinces (hereafter cited as SNP) 1/11/65, file KO 5458, vol. 3.

42. Nigeria, *Economic and Social Progress*, 50.

43. Complaints ranging from inability to pay for utilities due to dwindling incomes, general unemployment, the exemption of non-European immigrants (Arabs) from taxation, and European produce buyers shortchanging local producers appeared frequently in the local press during the Depression. For an in-depth analysis of the widening frontiers of discursive protest during the Depression, see chap. 4.

44. See for instance, NAK, SNP/1/11/65, file KO 5458, vol. 3, p. 465. See also p. 358 for a specific protest against the "Syrians," who local traders and middlemen alleged were charging lower prices for services because the former were not taxed enough. Local traders claimed that the Syrians were running them out of business and urged the government to tax them harder.

45. Nigeria, *Economic and Social Progress*, 30.

46. See Sara Berry, *Fathers Work for Their Sons: Accumulation, Mobility, and Class Formation in an Extended Yorùbá Community* (Berkeley: University of California Press, 1985).

47. Nigeria, *Economic and Social Progress*, 31.

48. Ibid., 29.

49. Ibid. The number of acres planted in oil palm increased from 180 in 1929 to 695 in 1932.

50. Mixed farming entailed the grazing of livestock on cultivable land to supply the land with natural manure in order to cut cost and increase yield. It also entailed, in some cases, the mixed cultivation of food and export crops on the same plot.

51. The agricultural extension and research station at Gboko, in Benue Province, served as the hub of these extension activities. It was one of many agricultural stations either set up or reactivated during the Depression to facilitate the massive intervention in agriculture that the British envisioned as an important component of their anti-Depression effort.

52. Nigeria, *Economic and Social Progress*, 34.

53. Ibid.

54. Ibid., 37.

55. Ibid., 53.

56. Ibid. The Egbe society is a mutual assistance fraternity popular in southwestern Nigeria. Members care for one another through soft loans, assistance with funerary and celebratory ceremonies, and other needs. Esusu is a community

savings and banking system practiced mostly but not exclusively by women in Eastern Nigeria. In the Esusu system, traders deposit agreed sums with esusu operators who are paid commissions for their services. The operators make soft loans to depositors who need capital for expansion or to tide them over hard times.

57. *Comet*, November 18, 1933, 4, 24.

58. Ibid.

59. Ibid., 4.

60. Ibid.

61. So important was this project that the government, while not willing to commit the hundreds of thousands of pounds that it required—even though the money was available in Nigeria's reserve—took out a loan to carry out the work.

CHAPTER 2: THE DEPRESSION AND THE COLONIAL ENCOUNTER IN NORTHERN NIGERIA

1. James E. Genova, "Conflicted Missionaries: Power and Identity in French West Africa during the 1930s," *Historian* 66, no. 1 (2004): 53–54.

2. For information on the gradual but steady fall in the price of tin and the corresponding reduction in the quota allocated to Nigeria under the international tin agreement, see Bill Freund, *Capital and Labour in the Nigerian Tin Mines* (London: Longman, 1981). See also *Gazetteers of the Northern Provinces*, vol. 4, *The Highland Chieftancies* (London: Frank Cass, 1972), 303–6.

3. Export activities were conducted in the coastal regions of Southern Nigeria, and middlemen in the export trade were mostly Southern Nigerians. Also, the importation of commodities was controlled by European- and African-owned firms based in Southern Nigeria.

4. The taxation of women occurred only "in irregular patches in Abeokuta and Ijebu Ode Provinces . . . in the Southern Provinces" and in parts of Ekiti Province. Women were being taxed in Niger, Benue, and Kabba provinces long before the Native Revenue Ordinance of 1927. See RH, Afr. T. 16, S. M. Jacob, "Report on the Taxation and Economics of Nigeria, 1934," 24. In southeastern Nigeria, the attempt to introduce a women's tax was a major cause of the Aba Women's War of 1929. See A. E. Afigbo, *The Warrant Chiefs: Indirect Rule in Southeastern Nigeria, 1891–1929* (London: Longman, 1972), chap. 6.

5. Jacob, "Taxation and Economics," 34.

6. Ibid.

7. Ibid., 35, 37. Jacob refers to Frederick, Lord Lugard, *Political Memoranda: Revision of Instructions to Political Officers on Subjects Chiefly Political and Administrative, 1913 – 1918* (London: Frank Cass, 1970).

8. This is the administrative name for colonial Northern Nigeria.

9. Jacob, "Taxation and Economics," 35.

10. Ibid., 79.

11. See Polly Hill, *Rural Hausa: A Village and a Setting* (Cambridge: Cambridge University Press, 1972).

12. Robert Netting, *Hill Farmers of Nigeria: Cultural Ecology of the Kofyar of the Jos Plateau* (Seattle: University of Washington Press, 1968).

13. For a comprehensive discussion of this debate, see Louise Lennihan, "Critical Historical Conjunctures in the Emergence of Agricultural Wage Labor in Northern Nigeria," *Human Ecology* 12, no. 4 (1984): 465–81.

14. Even neo-Marxist scholars of Northern Nigeria like Michael Watts and Robert Shenton, who argue that there was a notable differentiation among rural peasants, concede that it was not significant enough to be described as an emergence of opposing rural classes.

15. Lennihan, "Critical Conjunctures."

16. NAK, SNP1/12/307, confidential circular 22, "The Financial Situation," 1931.

17. Ibid.

18. Ibid.

19. *Jarida Nijeria ta Arewa/Northern Provinces News*, November 1, 1935, 4. This was a bilingual newspaper published by the colonial government in Northern Nigeria between 1931 and 1937; sometimes only the Hausa title was used but other times both the Hausa and the English title appeared on the cover. On a few occasions, only the English title was used. In my references, I use the two titles together except where only one was used in the particular edition being cited.

20. NAK, Lokoja Provincial Office (hereafter cited as LOKOPROF), 95/1930, annual report, Igbirra Division, 1930, 8.

21. NAK, SNP20/1930, memorandum 11680/53, "Native Administration Reserve Funds," March 4, 1930.

22. Ibid., 4.

23. See chapter 1 for the set of instructions issued by the colonial bureaucracy in Lagos to regional and local colonial officials with respect to the Depression.

24. I use *progress* here in line with how the term was employed by Frederick Lugard and subsequently by other British officials—as the act of catering to the welfare of locals and building infrastructures that would facilitate the movement of people and goods, improve Northern Nigerians' standard of life, and increase their prosperity.

25. RH, Afr. S. 1358, W. L. Hogan, "The Development of Education in Nigeria 1920–1952," 33.

26. "Labarin Adamawa," *Jarida Nijeria ta Arewa*, November 1, 1935.

27. NAK, SNP1/18/116, 11096, vol. 2, Northern Provinces, Nigeria: Summary of Intelligence Reports for the Quarter Ending March 1930.

28. Ibid.

29. Frederick Cooper, "Africa and the World Economy," in *Confronting Historical Paradigms: Peasants, Labor, and the Capitalist World System in Africa and Latin America*, ed. Frederick Cooper, Allen F. Isaacman, Florencia E. Mallon, William Roseberry, and Steve J. Stern (Madison: University of Wisconsin Press, 1993), 88.

30. NAK, SNP1/18/116, 10096, Summary of Intelligence Reports for the Quarter Ending December 31, 1931, 10. See also NAK, SNP1/18/116, 10096, vol. 4, March 31, 1932, 12.

31. "Zaria," *Jarida Nijeria ta Arewa*, November 1931.

32. *Jarida Nijeria ta Arewa*, July 23, 1932.

33. "Kaduna," *Jarida Nijeria ta Arewa,* July 29, 1933, 14.

34. *Jarida Nijeria ta Arewa,* July 23, 1932, 10.

35. NAK, SNP1/18/116, 11096, vol. 2, Summary of Intelligence Reports for the Quarter Ending March 1930, 11.

36. NAK, SNP1/18/116, 11096, vol. 2, Summary of Intelligence Reports for the Quarter Ending September 1930.

37. Locusts invaded parts of Kabba Province in 1935. See *Jarida Nijeria ta Arewa/Northern Provinces News,* November 1, 1935, 12.

38. See Michael Watts, *Silent Violence: Food, Famine and Peasantry in Northern Nigeria* (Berkeley: University of California Press, 1983).

39. See NAK, SNP1/23/171, 14658A, 524/1926/69, Memo from Resident, Benue Province, to Secretary, Northern Provinces, "Locust Destruction and Famine Relief." See also NAK, SNP1/23/171, C12/1931/21, Resident, Niger Province, to Secretary, Northern Provinces, "Food Shortage in Kontagora."

40. NAK, SNP1/23/171, 1465819, "Food Shortage in the Northern Provinces: 1931."

41. NAK, SNP1/23/171, 10/1920/43, Resident, Plateau Province, to Secretary, Northern Provinces, "Famine in the Northern Provinces."

42. See NAK, SNP1/23/171, 7/1931/6, "Famine in Wana District, Southern Division." See also no. 14658/22, "Food Shortages in the NP, 1931."

43. Watts, *Silent Violence,* 320.

44. NAK, SNP1/23/171, 7/1931/6, 55/9, "Food Situation Northern Provinces, 1931."

45. Watts, *Silent Violence,* 317.

46. Ibid.

47. Lennihan, "Critical Conjunctures," 477–78.

48. Shenton details and discusses the origins and development of this trade and the competition that resulted between Arab and European buyers. Robert Shenton, *The Development of Capitalism in Northern Nigeria* (London: James Currey, 1986).

49. One of the propaganda items of the middlemen was the claim that the UAC wanted to turn them all into laborers by eliminating them from the produce-buying business. See SNP1/18/116, 11096, Summary of Intelligence Reports for the Quarter Ending December 1932, 9.

50. Farmers had always been suspicious of the practices of European produce-buying firms, which often took advantage of location, transport difficulty, price fixing, and oligopolistic advantages to shortchange farmers.

51. NAK, SNP1/18/116, 11096, Summary of Intelligence Reports for the Quarter Ending December 1932.

52. NAK, file 13447, "The United Africa Company: Dealings in Local Foodstuffs."

53. Ibid.

54. NAK, file 13447, Chief Secretary's Office to General Manager, United Africa Company.

55. Ibid.

56. For big colonial merchant firms, the colonial bureaucracy was not always a pillar of support. See, for instance, Jacques Marseille, *Empire colonial et capitalisme français: Histoire d'un divorce* (Paris: A. Michel, 1984).

57. NAK, SNP1/18/116, 11096, Summary of Intelligence Reports for the Quarter Ending September 30, 1931, 10.

58. NAK, file 13447, Senior General Manager, UAC, to Chief Secretary to the Government.

59. Ibid.

60. Ibid.

61. Shenton, *Development of Capitalism*. A similar argument about the persecution of African middlemen by colonial authorities in favor of British firms during the Depression has been made by Anthony Nwabughuogu with respect to Eastern Nigeria. Nwabughuogu, "From Wealthy Entrepreneurs to Petty Traders: The Decline of African Middlemen in Eastern Nigeria, 1900–1950," *Journal of African History*, 23, no. 3 (1982): 365–79.

62. NAK, SNP1/23/171, 14658A, Extract from Resident Niger's Intelligent Report September Quarter: 1931.

63. Ibid.

64. Watts, *Silent Violence*, 317.

65. Amartya Sen, *Poverty and Famines: An Essay on Entitlement and Deprivation* (New York: Oxford University Press, 1982).

66. NAK, SNP1/23/171, 14658A/51, "Food Shortage in Kontagora."

67. NAK, SNP1/23/171, C12/1931/21, Resident, Niger Province to Secretary, Northern Provinces, "Food Shortage in Kontagora." See also NAK, SNP1/23/171, "Report on Famine and Relief Measures."

68. Ibid.

69. Ibid.

70. NAK, SNP1/23/171, "Report on Famine and Relief Measures."

71. Ibid.

72. Ibid.

73. NAK, LOKOPROF, Kabba Distr., file 305, Petition of Ohimege Igu, Chief of Koton Karifi, to the District Officer of Koton Karifi.

74. NAK, LOKOPROF, file 305, divisional correspondence 9/1928/70, ADO i/c, Koton Karifi Division, to District Officer, i/c Kabba Division, "Tax Count, 1934–35 Complaint."

75. NAK, SNP1/18/116, 11096, vol. 4, Summary of Intelligence Reports for the Quarter Ending March 31, 1932.

76. NAK, SNP1/18/116, 11096, vol. 2, Summary of Intelligence Reports, December 31, 1931, 9.

77. "Ilorin," *Northern Provinces News*, July 23, 1932, 4.

78. NAK, LOKOPROF, 714, annual report, Igbirra Division, 1935, 3.

79. Ibid.

80. Watts, *Silent Violence*, 230.

81. For instance, Watts cites the case of Katsina, where twenty-eight officials were deposed for engaging in what officials termed revenue malpractices. Watts, *Silent Violence*, 230. For a discussion of the numerous depositions in the 1930s, see M. S. Abdulkadir, "An Economic History of Igalaland, 1896–1939" (PhD diss., Bayero University, Kano, 1990), chap. 8.

82. NAK, Zaria Provincial Office, 7/1, 125/1931, quoted in Watts, *Silent Violence*, 230.

83. NAK, SNP1/18/116, 11096, vol. 4, Summary of Intelligence Reports for the Quarter Ending March 31, 1932, "Civil Disturbances," 3.

84. Ibid., 4.

85. NAK, SNP17, 21349, annual report, Kabba Province, 1933.

86. NAK, LOKOPROF, provincial correspondence 59/1931, Divisional Office, Idah, "Bassa Komo Disturbances."

CHAPTER 3: SOCIAL TRANSFORMATIONS AND UNINTENDED
CONSEQUENCES IN A DEPRESSED ECONOMY

1. Bill Freund, *Capital and Labour in the Nigerian Tin Mines* (London: Longman, 1981), 121–26.

2. RH, MSS Brit. Empire, S443, W. R. Crocker, "Memoirs, 1902–75" (hereafter cited as Crocker, "Memoirs"), 138.

3. NAK, SNP1/18/116, 11096, Summary of Intelligence Reports for the Quarter Ending December 1931, 12.

4. For details of the quotas allocated to Nigeria under the international tin agreement and the fluctuation of those quotas in response to prices, see *Gazetteers of the Northern Provinces*, vol. 4, *The Highland Chieftaincies* (London: Frank Cass, 1972), 303–6.

5. NAK, SNP1/18/116, 11096, vol. 2, Summary of Intelligence Reports for the Quarter Ending March 1930, 22.

6. NAK, SNP1/18/116, 11096, Summary of Intelligence Reports for the Quarter Ending September 30, 1931, 11.

7. NAK, SNP1/18/116, 11096, Summary of Intelligence Reports for the Quarter Ending June 1930, 8.

8. NAK, SNP1/18/116, 11096, vol. 2, Summary of Intelligence Reports for the Quarter Ending January 1930.

9. RH, Afr. S. 1836, H. P. Elliot, "Reminiscence of Colonial Administrative Service in Nigeria," 4.

10. NAK, SNP1/18/116, 11096, Summary of Intelligence Reports for the Quarter Ending June 1930, 10.

11. Ibid.

12. NAK, SNP1/18/116, 11096, Summary of Intelligence Reports for the Quarter Ending September 30, 1931.

13. NAK, SNP1/18/116, 11096, Summary of Intelligence Reports for the Quarter Ending March 1931, 3. As Lamont King has argued, the *sabon garuruwa* (strangers' quarters), located along the railway in Northern Nigeria, became a haven for the unemployed during the Great Depression. It was at this time that "colonial officials began to complain about the presence of unemployed criminals and prostitutes." King, "From Caliphate to Protectorate: Ethnicity and the Colonial Sabon Gari System in Northern Nigeria," *Journal of Colonialism and Colonial History* 4, no. 2 (2003): 13, http://muse.jhu.edu/login?uri=/journals/journal_of_colonialism_and_colonial_history/v004/4.2king.html.

14. NAK, SNP1/18/116, 11096, Summary of Intelligence Reports for the Quarter Ending March 1931, 3.

15. For a discussion of how companies in British and French Africa secured cheap African labor during the Depression, see Frederick Cooper, *Decolonization and African Society: The Labor Question in French and British Africa* (Cambridge: Cambridge University Press, 1996), 43–51; Cooper, *On the African Waterfront: Urban Disorder and the Transformation of Work in Colonial Mombasa* (New Haven: Yale University Press, 1987), 33.

16. NAK, SNP1/18/116, 11096, Summary of Intelligence Reports for the Quarter Ending March 1931, 9.

17. Ibid., 3.

18. NAK, SNP1/18/116, 11096, Summary of Intelligence Reports for the Quarter Ending March 1931, 3.

19. NAK, SNP1/18/116, 11096, Summary of Intelligence Reports for the Quarter Ending June 2, 1930, 3.

20. NAK, SNP1/18/116, 11096, Summary of Intelligence Reports for the Quarter Ending September 30, 1931, 2.

21. On May 23, 1930, four NA policemen were attacked and robbed near the village of Delimi. See NAK, SNP1/18/116, 11096, Summary of Intelligence Reports for the Quarter Ending June 1930, 7.

22. Ibid.

23. Ibid.

24. NAK, Jos Magistrate Court, Criminal Record Book, 1/1/7.

25. Ibid., 1/1/8.

26. Ibid., 1/1/7.

27. Ibid.

28. See NAK, SNP1/18/116, 11096, Summary of Intelligence Reports for the Quarter Ending June 1930, 7.

29. See Walter R. Crocker, *Nigeria: A Critique of British Colonial Administration* (1936; repr., Freeport, New York: Books for Libraries, 1971), 69. The collapse was partly caused by the return of some retrenched tin miners to local agriculture, a return that created a glut in the agricultural market and further depressed prices. See Freund, *Capital and Labour*, 84.

30. NAK, SNP1/18/116, 11096, Summary of Intelligence Reports for the Quarter Ending September 30, 1931, 3.

31. Ibid.

32. Ibid.

33. See Paul Lovejoy and Jan Hogendorn, *Slow Death for Slavery: The Course of Abolition in Northern Nigeria, 1897–1936* (Cambridge: Cambridge University Press, 1993); Frederick Cooper, *From Slaves to Squatters: Plantation Labor and Agriculture in Zanzibar and Coastal Kenya, 1890–1925* (New Haven: Yale University Press, 1987). Lovejoy and Hogendorn in particular make a detailed assessment of the slow course of the death of slavery in Hausaland. According to them, legal status slavery and slave trafficking were all but dead by 1910, their gradual demise

happening through a process of negotiation and compromise with the slave-owning aristocracy.

34. The nonemirate parts of Northern Nigeria were those loosely contiguous areas that had never been part of the Sokoto caliphate, had less-organized political systems, and were religiously and ethnically diverse. Such areas include Kabba, Benue, and Plateau provinces.

35. This is evident from reading the annual reports of Benue, Kabba, and Plateau provinces. Zakariah Goshit makes a strong argument for Plateau Province in this regard. Goshit, "The Impact of the Great Depression on the Jos Plateau: A Case Study of the Tin Mine Fields in the 1930s," *Mandeng: Journal of Middle Belt History* 1, no. 1 (2001): 72–86

36. Ibid., 84.

37. NAK, SNP1/18/116, 11096, Summary of Intelligence Reports for the Quarter Ending September 30, 1932, 3.

38. Ibid.

39. One example of such official denials comes from W. R. Crocker, who wrote in his journal while serving in Benue Province in 1933, "I am convinced that despite the fall in the price of produce these people are very lightly taxed and suffer no hardship."

40. NAK, SNP1/18/116, 11096, Summary of Intelligence Reports for the Quarter Ending September 30, 1932, 8.

41. Debt was one of the biggest problems of the Depression in Northern Nigeria. The explosion in the number of moneylenders—indicated by the unprecedented increase in the application for money-lending licenses—was one indicator of the poverty and debt problem. A survey conducted by the *Nigeria Gazette*, a publication of the Nigerian secretariat in Lagos from the 1920s through the 1930s, shows quite clearly that the 1930s marked a boom in the money-lending business. Pawning has always been an aspect of life in southwestern Nigeria and the Niger Delta. See Kenneth Onwuka Dike, *Trade and Politics in the Niger Delta, 1830–1885* (Oxford: Clarendon Press, 1956). However, colonial complaints and outrage over the practice reached a crescendo in the 1930s. See Judith Byfield, *The Bluest Hands: A Social and Economic History of Women Dyers in Abeokuta (Nigeria), 1890–1940* (Portsmouth, NH: Heinemann; Oxford: James Currey, 2002). Officials often called the pawned children slaves and liked to view the practice as a vestige of an ancient local custom. See, for instance, Crocker, "Memoirs," 142.

42. Railway workers were a perennially militant segment of the colonial workforce in Nigeria and West Africa. See Lisa Lindsay, *Working with Gender: Wage Labor and Social Change in Southwestern Nigeria* (Portsmouth, NH: Heinemann, 2003); Cooper, *Decolonization*, 134–35.

43. I have been told by informants in the Idoma area, a major supplier of railway labor, that this practice was quite common.

44. NAK, SNP1/18/116, 11096, Summary of Intelligence Reports for the Quarter Ending June 1930, 3. The report laments the prevalence of railway keys in

Southern Division, Plateau Province. It accuses the blacksmiths of the village of Wangibi of complicity in the crime.

45. NAK, SNP1/18/116, 11096, Summary of Intelligence Reports for the Quarter Ending September 30, 1931, 2.

46. Reports spoke of miserable conditions on the railway work camps and the bad workplace discipline that those conditions engendered.

47. NAK, SNP1/18/116, 11096, Summary of Intelligence Reports for the Quarter Ending September 30, 1932, 5.

48. NAK, SNP1/18/116, 11096, Summary of Intelligence Reports for the Quarter Ending March 31, 1932, 5.

49. NAK, SNP1/18/116, 11096, Summary of Intelligence Reports for the Quarter Ending September 30, 1931, 12.

50. Ibid.

51. Crocker, "Memoirs," 140.

52. NAK, SNP1/18/116, 11096, Summary of Intelligence Reports for the Quarter Ending September 30, 1931, 12. "Ibo" or "Ibos" (pl.) is the term preferred by the colonial authorities. It is a convenient corruption of "Igbo," which is the proper name for the people. Although "Ibo" is still used by uninformed people and by people copying colonial usage, the Igbo do not use it for themselves. In this work I have therefore used "Igbo" to reflect that preference.

53. Crocker, "Memoirs," 140.

54. NAK, SNP1/18/116, 11096, vol. 2, Summary of Intelligence Reports for the Quarter Ending June 1930, 8.

55. NAK, SNP1/116, 11096, Summary of Intelligence Reports for the Quarter Ending December 31, 1931, 12.

56. Crocker, "Memoirs," 140.

57. Ibid.

58. Ibid., 139.

59. NAK, SNP1/18/116, 11096, Summary of Intelligence Reports for the Quarter Ending September 30, 1931.

60. Crocker, "Memoirs," 142.

61. NAK, SNP1/18/116, 11096, Summary of Intelligence Reports for the Quarter Ending March 1932, 13

62. NAK, LOKOPROF, 390, annual report, Igbirra Division, 1932–33, pt. 1.

63. Alhaji Yusuf Utohu Dauda, interview, Okene, July 4, 2000. Alhaji Dauda is Western educated and was a commissioner in the old Kwara State. His father founded the Okene weaving center. According to the son, several Europeans visited Okene during the colonial period, taking samples and interviewing weavers, including his father. It was also during the period that cloth woven by Igbirra weavers, the Uba, was first used to sew school uniforms for Okene Middle School and to sew prison uniforms for prisoners in Okene. It is hard to assign a precise date to the founding of centers. During a research trip to Igbirraland in the summer of 2000, I was told by several informants within and around the centers that the centers were started at the same time that Hausa *mallams* (Islamic teachers) were

coming to Okene in unprecedented numbers, some for trade and some for religious activities. Ahmed Rufai Muhammad has dated the coming of these mallams to Okene to the early 1930s. Muhammad, "The History of the Spread of Islam in the Niger-Benue Confluence Area: Igalaland, Ebirraland and Lokoja, 1900–1960" (PhD diss., Bayero University, Kano, 1986). The beginning of the Ogaminana weaving center is linked with the activities of a European missionary in the area around the 1930s. But the center was started in its present form by a Roman Catholic priest in the 1970s. Mrs. Christiana Onusagba, interview, Ogaminana, Adavi LGA, July 4, 2000. The unseen force acting to sustain and promote this wave of local textile development was the expanding demand for the products.

64. The two major centers that have survived to date, the Ogaminana and Okene centers, now double as production and training centers; both are partially supported by the government, although the Ogaminana center is almost entirely owned by the family of Alhaji Yusuf Utohu Dauda.

65. Goshit, "Impact of the Great Depression," 80.

66. NAK, SNP1/18/116, 11096, vol. 4, Summary of Intelligence Reports for the Quarter Ending December 31, 1932, 9.

67. *Jarida Nijeria ta Arewa/Northern Provinces News*, November 1, 1935, 18.

68. *Jarida Nijeria ta Arewa/Northern Provinces News*, January 1, 1937, "Aikin Tonon Zinari," 26.

69. Ibid.

70. Ibid.

71. *Jarida Nijeria ta Arewa/Northern Provinces News*, January 7, 1934, 1.

72. Crocker, "Memoirs," 139.

73. *Jarida Nijeria ta Arewa/Northern Provinces News*, October 15, 1934, 1.

74. Ibid.

75. NAK, LOKOPROF, divisional correspondence 34/211, "General Notes on the Social and Economic Progress of the People of Nigeria, 1938."

76. NAK, SNP 17, annual report, Kabba Province, 1933.

77. Ibid.

78. Ibid.

79. Ibid.

80. NAK, LOKOPROF, Kabba Dist., divisional correspondence 68, General Notes on the Social and Economic Progress of the People of Nigeria, 1938 (Kabba Division).

81. A good example here is the population of "vagrant" tin workers on the Jos Plateau described by Freund, *Capital and Labour*, 78. For parallels in other African colonies, see John Higginson, *A Working Class in the Making: Belgian Colonial Labor Policy, Private Enterprise, and the African Mineworker, 1907–1951* (Madison: University of Wisconsin Press, 1989), 118–29; Cooper, *African Waterfront*, 32–33.

82. NAK, LOKOPROF, provincial correspondence 435/1927/54, Annual Report on the Social and Economic Progress of the People of Nigeria, Kabba Division, 1934.

83. Sara Berry, "Cocoa in Western Nigeria, 1890–1940: A Study of an Innovation in a Developing Economy" (PhD diss., University of Michigan, 1967), 195–202.

84. Ibid., 202.

85. Pa David Adeolaojo, interview, Akure, April 21, 2002.

86. I got a sense from the interviews that the 1937 date stuck because it was about then that migrants began to settle down in Western Nigeria, building temporary houses and bringing wives over. Earlier migrants may have started going to the cocoa plantations in about 1930, as suggested by G. E. Ode in the case of migrants from the Agatu area of Idoma Division. Ode, "Impact of British Colonialism on the People of Idoma Division, 1908–1950" (master's thesis, Ahmadu Bello University, Zaria, June 1981). See also James Aliu Ohiare, "The History of Migration from the Okene Area to the Cocoa Belt of Western Nigeria, 1923–1970" (bachelor's thesis, Ahmadu Bello University, Zaria, 1977). Ohiare dates the migration of young Igbirra men to the cocoa belt to the late 1920s. The earlier migrants were seasonal and were fewer, hence they may not have registered in the minds of locals.

87. RH, Afr. T. 16, S. M. Jacob, "Report on the Taxation and Economics of Nigeria, 1934," 114.

88. Ibid., 115. Jacob himself quoted "administrative and business sources."

89. M. S. Abdulkadir, "Currency Problems in Igalaland, Central Nigeria: 1930–1934." *Transafrican Journal of History* 24 (1995): 178–85. My own research in Idoma Division has revealed that precolonial currencies and trade by barter reemerged during the Depression, to the disappointment of colonial officials who spilled an enormous amount of ink lamenting the development. For a detailed analysis of this currency conundrum, see chapters 5 and 6.

90. NAK, LOKOPROF, file 366, "Taxation in Igala Division," quoted in M. Abdulkadir, "Currency Problems," 181.

91. See NAK, 12,072, vol. 2, Resident, Plateau Province, to Secretary, Northern Provinces, "Counterfeit Coinage."

92. Ayodeji Olukoju, "Self-Help Criminality as Resistance: Currency Counterfeiting in Colonial Nigeria," *International Review of Social History* 45, no. 3 (2000): 403. Although, as Olukoju demonstrates, currency counterfeiting and colonial anxieties over it predated the Depression, the economic crisis and the currency shortages that followed the withdrawal of currency from the Nigerian economy turned the practice into a major colonial problem.

93. NAK, SNP1/18/116, 11096, Summary of Intelligence Reports for the Quarter Ending September 1930, 13.

94. The Maria Theresa dollar, a currency that was quite popular in precolonial Northern Nigeria, made its return during the Depression; this time its origin was traced to Czechoslovakia. Silver coins imported into Nigeria were said to have come from diverse international sources.

95. NAK, SNP1/18/116, 11096, Summary of Intelligence Reports for the Quarter Ending September 1930, 13.

96. NAK, SNP1/18/116, 11096, Summary of Intelligence Reports for the Quarter Ending March 1930.

97. NAK, SNP1/18/116, 11096, Summary of Intelligence Reports for the Quarter Ending December 31, 1932, 10.

98. NAK, SNP1/18/116, 11096, Summary of Intelligence Reports for the Quarter Ending December 1931, 13.

99. See NAK, SNP/18/116, 11096, Summary of Intelligence Reports for the Quarter Ending September 30, 1932, 13.

100. Intelligence reports up to 1934 cited these areas as centers where counterfeit coins circulated heavily.

101. See, for instance, NAK, D1221, "Bank of British West Africa to the D. O. Daura Native Administration."

102. Ibid.

103. NAK, SNP 11668, CR4: "Financial Memoranda for Guidance in Native Authorities," April 1931.

104. NAK, 12,072, vol. 2, Resident, Sokoto Province, to Secretary, Northern Provinces, "Native Treasuries—Counterfeit Coinage."

105. NAK, 12,072, vol. 2, Auditor, Lagos, to Chief Secretary to the Government, 5.

106. NAK, 12,072, vol. 2, Secretary, Northern Provinces, to Residents, All Provinces, "Counterfeit Coinage."

107. The government's auditor expressed this sentiment in his report to the government. See NAK, 12,072, vol. 2, p. 3.

108. Ibid.

109. NAK, 12,072, vol. 2, p. 3, Secretary, Northern Provinces, to Residents, All Provinces, p. 2.

110. Ibid.

111. NAK, LOKOPROF, 48/1923, Secretary, Northern Provinces, to Resident, Kabba Province, "Counterfeit Coins," July 1939.

CHAPTER 4: PROTESTS, PETITIONS, AND POLEMICS
ON THE ECONOMIC CRISIS

1. AH, SNP1/23/171, file 14658A, "Elder Dempster and Co. and the United Africa Company," *Nigerian Protectorate Ram*, Lokoja, September 2, 1930.

2. AH, SNP1/23/171, file 14658A, Cole-Edwards to Resident, Kabba Province, October 17, 1932.

3. Ibid.

4. Ibid.

5. AH, SNP1/23/171, file 14658A, Cole-Edwards to Secretary, Northern Provinces, October 21, 1933.

6. Ibid.

7. AH, SNP1/23/171, file 14658A, Cole-Edwards to Resident, Kabba Province, October 1932.

8. AH, SNP1/23/171, file 14658A, Cole-Edwards to Lieutenant Governor, October 1933.

9. AH, SNP1/23/171, file 14658A, "To All Classes of My People," *Nigerian Protectorate Ram*, September 22, 1930.

10. AH, SNP1/23/171, file 14658A, "Progress of the People of the Northern Provinces," *Nigerian Protectorate Ram*, September 22, 1930.

11. The discovery by a secret British investigation that several workers in the Northern Nigerian colonial bureaucracy were contributing money toward the paper's viability and that a senior African civil servant, the head of the mail and telegrams in Jos, had contributed £30 alerted British officials to just how clandestine and amorphous the newspaper's tentacles of support and readership were. See AH, SNP1/23/171, file 14658A, Resident, Kabba Province, to Secretary, Northern Provinces, November 1, 1930.

12. Ibid.

13. Like all colonial governments, the Nigerian government, even before the amalgamation of the Northern and Southern protectorates in 1914, regarded educated Africans with a mixture of suspicion and disdain. They were seen as carriers of subversive ideologies and perennial agitators. When groups of these Africans added newspaper publishing to their repertoire in the late 1890s, the Lagos government grew more suspicious. For a full account of the emergence of the so-called Lagos press and of the evolution of their tradition of journalistic anticolonial activism, see Philip S. Zachernuk, *Colonial Subjects: An African Intelligentsia and Atlantic Ideas* (Charlottesville: University Press of Virginia, 2000).

14. AH, SNP1/23/171, file 14658A, Resident, Kabba Province, to Secretary, Northern Provinces.

15. Ibid.

16. Ibid.

17. Ibid. At the beginning of the Depression, the United Africa Company and John Holt, the two biggest British trading firms, merged in order to eliminate competition and control prices. The result of the merger was that the new conglomerate fixed produce prices across all its trading territories in Northern Nigeria.

18. AH, SNP1/23/171, file 14658A, Resident, Kabba Province, to Secretary, Northern Provinces.

19. AH, SNP1/23/171, file 14658A, Cole-Edwards to Secretary to the Government, October 21, 1933.

20. Officials discovered that most of the freelance writers for the *Nigerian Protectorate Ram* and the writers of anticolonial petitions had lost their jobs in the retrenchments of the 1930s and that even Africans who retained their jobs but had to take pay cuts supported the league of petition writers and the *Ram* financially and logistically. AH, SNP1/23/171, file 14658A, Resident, Kabba Province, to Secretary, Northern Provinces, November 1, 1930.

21. "The Progress of the People of the Northern Provinces," *Nigerian Protectorate Ram*, September 22, 1930, 1.

22. Ibid.

23. *Nigerian Protectorate Ram*, September 22, 1930. Response of the Chief Secretary to the Government on behalf of the Governor of Nigeria.

24. *Nigerian Protectorate Ram*, September 22, 1930. Petition signed by Samuel Cole-Edwards.

25. Incidentally, it was Frederick Lugard, the first governor of Northern Nigeria, who intervened decisively in this debate and inscribed the concept of dual mandate on British colonialism. See Lugard's canonical work *The Dual Mandate in British Tropical Africa* (Edinburgh: W. Blackwood and Sons, 1922).

26. "Street Lights Should Be Provided in the Township and the Native Town," *Nigerian Protectorate Ram*, September 22, 1930, 5.

27. Ibid.

28. AH, SNP1/23/171, file 14658A, *Nigerian Weekly Despatch*, August 15, 1931.

29. I have assumed here that the anonymous author was a man, a safe assumption considering that there were few Western-educated women in Northern Nigeria who participated in public erudition in the 1930s. Newspaper publishing and punditry was a male-dominated institution, especially in culturally conservative Northern Nigeria. For a previous anonymous article in this chapter, I was less certain of the gender of the author because of the focus of the author's critique on the question of women taxation in Northern Nigeria. Except for those kinds of situations, it is safe to assume that anonymous commentaries in Northern Nigerian newspapers of the 1930s were written by men. This assumption is less safe for the period after 1945, when there was a growth in female education in the non-Muslim parts of Northern Nigeria and when some women began playing open roles in the civil service and even in the proto-nationalist politics of the period.

30. "A Call to Service," *Nigerian Protectorate Ram*, September 22, 1930, 6.

31. For details of the role of the two companies in produce buying in Northern Nigeria, the ways that they sought to position themselves during the Depression, and their struggle to capture a share of local produce and anchor their own recovery on the backs of local peasants, see chapter 2.

32. "A Call to Service," *Nigerian Protectorate Ram*, September 22, 1930, 6.

33. Ibid.

34. AH, SNP1/23/171, file 14658A, Secretary, Northern Provinces, to Resident, Kabba Province, October 1930.

35. The paper was published in English, Hausa, and Arabic. A few editions also carried articles in Tiv and Kanuri, Northern Nigeria's two most widely spoken languages after Hausa.

36. Dan Zaki, "About Men and Affairs," *Daily Telegraph*, July 31, 1934, 11.

37. "Economy and the Levy," *Northern Provinces News*, July 29, 1933.

38. Ibid.

39. *Northern Provinces News*, April 9, 1932, 18.

40. "The King's Message to His People," *Northern Provinces News*, March 18, 1933, 1.

41. Moses Ebe Ochonu, "Articulation, Dissemination, and Implications of the Hausa Imaginary in Colonial Northern Nigeria," paper presented at the Annual Southeast Regional Seminar on African Studies, Norfolk, Virginia, April 15–16, 2005.

42. Steven Pierce, "Punishment and the Colonial Body: Flogging and Colonialism in Northern Nigeria," *Interventions* 3, no. 2 (2001): 213.

43. Alex Schmid and Janny de Graaf, eds., *Violence as Communication: Insurgent Terrorism and the Western News Media* (London: Sage, 1982), 184–85, cited in

Kumar Ramakrishna, *Emergency Propaganda: The Winning of Malaysian Hearts and Minds, 1948–1958* (Richmond, UK: Curzon, 2002), 13.

44. Rosaleen Smyth, "Britain's African Colonies and British Propaganda during the Second World War," *Journal of Imperial and Commonwealth History* 14, no. 1 (1985): 65–82.

45. "The Reign of Our King: 1910–1935 (A Twenty-Five-Year Review of the Northern Provinces)," *Jarida Nijeria ta Arewa/Northern Provinces News*, November 1, 1935, 1.

46. Ibid.

47. "Rashin Sani ya fi dare duhu," *Northern Provinces News*, October 15, 1934, 4.

48. Ibid.

49. "Nigeria a yau," *Jarida Nijeria ta Arewa/Northern Provinces News*, January 1, 1937, 19.

50. Ibid., 20.

51. Ibid.

52. For a full account of Zungur's life and intellectual activities, see Sa'adu Zungur, *Sa'adu Zungur: An Anthology of the Social and Political Writings of a Nigerian Nationalist*, ed. Alhaji Mahmood Yakubu (Kaduna: Nigerian Defence Academy Press, 2000). For his poetry and literary legacy, see Dandatti Abdulkadir, *The Poetry, Life, and Opinions of Sa'adu Zungur* (Zaria: Northern Nigerian Publishing, 1974). For his political thinking and legacy, see Ahmadu U. Jalingo, "The Radical Tradition in Northern Nigeria" (PhD thesis, University of Edinburgh, 1980); Billy Dudley, *Parties and Politics in Northern Nigeria* (London: Frank Cass, 1968). The BDC spawned several radical anticolonial populist offshoots, which intermeshed with other emirate Muslim anticolonial populist political movements to produce a virulent strain of mass popular protest politics that came to be symbolized by Aminu Kano's Northern Elements Progressive Union.

CHAPTER 5: THE PERIPHERY STRIKES BACK

1. The term Idoma Division is used here to denote the colonial administrative unit encompassing the areas of colonial Northern Nigeria settled by the Idoma people. This was how the British designated it. In this and the next chapter I will use the term only as an administrative appellation. I will use Idomaland to denote the precolonial Idoma territory, which corresponds fairly accurately to colonial Idoma Division. Finally, I use Idoma (or the Idoma) to refer to the people who speak the Idoma language (in whatever dialect).

2. To be sure, the colonial economic, political, and educational intervention in Idoma Division in the 1920s was limited, short-lived, and ran against the grain of metropolitan colonial policy consensus, which focused not on transformation but preservation because the former was expensive. The intervention was never designed for total cultural transformation, although officials' rhetoric embraced those aims. The aim of bringing Idoma Division within the economic mainstream of Northern Nigeria through a process of colonial education and the engineering of chieftaincy institutions was more preparatory than developmental. It was

conceived merely as a way of facilitating the transition of the Idoma into the normative economic and political order in Northern Nigeria. Thus, the Depression did not mark a radical departure from earlier colonial policy. It was merely a small, largely rhetorical departure from pre-Depression colonial commitments.

3. V. G. O'kwu, "The Establishment of Colonial Administration in Idomaland, 1921–1930," *Savanna* 5, no. 1 (June 1976): 37.

4. I arrived at this figure from the 1921 colonial census numbers published by C. K. Meek. By those numbers the Idoma population in Munshi (later Benue) Province was 91,750. Since the Agatu branch of the Idoma was classified differently and was evenly divided between Munshi (Benue) Province and Nasarawa Province, I have added half the total population of the Agatu (which comes to 21,185) to the Idoma population figure. See Meek, *The Northern Tribes of Nigeria: An Ethnographical Account of the Northern Provinces of Nigeria Together with a Report on the 1921 Decennial Census* (New York: Negro Universities Press, 1969), 181, 185. In 1976 the population of the Idoma stood at half a million. See O'kwu, "Colonial Administration," 29.

5. For a full account of the conquest of Idomaland by the British, see O'kwu, "Colonial Administration."

6. O'kwu has attributed this thinking ultimately to a variant of the infamous Hamitic hypothesis, which ascribes preeminence, sophistication, higher social and economic evolution, and political suzerainty in Sudanic Africa to the influence and direct agency of polities and peoples of the Near East, who were influenced by Islam and traditions of the Near East.

7. Timothy Mitchell, *Rule of Experts: Egypt, Techno-politics, Modernity* (Berkeley: University of California Press, 2002), chap. 3.

8. See Mahdi Adamu, *The Hausa Factor in West African History* (Zaria: Ahmadu Bello University Press; Ibadan: Oxford University Press, 1978), 37–52; esp. 43.

9. NAK, Otudist., ACC 26, N. J. Brooke, "Eastern District of Okwoga."

10. O'kwu, "Colonial Administration," 42.

11. For a comprehensive history of the Ogbuloko rebellion, see A. P. Anyebe, *Man of Courage and Character: The Ogbuloko War in Colonial Idomaland of Nigeria* (Enugu: Fourth Dimension, 2002).

12. Walter R. Crocker, *Nigeria: A Critique of British Colonial Administration* (1936; repr., Freeport, NY: Books for Libraries, 1971), 31. This statement was an entry in Crocker's official diary, which was submitted to his superiors and would later form the basis of official policies toward the Idoma and other peoples in the Lower Benue Valley.

13. Alvin Magid, *Men in the Middle: Leadership and Role Conflict in a Nigerian Society* (Manchester: Manchester University Press, 1976), 45. I prefer the term *emirate model* to *Fulani system* because it is ethnically neutral and does not suggest that only the areas conquered and dominated by the Fulani warrior-ideologues of the 1804 jihad practiced the system of Islamic autocracy that characterized the Sokoto caliphate. A parallel program of colonial administrative outsourcing that involved the superimposition of "alien" chiefs on "backward" people was imple-

mented in Buganda. See Lloyd Fallers, *Bantu Bureaucracy: A Century of Political Evolution among the Basoga of Uganda* (Chicago: University of Chicago Press, 1965), 145–46.

14. RH, Afr. S. 1836, H. P. Elliot, "Reminiscence of Colonial Administrative Service in Nigeria," 1.

15. The removal of the superstructure of Hausa rulers was not complete until about 1919. See Magid, *Men in the Middle*, 43. But even after that, some Hausa administrative officials working in the clerical cadre of the colonial bureaucracy were retained.

16. The essentials of this belief in the exceptional difficulty of Idoma Division, its backwardness, and its aversion to taxation and other forms of colonial control were outlined by J. C. Sciortino, a colonial official who averred that the Idoma colonial subjects were "probably the most difficult in the Northern Provinces"; by A. C. Francis, an assistant district officer at Okpoga in 1926; and by both W. R. Crocker and H. P. Elliot, both of whom served in Idoma Division as ADOs. The first two articulations of the notion of Idoma notoriety are contained in file 109 of the ACC group of NAK; the last two are in the diaries of the two officers. See RH, Afr. S. 1336, Afr. S. 1073, respectively. H. P. Elliot spent three years (1935–38) in Idoma Division. He describes the Idoma as headhunters, witch doctors, and as a collection of "largely backward [and] animist tribes." See Elliot, "Reminiscence," 6.

17. The use of brass rods and the nonavailability of colonial currencies in Idoma Division were appropriated as part of the discourse of backwardness, not necessarily as a result of the lack of cash-earning opportunities in the division and the activities of itinerant non-Idoma traders. In 1923, N. J. Brooke, an ADO in Idoma Division (then known as Okwoga Division), had warned that the division was becoming a dumping ground for brass rods from neighboring divisions, but his warning seems to have been lost in the iron-clad conviction of colonial authorities about the desire of the Idoma to be excluded from colonial schemes, including monetization. See NAK, Otudist., ACC 26, N. J. Brooke, "Eastern District of Okwoga."

18. The colonial intelligence reports lamented the abnormal fall in the price of food crops. See NAK, SNP1/18/116, 10096, "Intelligence Report for the Quarter Ending December 1931."

19. *Jarida Nijeria ta Arewa/Northern Provinces News*, November 1, 1935, 6–7.

20. Ibid.

21. Elliot, "Reminiscence," 7.

22. Ibid., 7–8.

23. NAK, Otudist., Idoma Division Half-Yearly Report for June 1932.

24. *Jarida Nijeria ta Arewa/Northern Provinces News*, November 1, 1935, 6–7. See also M. S. Abdulkadir, "Currency Problems in Igalaland, Central Nigeria: 1930–1934," *Transafrican Journal of History* 24 (1995): 178–85.

25. Road tolls and informal communal contributions toward teachers' salaries fall in this category.

26. Brass rods and other precolonial currency had technically ceased to be legal tender, but officials had generally acquiesced in the inevitability of their utility as

the means of exchange in Idoma Division. W. R. Crocker's statement sums up the attitude of the colonial regime to brass rods: "the money is not our legal currency, but. . . . despite their cumbersomeness, and though they are not legal tender, [they] are still used."

27. For a discussion of the crisis in the tin industry during the Depression and the cost-cutting measures that the industry adopted, see Bill Freund, *Capital and Labour in the Nigerian Tin Mines* (London: Longman, 1981), 121–26. Closures were common, but the few mines that remained in business had to lay off workers and reduce the wages of those retained.

28. Nigeria joined the agreement in 1931. For information on Nigeria's participation in the tin quota agreement of the 1930s, see *Gazetteers of Northern Provinces*, vol. 4, *The Highland Chieftancies* (London: Frank Cass, 1972), 303–6.

29. Crocker, *Nigeria*, 69.

30. I use *development* here (as elsewhere in this book) purely in an elemental sense to denote infrastructural improvements and the provision of basic social amenities and social services. Development as a concept and as a philosophy of rule did not become operative in policy terms within British colonialism until after World War II, when pressures to improve the quality of lives of colonial peoples increased.

31. NAK, ACC 26, response of resident to annual report of Idoma Division, 1932.

32. NAK, ACC 26, response of resident to Idoma Division half-yearly report for June 1932.

33. Ibid., 23.

34. Elliot, "Reminiscence," 28.

35. NAK, ACC 26, Otukpo Division (hereafter cited as Otudiv.), annual report, Idoma Division, 1932.

36. Ibid.

37. Ibid.

38. Ibid., sec. 3, "Revenue and Taxation."

39. This situation seems to differ somewhat from the infamous Rwanda case, where the imposition and codification of Tutsi leadership and, for all practical purposes, superiority, was naturalized and anthropologically reified as a precolonial verity. See Mahmood Mamdani, *When Victims Become Killers: Colonialism, Nativism, and the Genocide in Rwanda* (Princeton: Princeton University Press, 2001).

40. O'kwu, "Colonial Administration," 32.

41. O'kwu has suggested that the division was in fact seen as a place of punishment for insubordinate officials and a dumping ground for incompetent ones. Crocker's own observations support the former contention. In fact Crocker grumbled his way through Idoma Division during his service there and would later bemoan his transfer to the division in 1933 as a ploy to get rid of him because of his outspokenness. O'kwu, "Colonial Administration."

42. Norcross Memorial Methodist Diocese Archives (hereafter cited as NMMDA) Otukpo, Benue State (uncataloged), general correspondence, Rev. Hutchinson, August 29, 1930.

43. For a comprehensive history of missionary activities and of the educational work of the Methodist mission in Idoma Division, see Timothy Andrew Ikoja, "The History of Methodist Mission in Idomaland of Benue State" (NCE thesis, Federal College of Education, Abeokuta, 1991).

44. Albert Ozigi and Lawrence Ocho have analyzed the unwillingness of the colonial authorities to support missionary education in the Moslem emirate areas as a political decision founded on a British promise not to interfere with the emirates' Islamic religion. Ozigi and Ocho, *Education in Northern Nigeria* (London: Allen and Unwin, 1981).

45. The kind of hostility that existed between missionary educators and colonial officials in emirate Northern Nigeria never existed in Idoma Division. They saw each other as mutually reinforcing entities.

46. School of Oriental and African Studies Library, London (hereafter cited as SOAS), Primitive Methodist Mission Collection (hereafter cited as PMMC), H-2734, box 9, 327 (6–10), Mr. Ayre to Rev. Dodds, "Re: Education Matters," August 21, 1930.

47. Ibid.

48. NMMDA, Rev. Hutchinson's diary, February 24, 1930.

49. Ibid.

50. NMMDA, Rev. Hutchinson's diary, September 30, 1933.

51. NMMDA, Rev. Hutchinson's diary, November 6, 1930.

52. NMMDA, Rev. Hutchinson's diary, October 30, 1931.

53. SOAS, PMMC, 364, box 10, Hutchinson to Mrs. McKenzie.

54. SOAS, PMMC, Ayre to Rev. Dodds, May 3, 1935.

55. Ibid.

56. Ibid.

57. SOAS, PMMC, 1762, Rev. Dodds to Mr. Chairman, "Retrenchment."

58. See Bengt Sundkler, *Bantu Prophets in South Africa* (London: Oxford University Press, 1961); Sundkler and Christopher Steed, *A History of the Church in Africa* (Cambridge: Cambridge University Press, 2000); Emmanuel Ayandele, *The Missionary Impact on Modern Nigeria, 1842–1914: A Political and Social Analysis* (New York: Humanities Press, 1967).

59. NMMDA, Hutchinson, October 30, 1931.

60. SOAS, PMMC, reply by Rev. Dodds to Rev. Norcross's letter of August 17, 1934.

61. Ibid.

62. SOAS, PMMC, H-2734, 327 (7–10), Local Correspondence between Mission Stations and Mission Headquarters in Port Harcourt.

63. NMMDA, Rev. Hutchinson's diary, September 30, 1933.

64. SOAS, PMMC, Hutchinson to Ayre, July 13, 1936.

65. Ibid.

66. NMMDA, Rev. Hutchinson's diary, May 26, 1930.

67. Ibid.

68. NMMDA, Rev. Hutchinson's diary, September 30, 1933.

69. Philip S. Zachernuk, *Colonial Subjects: An African Intelligentsia and Atlantic Ideas* (Charlottesville: University Press of Virginia, 2000), 82.

70. SOAS, PMMC, Rev. Hutchinson to Mr. Ayre, November 6, 1935.

71. NMMDA, Rev. Hutchinson's diary, August 29, 1930.

72. NMMDA, Rev. Hutchinson's diary, June 15, 1933.

73. NAK, Otukpo District (hereafter cited as Otudist.), annual report, Idoma Division, 1932.

74. Ibid.

75. Ibid.

76. Ibid.

77. Interviews in both Idoma Division and the cocoa fields have confirmed this. Interviews with cocoa farm owners like Pa David Adeolaojo (Akure, April 20, 2002) and former migrants like Egwurube Ubah (Otukpo, April 5, 2001) point to the 1930s as the beginning of a significant migration of Idoma youths to the cocoa fields. James Ohiare, in his study of Igbirra migration to the cocoa belt, also points to the 1930s as a watershed in the migration of Ebira youths to Western Nigeria. Ohiare, "The History of Migration from the Okene Area to the Cocoa Belt of Western Nigeria, 1923–1970" (BA thesis, Ahmadu Bello University, Zaria, 1977).

78. Sara Berry, "Cocoa in Western Nigeria, 1890–1940: A Study of an Innovation in a Developing Economy" (PhD diss., University of Michigan, 1967), 200–205. Berry documents the cocoa boom of the 1930s.

79. Pa David Adeolaojo, whose father (and later he himself) made extensive use of the labor recruiters, described how labor demands in the boom years and the recruiters' willingness to travel to far flung provinces and districts ensured the constant supply of affordable labor, which in turn sustained profitability and prosperity. Adeolaojo, interview, Akure, April 20, 2001.

80. NAK, SNP1/18/116, 11096, Summary of Intelligence Reports for the Quarter Ending September 30, 1932.

81. Pa David Adeolaojo, interview.

82. I heard this first from Pa David Adeolaojo, and my interviews with former migrants in Idoma Division confirmed it, although they maintained that only a minority of migrants experienced such deprivation.

83. Sources point to the Igedde people as the pioneers of this process, but they were by no means the biggest participants in it. Sources told me that it took a while for gerontocracies in different districts to accept this practice as a career path for young men. As both itinerant and situated laborers also cultivated their own plots on alternate days and continued to help their wives, mothers, and fathers, the practice soon found acceptance.

CHAPTER 6: ECONOMIC RECOVERY AND GRASSROOTS REVENUE OFFENSIVES

1. The use of taxation as a technique of colonial control has been analyzed and documented by both historians and scholars engaged in a postmodern unpacking

of empire. In "normal" colonial times, the deployment of revenue schemes and accounting procedures was invested with the task of raising revenue for the state, schooling locals in the fiscal obligations of responsible imperial subjecthood, and consolidating control. They were also crafted as a means of projecting imperial power and reach. See Colin Newbury, "Accounting for Power in Northern Nigeria," *Journal of African History* 45, no. 2 (2004): 257–77; Barbara Bush and Josephine Maltby, "Taxation in West Africa: Transforming the Colonial Subject into a 'Governable Person,'" *Critical Perspectives on Accounting* 15, no. 1 (2004): 5–34; P. Miller and T. O'Leary, "Accounting and the Construction of the Governable Person," *Accounting, Organizations, and Society* 12, no. 3 (1987): 235–65.

2. NAK, Otudist., provincial report 56/1932/1, Idoma Division Half-Yearly Report for June 1932.

3. Ibid.

4. Steven Pierce has argued that the colonial obsession with revenue led to a series of reforms that established certain baselines and standards for revenue collection. The failure of individual chiefs and other colonial auxiliaries to satisfy these artificial standards attracted the label of corruption. See Steven Pierce, "Looking Like a State: Colonialism and the Discourse of Corruption in Northern Nigeria," *Comparative Studies in Society and History* 48, no. 4 (2006): 887–914.

5. Ibid.

6. NAK, Makurdi Provincial Office (hereafter cited as MAKPROF), provincial correspondence 8/1932/4, DO, Idoma Division, to Resident, Benue Province, Makurdi.

7. NAK, Otudist., Idoma Division, Capt. R. J. Lynch, ADO, Annual Report for the Year Ending December 31, 1932, "Native Administration and Organization."

8. NAK, MAKPROF, resident's memo 96B/1932, January 31, 1933, Comments on Annual Report.

9. NAK, Otudist., Annual Report on Idoma Division for the Year Ending December 1932.

10. Bill Freund, *Capital and Labour in the Nigerian Tin Mines* (London: Longman, 1981), 80.

11. NAK, MAKPROF, Annual Report on Idoma Division for the Year Ending December 31, 1932.

12. Ibid.

13. NAK, MAKPROF, report 17, Idoma Division, Capt. G. D. C. Money, ADO, Report for Half-Year Ending June 30, 1932.

14. Felicia Ekejiuba, "Currency Instability and Social Payments among the Igbo of Eastern Nigeria, 1890–1990," in *Money Matters: Instability, Values, and Social Payments in the Modern History of West African Communities*, ed. Jane Guyer (Portsmouth, NH: Heinemann; London: James Currey, 1995), 141.

15. Ekejiuba, "Currency Instability." In fact, as Walter Ofonagoro shows, it was not until 1948 that the colonial government took decisive action against manillas, launching the infamous Operation Manilla, which was aimed at ridding the country of manillas, the predominant local currency in Eastern Nigeria. See

Ofonagoro, "From Traditional to British Currency in Southern Nigeria: Analysis of the Currency Revolution, 1880–1948," *Journal of Economic History* 39, no. 3 (1979): 623–54. Eno J. Usoro has suggested that in the palm oil trade the colonial government intentionally encouraged the proliferation of multiple currencies in order to prevent price fixing by African palm produce sellers and middlemen. Usoro, *The Nigerian Oil Palm Industry: Government Policy and Export Production, 1906–1965* (Ibadan: Ibadan University Press, 1974).

16. NAK, MAKPROF, Annual Report on Idoma Division for the Year Ending December 31, 1932.

17. Ibid.

18. NAK, 12, 072, vol. 2, Auditor to Chief Secretary to the Government, Lagos, "Counterfeit Coin."

19. Ibid.

20. Ibid. Although the auditor-general argued that the "sudden flooding of these [Idoma] districts with counterfeit coins" was the work of Ibo traders, other sources speak of other syndicates operating from the North.

21. Crocker's journal, December 1, 1933.

22. Crocker's journal, October 22, 1933.

23. Crocker acknowledges the impact of the Depression on the taxpaying capacity of the Idoma but in the same breath argues that the inability of the Idoma to pay taxes was due to "their unwillingness to make any effort to come by the money." See Crocker, *Nigeria: A Critique of British Colonial Administration* (1936; repr., Freeport, NY: Books for Libraries, 1971), 69.

24. Ibid.

25. Ibid.

26. Crocker's journal, November 14, 1933. Elsewhere, Crocker estimated the number of goats confiscated at "about eighty" and fowls at sixty. Also confiscated were "yams, oil nuts, and odds-and-ends like cloth." Crocker, *Nigeria*, 79.

27. Ibid.

28. Crocker's journal, November 23, 1933.

29. Ibid.

30. Crocker's journal, November 24, 1933.

31. Crocker's journal, December 14, 1933.

32. Crocker, *Nigeria*, 81.

33. Ibid., 80.

34. RH, Afr. S. 1836, H. P. Elliot, "Reminiscence of Colonial Administrative Service in Nigeria," 18.

35. RH, Afr. S. 1336, journal of H. P. Elliot, assistant district officer (hereafter cited as Elliot's journal), October 11, 1935.

36. Elliot, "Reminiscence," 17.

37. Ibid., 1.

38. Elliot's journal, November 24, 1935.

39. Elliot, "Reminiscence," 18.

40. Elliot's journal, November 24, 1935.

41. Elliot's journal, November 26, 1935.

42. Elliot, "Reminiscence," 16.

43. Ibid., 28.

44. Crocker's journal, November 18, 1933.

45. Crocker's journal, December 1, 1933.

46. Crocker's journal, December 14, 1933.

47. Elliot's journal, August 23, 1935.

48. Elliot's journal, November 19, 1935.

49. Elliot's journal, January 17, 1936.

50. Crocker's journal, November 17, 1933.

51. Elliot's journal, August 6, 1935.

52. Elliot's journal, October 29, 1936.

53. Jane Guyer, "The Depression and the Administration in South-Central Cameroun," *African Economic History* 10 (1981): 74–75.

54. Crocker's journal, November 19, 1933. See also Crocker, *Nigeria*, 83.

55. During my fieldwork in Idoma Division I was told stories of Hausa-speaking colonial messengers raiding farms and villages for taxes, purportedly on behalf of colonial authorities, as late as the early 1950s.

56. Constance Larymore, *A Resident's Wife in Nigeria*, 2nd ed., rev. (London: George Routledge and Sons; New York: E. P. Dutton, 1911).

57. Amadou Hampaté Bâ, *The Fortunes of Wangrin*, trans. Aina Pavolini Taylor (Bloomington: Indiana University Press, 1999). See also Benjamin Lawrence, Emily Osborn, and Richard Roberts, eds., *Intermediaries, Interpreters, and Clerks: African Employees in the Making of Colonial Africa* (Madison: University of Wisconsin Press, 2006).

58. NAK, MAKPROF, Capt. G. D. C. Money, assistant district officer, report 17, for the half-year ending June 30, 1932.

59. NAK, MAKPROF, provincial correspondence 8/1932/4, Idoma Division Financial Report, 1931–32.

60. Overall, fines were overwhelmingly preferred during the Depression. The statistical appendix to the 1932 annual report for Idoma Division shows that the number of fines imposed almost equaled the number of all other punishments combined. NAK, MAKPROF, Annual Report for Idoma Division, 1932.

61. NAK, MAKPROF, Annual Report on Idoma Division for the Year Ending December 1932, "Judicial."

EPILOGUE

1. Niall Ferguson, *Empire: The Rise and Demise of the British World Order and the Lessons for Global Power* (New York: Basic Books, 2003).

2. See Catherine Coquery-Vidrovitch, "'L'Afrique coloniale française et la crise de 1930: Crise structurelle et genèse du sous-développement,' l'Afrique et la crise de 1930," *Revue d'histoire d'outre-mer* 63, numéro spécial (1976). See a fuller bibliographical reference of this paradigm in the introduction to this volume.

3. Jane Guyer, "The Depression and the Administration in South-Central Cameroun," *African Economic History* 10 (1981): 68.

4. NAK, LOKOPROF, 48/1923, Secretary, Northern Provinces, to Resident, Kabba Province, "Counterfeit Coins," July 1939.

5. See Sa'adu Zungur, *Sa'adu Zungur: An Anthology of the Social and Political Writings of a Nigerian Nationalist,* ed. Alhaji Mahmood Yakubu (Kaduna: Nigerian Defence Academy Press, 2000), 106. See also http://Saaduzungur.tripod.com.

6. Zungur, *Sa'adu Zungur.*

7. Ibid., 39.

8. Ibid., 41.

9. See Ahmadu U. Jalingo, "The Radical Tradition in Northern Nigeria" (PhD thesis, University of Edinburgh, 1980); Zungur, *Sa'adu Zungur.*

10. Zungur, *Sa'adu Zungur,* 57.

11. Frederick Cooper, *Decolonization and African Society: The Labor Question in French and British Africa* (Cambridge: Cambridge University Press, 1996), 111–50; Michael Havinden and David Meredith, *Colonialism and Development: Britain and Its Tropical Colonies, 1850–1960* (London: Routledge, 1993). For an analysis of how the postwar British Colonial Development and Welfare Fund operated and of the fortunes of its projects in British Africa, see Mike Cowen, "Early Years of the Colonial Development Corporation: British State Enterprise Overseas during Late Colonialism," *African Affairs* 83, no. 330 (1984): 63–75.

12. See Cooper, *Decolonization.*

13. The groundnut pyramids of Kano were the most visible symbols of Northern Nigerian colonial export agricultural prosperity. Represented in several visual mediums as iconic landmarks in the economic landscape of Northern Nigeria, they represented the "success" of British efforts to promote agricultural exports as a pathway to a steady stream of incomes for Northern Nigerians and raw materials for British factories. The pyramids are all gone now as groundnut exports have dwindled to a stop in the postcolonial period largely as a result of the rise of oil as Nigeria's principal foreign exchange earner.

Bibliography

ARCHIVES

Northern Nigeria

Arewa House: Centre for Historical Research and Documentation, Kaduna (AH)
  Nigerian Protectorate Ram (weekly, Kaduna, October–December 1930)
  Nigerian Daily Telegraph (weekly)
  Jarida Nijeria ta Arewa/Northern Provinces News (weekly, Kaduna, November 1931–January 1937)
  Nigerian Gazette Extraordinary (irregular, 1930–36)
National Archives of Nigeria, Kaduna (NAK)
Norcross Memorial Methodist Diocese Archives (NMMDA) (uncataloged), Otukpo

United Kingdom

British Library Newspaper Archive, Collingdale
  Empire Illustrated: The National Review (monthly)
  Imperial Review
  The Comet: A Weekly News Magazine of West Africa
  The West African Mail and Trade Gazette
Primitive Methodist Mission Collection (PMMC), School of Oriental and African Studies (SOAS), London
Rhodes House Archives, Oxford

United States

Alexander Sachs Papers, Franklin and Eleanor Roosevelt Institute, Hyde Park, New York
University of Michigan Library

BOOKS, ARTICLES, AND DISSERTATIONS

Abdulkadir, Dandatti. *The Poetry, Life, and Opinions of Sa'adu Zungur.* Zaria: Northern Nigerian Publishing, 1974.
Abdulkadir, M. S. "Currency Problems in Igalaland, Central Nigeria: 1930–1934." *Transafrican Journal of History* 24 (1995): 178–85.
———. "An Economic History of Igalaland, 1896–1939." PhD diss., Bayero University, Kano, 1990.
Adamu, Mahdi. *The Hausa Factor in West African History.* Zaria: Ahmadu Bello University Press; Ibadan: Oxford University Press, 1978.

Afigbo, A. E. *The Warrant Chiefs: Indirect Rule in Southeastern Nigeria, 1891–1929.* London: Longman, 1972.

Almeida-Topor, Hélène d'. *Les jeunes en Afrique.* Paris: L'Harmattan, 1982.

Amin, Samir. *Accumulation on a World Scale: A Critique of the Theory of Development.* Trans. Brian Pearce. New York: Monthly Press, 1974.

Ampiah, Kweku. "British Commercial Policies against Japanese Expansionism in East and West Africa, 1932–1935." *International Journal of African Historical Studies* 23, no. 4 (1990): 619–41.

Anderson, David, and David Throup. "The Agrarian Economy of Central Province, Kenya, 1918 to 1939." In *The Economies of Africa and Asia in the Inter-war Depression,* edited by Ian Brown, 8–28. London: Routledge, 1989.

Anyebe, A. P. *Man of Courage and Character: The Ogbuloko War in Colonial Idomaland of Nigeria.* Enugu: Fourth Dimension, 2002.

August, Thomas. *The Selling of the Empire: British and French Imperial Propaganda, 1890–1940.* Westport, CT: Greenwood, 1985.

Austen, Ralph. *African Economic History.* London: James Currey; Portsmouth, NH: Heinemann, 1987.

Ayandele, Emmanuel. *The Missionary Impact on Modern Nigeria, 1842–1914: A Political and Social Analysis.* New York: Humanities Press, 1967.

Bâ, Amadou Hampaté. *The Fortunes of Wangrin.* Trans. Aina Pavolini Taylor. Bloomington: Indiana University Press, 1999.

Berry, Sara. "Cocoa in Western Nigeria, 1890–1940: A Study of an Innovation in a Developing Economy." PhD diss., University of Michigan, 1967.

———. *Fathers Work for Their Sons: Accumulation, Mobility, and Class Formation in an Extended Yorùbá Community.* Berkeley: University of California Press, 1985.

Bhattacharya, Sanjoy. *Propaganda and Information in Eastern India, 1939–1945: A Necessary Weapon of War.* Richmond, Surrey: Curzon, 2001.

Bissel, William Cunningham. "Colonial Constructions: Historicizing Debates on Civil Society in Africa." In *Civil Society and the Political Imagination: Critical Perspectives,* edited by John L. Comaroff and Jean Comaroff, 124–59. Chicago: University of Chicago Press, 1999.

Boone, Catherine. *Merchant Capital and the Roots of State Power in Senegal, 1930–1985.* Cambridge: Cambridge University Press, 1992.

Brown, Ian, ed. *The Economies of Africa and Asia in the Inter-war Depression.* London: Routledge, 1989.

Bugaje, Usman. "Questioning the National Question: A Response to the First *Citizen* Annual Dialogue, Held at Abuja Sheraton Hotel and Towers, August 20, 1992." http://www.webstar.co.uk/~ubugaje/nationalquestion.html. Accessed June 23, 2008.

Bush, Barbara, and Josephine Maltby. "Taxation in West Africa: Transforming the Colonial Subject into a 'Governable Person.'" *Critical Perspectives on Accounting* 15, no. 1 (2004): 5–34.

Byfield, Judith. *The Bluest Hands: A Social and Economic History of Women Dyers in Abeokuta (Nigeria), 1890–1940.* Portsmouth, NH: Heinemann; Oxford: James Currey, 2002.

———. "Innovation and Conflict: Cloth Dyers and the Interwar Depression in Abeokuta, Nigeria." *Journal of African History* 38, no. 1 (1997): 77–99.

Chayanov, A. V. *On the Theory of Peasant Economy.* Edited by Daniel Thorner, Basile Kerblay, and R. E. F. Smith. Homewood, IL: Published for the American Economic Association by R. D. Irwin, 1966.

Clarence-Smith, Gervase. "The Effects of the Great Depression on Industrialization in Equatorial and Central Africa." In *The Economies of Africa and Asia in the Inter-war Depression*, edited by Ian Brown, 170–202. London: Routledge, 1989.

Comaroff, John L., and Jean Comaroff. Introduction to *Civil Society and the Political Imagination in Africa: Critical Perspectives*, edited by John L. and Jean Comaroff. Chicago: University of Chicago Press, 1999.

Connelly, Matthew. "The New Imperialists." In *Lessons of Empire: Imperial Histories and American Power*, edited by Craig Calhoun, Frederick Cooper, and Kevin W. Moore, 19–33. New York: New Press, 2006.

Conklin, Alice. *A Mission to Civilize: The Republican Idea of Empire in France and West Africa, 1895–1930.* Stanford: Stanford University Press, 1997.

Cooper, Frederick. "Africa and the World Economy." In *Confronting Historical Paradigms: Peasants, Labor, and the Capitalist World System in Africa and Latin America*, edited by Frederick Cooper, Allen F. Isaacman, Florencia E. Mallon, William Roseberry, and Steve J. Stern, 84–201. Madison: University of Wisconsin Press, 1993.

———. *Africa since 1940: The Past of the Present.* Cambridge: Cambridge University Press, 2002.

———. *Decolonization and African Society: The Labor Question in French and British Africa.* Cambridge: Cambridge University Press, 1996.

———. "Empire Multiplied: A Review Essay." *Comparative Study of History and Society* 46, no. 1 (2004): 247–72.

———. *From Slaves to Squatters: Plantation Labor and Agriculture in Zanzibar and Coastal Kenya, 1890–1925.* New Haven: Yale University Press, 1987.

———. *On the African Waterfront: Urban Disorder and the Transformation of Work in Colonial Mombasa.* New Haven: Yale University Press, 1987.

———. "What Is the Concept of Globalization Good For? An African Historian's Perspective." *African Affairs* 100, no. 399 (2001): 189–213.

Cooper, Frederick, and Randall Packard, eds. *International Development and the Social Sciences: Essays on the History and Politics of Knowledge.* Berkeley: University of California Press, 1997.

Coquery-Vidrovitch, Catherine. *Africa: Endurance and Change South of the Sahara.* Trans. David Maisel. Berkeley: University of California Press, 1985.

———. "'L'Afrique coloniale française et la crise de 1930: Crise structurelle et genèse du sous-développement,' l'Afrique et la crise de 1930." *Revue d'histoire d'outre-mer* 63: 3–4, numéro spécial (1976), 386–424.

———. "Mutation de l'impérialisme colonial français dans les années 30." *African Economic History* 4 (1977): 103–52.

Cowen, Mike. "Early Years of the Colonial Development Corporation: British State Enterprise Overseas during Late Colonialism." *African Affairs* 83, no. 330 (1984): 63–75.

Crocker, Walter R. *Nigeria: A Critique of British Colonial Administration.* 1936. Reprint, Freeport, NY: Books for Libraries, 1971.

Cunningham, Stanley B. *The Idea of Propaganda: A Reconstruction.* Westport, CT: Praeger, 2002.

Davis, Lance E., and Robert A. Huttenback. *Mammon and the Pursuit of Empire: The Political Economy of British Imperialism, 1860–1912.* Cambridge: Cambridge University Press, 1986.

Davis, Mike. *Late Victorian Holocausts: El Niño Famines and the Making of the Third World.* London: Verso, 2002.

Dike, Kenneth Onwuka. *Trade and Politics in the Niger Delta, 1830–1885.* Oxford: Clarendon Press, 1956.

Dopcke, Wolfgang. "'Magomo's Maize': State and Peasants during the Depression in Colonial Zimbabwe." In *The Economies of Africa and Asia in the Inter-war Depression,* edited by Ian Brown, 29–53. London: Routledge, 1989.

Dudley, Billy. *Parties and Politics in Northern Nigeria.* London: Frank Cass, 1968.

Egwu, Samuel. *Structural Adjustment, Agrarian Change, and Rural Ethnicity in Nigeria.* Research report 103. Uppsala: Nordiska Afrikainstitutet, 1998.

Ekejiuba, Felicia. "Currency Instability and Social Payments among the Igbo of Eastern Nigeria, 1890–1990." In *Money Matters: Instability, Values, and Social Payments in the Modern History of West African Communities,* edited by Jane Guyer, 133–61. Portsmouth, NH: Heinemann; London: James Currey, 1995.

Ekundare, R. O. *An Economic History of Nigeria, 1860–1960.* London: Methuen, 1973.

Engels, Dagmar, and Shula Marks, eds. *Contesting Colonial Hegemony: State and Society in Africa and India.* London: British Academic Press, 1994.

Fallers, Lloyd. *Bantu Bureaucracy: A Century of Political Evolution among the Basoga of Uganda.* Chicago: University of Chicago Press, 1965.

Ferguson, Niall. *Empire: The Rise and Demise of the British World Order and the Lessons for Global Power.* New York: Basic Books, 2003.

Flint, John. *Sir George Goldie and the Making of Nigeria.* London: Oxford University Press, 1960.

Frank, Andre Gunder. *Capitalism and Underdevelopment in Latin America: Historical Studies of Chile and Brazil.* New York: Monthly Review Press, 1967.

Freund, Bill. *Capital and Labour in the Nigerian Tin Mines.* London: Longman, 1981.

Geertz, Clifford. *Agricultural Involution: The Process of Ecological Change in Indonesia.* Berkeley: University of California Press, 1963.

Genova, James E. "Conflicted Missionaries: Power and Identity in French West Africa during the 1930s." *Historian* 66, no. 1 (2004): 45–66.

Goshit, Zakariah. "The Impact of the Great Depression on the Jos Plateau: A Case Study of the Tin Mine Fields in the 1930s." *Mandeng: Journal of Middle Belt History* 1, no. 1 (2001): 72–86.

Guyer, Jane. "The Depression and the Administration in South-Central Camer-oun." *African Economic History* 10 (1981): 67–79.

Habermas, Jürgen. *The Structural Transformation of the Public Sphere: An Inquiry into a Category of Bourgeois Society.* Translated by Thomas Burger and Freder-ick Lawrence. Cambridge, MA: MIT Press, 1989.

Hardt, Michael, and Antonio Negri. *Empire.* Cambridge, MA: Harvard University Press, 2000.

Harrison, Richard. "A Presidential *Démarche*: Franklin D. Roosevelt's Personal Diplo-macy and Great Britain, 1936–37." *Diplomatic History* 5, no. 3 (1981): 245–72.

Havinden, Michael, and David Meredith. *Colonialism and Development: Britain and Its Tropical Colonies, 1850–1960.* London: Routledge, 1993.

Helleiner, Gerald. *Peasant Agriculture, Government, and Economic Growth in Ni-geria.* Homewood, IL: Richard D. Irwin, 1966.

Higginson, John. *A Working Class in the Making: Belgian Colonial Labor Policy, Private Enterprise, and the African Mineworker, 1907–1951.* Madison: University of Wisconsin Press, 1989.

Hill, Polly. *Rural Hausa: A Village and a Setting.* Cambridge: Cambridge Univer-sity Press, 1972.

Hiskett, M. "The Development of Sa'adu Zungur's Political Thought from *Maraba da soja* through *Arewa jamhuuriyaa koo muluukiyaa* to *waakar yanci.*" *African Language Studies* 16 (1975): 1–23.

Hogendorn, Jan. *Nigerian Groundnut Exports: Origins and Early Development.* Zaria: Ahmadu Bello University Press, 1978.

Hopkins, A. G. *An Economic History of West Africa.* New York: Columbia Univer-sity Press, 1973.

Ihonvbere, Julius. *Nigeria: The Politics of Adjustment and Democracy.* New Bruns-wick, NJ: Transaction, 1994.

Ikime, Obaro. *The Fall of Nigeria: The British Conquest.* London: Heinemann, 1977.

Ikoja, Timothy Andrew. "The History of the Methodist Mission in Idomaland of Benue State." NCE thesis, Social Studies/Christian Religious Studies, Federal College of Education, Abeokuta, Nigeria, 1991.

Jalingo, Ahmadu U. "The Radical Tradition in Northern Nigeria." PhD thesis, University of Edinburgh, 1980.

James, Harold. *The End of Globalization: Lessons from the Great Depression.* Cambridge, MA: Harvard University Press, 2001.

Jewsiewicki, Bogumil. "The Great Depression and the Making of the Colonial Eco-nomic System in the Belgian Congo." *African Economic History* 4 (1977): 153–76.

Johnson, Marion. "Cotton Imperialism in West Africa." *African Affairs* 73, no. 291 (1974): 178–87.

Kaniki, M. H. Y. "The Impact of the Great Depression on Northern Rhodesia." *Transafrican Journal of History* 24 (1995): 131–150.

King, Lamont. "From Caliphate to Protectorate: Ethnicity and the Colonial Sabon Gari System in Northern Nigeria." *Journal of Colonialism and Colonial History* 4, no. 2 (2003): 1–20.

Lakroum, Monique. *Le travail inégal: Paysans et salariés sénégalais face à la crise des années trente*. Paris: L'Harmattan, 1982.

Larymore, Constance. *A Resident's Wife in Nigeria*. 2nd ed., rev. London: George Routledge and Sons; New York: E. P. Dutton, 1911.

Lawrence, Benjamin, Emily Osborn, and Richard Roberts, eds. *Intermediaries, Interpreters, and Clerks: African Employees in the Making of Colonial Africa*. Madison: University of Wisconsin Press, 2006.

Lennihan, Louise. "Critical Historical Conjunctures in the Emergence of Agricultural Wage Labor in Northern Nigeria." *Human Ecology* 12, no. 4 (1984): 465–81.

Lindsay, Lisa. *Working with Gender: Wage Labor and Social Change in Southwestern Nigeria*. Portsmouth, NH: Heinemann, 2003.

Lonsdale, John. "The Depression and the Second World War in the Transformation of Kenya." In *Africa and the Second World War*, edited by David Killingray and Richard Rathbone, 119–36. New York: St. Martin's, 1986.

Lovejoy, Paul, and Jan Hogendorn. *Slow Death for Slavery: The Course of Abolition in Northern Nigeria, 1897–1936*. Cambridge: Cambridge University Press, 1993.

Lugard, Frederick. *The Dual Mandate in British Tropical Africa*. Edinburgh: W. Blackwood and Sons, 1922.

Magid, Alvin. *Men in the Middle: Leadership and Role Conflict in a Nigerian Society*. Manchester: Manchester University Press, 1976.

Mamdani, Mahmood. *Citizen and Subject: Contemporary Africa and the Legacy of Late Colonialism*. Princeton: Princeton University Press, 1996.

———. *When Victims Become Killers: Colonialism, Nativism, and the Genocide in Rwanda*. Princeton: Princeton University Press, 2001.

Manning, Patrick. *Francophone Sub-Saharan Africa, 1880–1995*. 2nd ed. Cambridge: Cambridge University Press, 1998.

Marseille, Jacques. *Empire colonial et capitalisme français: Histoire d'un divorce*. Paris: A. Michel, 1984.

Martin, Susan M. "The Long Depression: West African Export Producers and the World Economy, 1914–45." In *The Economies of Africa and Asia in the Inter-war Depression*, edited by Ian Brown, 75–94. London: Routledge, 1989.

Mbembe, Achille. *On the Postcolony*. Berkeley: University of California Press, 2001.

Meek, C. K. *The Northern Tribes of Nigeria: An Ethnographical Account of the Northern Provinces of Nigeria Together with a Report on the 1921 Decennial Census*. New York: Negro Universities Press, 1969.

Miller, Peter, and Ted O'Leary. "Accounting and the Construction of the Governable Person." *Accounting, Organizations, and Society* 12, no. 3 (1987): 235–65.

Mitchell, Timothy. *Rule of Experts: Egypt, Techno-politics, Modernity*. Berkeley: University of California Press, 2002.

Muhammad, Ahmed R. "The History of the Spread of Islam in the Niger-Benue Confluence Area: Igalaland, Ebirraland and Lokoja, 1900–1960." PhD diss., Bayero University, Kano, 1986.

Mustapha, A. R. "Structural Adjustment and Agrarian Change in Nigeria." In *The Politics of Structural Adjustment in Nigeria*, edited by Adebayo Olukoshi. London: James Currey, 1993.

Nadel, S. F. A *Black Byzantium: The Kingdom of Nupe in Nigeria*. London: Oxford University Press, 1942.

Nash, June. "Ethnographic Aspects of the Capitalist World System." *Annual Review of Anthropology* 10 (1981): 393–423.

Netting, Robert. *Hill Farmers of Nigeria: Cultural Ecology of the Kofyar of the Jos Plateau*. Seattle: University of Washington Press, 1968.

Newbury, Colin. "Accounting for Power in Northern Nigeria." *Journal of African History* 45, no. 2 (2004): 257–77.

Nwabughuogu, Anthony I. "From Wealthy Entrepreneurs to Petty Traders: The Decline of African Middlemen in Eastern Nigeria, 1900–1950." *Journal of African History* 23, no. 3 (1982): 365–79.

Ode, G. E. "The Impact of British Colonialism on the People of Idoma Division, 1908–1950." Master's thesis, Ahmadu Bello University, Zaria, 1981.

Ofonagoro, Walter. "From Traditional to British Currency in Southern Nigeria: An Analysis of the Currency Revolution, 1880–1948." *Journal of Economic History* 39, no. 3 (1979): 623–54.

Ohiare, James Aliu. "The History of Migration from the Okene Area to the Cocoa Belt of Western Nigeria, 1923–1970." Bachelor's thesis, Ahmadu Bello University, Zaria, 1977.

Okediji, Florence Adebisi. "An Economic History of Hausa-Fulani Emirates of Northern Nigeria: 1900–1939." PhD diss., Indiana University, 1970.

O'kwu, V. G. "The Establishment of Colonial Administration in Idomaland, 1921–1930." *Savanna* 5, no. 1 (1976): 29–44.

Olukoju, Ayodeji. "Self-Help Criminality as Resistance: Currency Counterfeiting in Colonial Nigeria." *International Review of Social History* 45, no. 3 (2000): 385–407.

Ozigi, Albert, and Lawrence Ocho. *Education in Northern Nigeria*. London: Allen and Unwin, 1981.

Pearce, Richard D. *The Turning Point in Africa: British Colonial Policy, 1938–48*. London: Frank Cass, 1982.

Phillips, Anne. *The Enigma of Colonialism: British Policy in West Africa*. London: James Currey; Bloomington: Indiana University Press, 1989.

Pierce, Steven. "Looking for the Legal: Land, Law, and Colonialism in Kano Emirate, Nigeria." PhD diss., University of Michigan, 2000.

——. "Punishment and the Colonial Body: Flogging and Colonialism in Northern Nigeria." *Interventions* 3, no. 2 (2001): 206–21.

Ramakrishna, Kumar. *Emergency Propaganda: The Winning of Malayan Hearts and Minds, 1948–1958*. Richmond, UK: Curzon, 2002.

Renne, Elisha. *Cloth That Does Not Die: The Meaning of Cloth in Bùnú Social Life*. Seattle: University of Washington Press, 1995.

Rhodie, Sam. "The Gold Coast Cocoa Hold-up of 1930–31." *Transactions of the Historical Society of Ghana* 10 (1968): 105–18.

Skocpol, Theda. "Wallerstein's World Capitalist System: A Theoretical and Historical Critique." *American Journal of Sociology* 82, no. 6 (1977): 1075–90.

Scott, James. *Domination and the Arts of Resistance: Hidden Transcripts*. New Haven: Yale University Press, 1990.

Sen, Amartya. *Poverty and Famines: An Essay on Entitlement and Deprivation.* New York: Oxford University Press, 1982.

Shenton, Robert. *The Development of Capitalism in Northern Nigeria.* London: James Currey, 1986.

Smyth, Rosaleen. "Britain's African Colonies and British Propaganda during the Second World War." *Journal of Imperial and Commonwealth History* 14, no. 1 (1985): 65–82.

Sundkler, Bengt. *Bantu Prophets in South Africa.* London: Oxford University Press, 1961.

Sundkler, Bengt, and Christopher Steed. *A History of the Church in Africa.* Cambridge: Cambridge University Press, 2000.

Thompson, Alvin O. *Economic Parasitism: European Rule in West Africa, 1880–1960.* Barbados: University of the West Indies Press, 2006.

Usoro, Eno J. *The Nigerian Oil Palm Industry: Government Policy and Export Production, 1906–1965.* Ibadan: Ibadan University Press, 1974.

Van Onselen, Charles. *Chibaro: African Mine Labour in Southern Rhodesia, 1900–1933.* London: Pluto Press, 1976.

———. *The Seed Is Mine: The Life of Kas Maine, a South African Sharecropper, 1894–1985.* New York: Hill and Wang, 1997.

Wallerstein, Immanuel. "Africa in a Capitalist World." *Issue* 3, no. 3 (1973): 1–11.

———. *The Capitalist World-Economy: Essays.* Cambridge: Cambridge University Press, 1979.

Welsh, David J. *The Roots of Segregation: Native Policy in Colonial Natal, 1845–1910.* Cape Town: Oxford University Press, 1992.

Watts, Michael. *Silent Violence: Food, Famine, and Peasantry in Northern Nigeria.* Berkeley: University of California Press, 1983.

Wilson, Henry S. *African Decolonization.* London: Edward Arnold, 1994.

Zachernuk, Philip S. *Colonial Subjects: An African Intelligentsia and Atlantic Ideas.* Charlottesville: University Press of Virginia, 2000.

Zolberg, Aristide. *Creating Political Order: The Party-States of West Africa.* Chicago: Rand McNally, 1966.

Zungur, Sa'adu. *Sa'adu Zungur: An Anthology of the Social and Political Writings of a Nigerian Nationalist.* Edited by Alhaji Mahmood Yakubu. Kaduna: Nigerian Defence Academy Press, 2000.

Index

counterfeiting. *See* currency
counterfeiting
crafts, local, 86
criminality: fight against, 77; railway and,
80–85; self-help and, 23, 71–72, 98;
unemployment and, 75–78, 186n13
Crocker, W. R., 1, 84–85, 126, 152–56,
156–61, 188n39
currency counterfeiting, 16, 23, 72,
93–99, 130, 150–51, 169

Dauda, Yusuf Utohu, 189n63
Davies, Mike, 3
diamonds. *See under* mining industry
direct rule. *See under* indirect rule
Dodds, Rev., 134–35, 137
dual-mandate principle. *See under*
exploitation

economic recovery policy: British,
15, 23, 25, 28–32, 45, 93, 113–15,
131–32; chiefly privilege and, 15–16,
160; contradictory policies, 113–14;
core activities, 34; crisis in, 18, 113;
criticism of, 23, 107–12, 119–20,
170; currency scarcity and, 169;
elements, 7, 15; exploitation and,
12; export and, 71; famine and, 3,
63; goal of, 23, 32, 34–35; Idoma
reactions, 141–45; implementation,
18, 23, 63; isolationism and, 28; local
responses, 85–90; mise en valeur, 11;
nativism as, 114; official response to
Depression, 32–37, 45; retrenchment
and, 34–36, 72; revenue generation
and, 23, 47; self-preservation and, 13;
staff reduction, 51–52; suspension of
public works under, 12–13, 39, 53,
131–32; taxation and, 39, 49, 70, 164;
territorialism and, 28; unemployment
and, 35; unintended consequences,
23, 46, 71, 85–90, 99, 168
education project. *See* missionary
education project
egbe societies, 42
Ekejuiba, Felicia, 149
Elder Dempster Lines, 31
Elliot, H. P., 1, 73, 129, 132, 155–58, 160,
178n32
Empire Illustrated, The (journal), 179n5
esusu cooperative-credit system, 42, 44
expenditures, productive/nonproductive,
44–45

exploitation: agricultural interventions
and, 39–42; colonial, 4–5, 10–14, 25;
dual-mandate principle and, 11–13,
16, 110, 172; economic principles of, 2;
failure of, 4–5, 166–67; suffering and,
4, 167
exports: duties, 30; imperial economy
and, 32, 121; world market and, 8–9.
See also imperial preference policy;
specific goods

famine: causes, 16, 47, 55–57, 62–64;
response to, 3, 63; taxation and, 63,
167
farm raider. *See sojan gona*
Ferguson, Niall, 176n10
food shortage causes, 16, 47, 57–58,
62–64
Freund, Bill, 72, 149

Geertz, Clifford, 10
Genova, James, 46
geography of Northern Nigeria, 26, 47,
48–51, 177n19
Girouard, Percy, 6
global economics. *See* world markets
gold mining. *See under* mining industry
Goshit, Zakariah, 87
grasshopper invasion, 55–56
groundnut cultivation. *See* agricultural
production/exports
gum cultivation. *See* agricultural
production/exports
Guyer, Jane, 160

Hardt, Michael, 2
Hausa-British modernity, 114
Hausa language, 161–62
Hausa traders, 125–27, 141
Hogendorn, Jan, 78
Holt, John, 110
human trafficking, 78–80
Hutchinson, Rev., 135, 137–38, 140

Ibn Sanda, Mustapha, III, 170
Idoma Division, 19–21, 24; as backward,
18, 42, 122, 125, 128, 146, 164, 179n32;
colonial policy, 124–27; currency
scarcity, 129–30; economic crisis,
122–23, 127–33; food crop cultivation
in, 128–29; Hausa traders in, 125–27,
141; map, 122; marginality of, 121, 146;
migration and, 123, 143–45; mining

Watts, Michael, 56, 63
weavers, women, 17, 22, 72, 86–87
welfare: colonial failure and, 100;
    projects, cancellation, 37; self-help
    and, 43–44; transfer of obligations, 2,
    23, 42–45
women: source material on, 22;
    migration and, 91; roles of, 16–17,
    21–22; taxation and, 49–50; weavers,
    17, 22, 72, 86–87
world markets: African middlemen and,
    62; British pound value and, 26;
    dependence on, 49, 71; forces shaping
    Depression events, 19–21; integration
into, 8–9, 10, 45, 145; intervention
and, 42; loss of confidence in, 71;
recovery and, 173; self-preservation
and, 17; turbulence in, 2

xenophobia, 20, 123, 141–43

yam cultivation. *See* agricultural
    production/exports

Zachernuk, Philip, 139
Zaki, Dan, 113
Zukogi, Abubakar Sadiq, 170
Zungur, Mallam Sa'adu, 119, 170–71